ASSESSMENT:

Time-Saving Procedures

- F O R -

Busy Teachers

THIRD EDITION 3

BERTIE KINGORE
AUTHOR

Jeffery Kingore
GRAPHIC DESIGN

Professional Associates Publishing
www.kingore.com

Current Publications by
Bertie Kingore, Ph.D.

Alphabetters: Thinking Adventures with the Alphabet (Task Cards)
Assessment Interactive CD-ROM
Centers in Minutes!
Centers in Minutes! CD-ROM Volume 1: Grades K-8
Centers in Minutes! CD-ROM Volume 2: Learners with Limited Reading and Writing Skills
Differentiation Interactive CD-ROM
Differentiation: Simplified, Realistic, and Effective
Engaging Creative Thinking: Activities to Integrate Creative Problem Solving
Integrating Thinking: Practical Strategies and Activities
Just What I Need! Learning Experiences to Use on Multiple Days in Multiple Ways
Kingore Observation Inventory (KOI), 2nd ed.
Literature Celebrations: Catalysts for High-Level Book Responses, 2nd ed.
*Reading Strategies for Advanced Primary Readers: Texas Reading Initiative Task Force for the
        Education of Primary Gifted Children*
Reading Strategies for Advanced Primary Readers: Professional Development Guide
Teaching Without Nonsense: Activities to Encourage High-Level Responses
We Care: A Curriculum for Preschool Through Kindergarten, 2nd ed.

FOR INFORMATION OR ORDERS CONTACT:
PROFESSIONAL ASSOCIATES PUBLISHING
PO Box 28056
Austin, Texas 78755-8056
Toll free phone/fax: 866-335-1460

ASSESSMENT: Time Saving Procedures for Busy Teachers
THIRD EDITION

Table of Contents

Reproducible Figures

Introduction

All glory comes from daring to begin.
—Eugene F. Ware

This implementation research began as I worked with districts interested in initiating or refining authentic assessment. The challenge in most cases was not to convince educators of the value of authentic assessment but rather to determine how the process could be accomplished in a more realistic and accountable manner that would benefit students, teachers, and schools.

Over the last fifteen years, I have worked with thousands of teachers and administrators to analyze authentic assessment needs, problem solve, increase efficiency and value, as well as celebrate successes. Two factors especially kept driving the work: 1) The observed value to students in terms of self-esteem and motivation to excel, and 2) The change authentic assessment invited in the way teachers teach.

The processes and products described here have been implemented with students in pre-kindergarten through college. The school districts included both rural and urban districts ranging in size from approximately 400 to 300,000 students. European-American, African-American, Asian-American, Native-American and Latin-American students whose socioeconomic status ranged from poverty level through upper-middle class were involved. In many classrooms, forms had to be translated by dedicated teachers into languages other than English so more students could be successful.

Rather than an academic discussion of assessment and evaluation, this book focuses on classroom applications and classroom instruments. The objective is to make assessment efficient and integrated with instruction.

This third edition expands and reorganizes previous editions in significant ways.
- A new chapter, Developing a Background in Assessment and Evaluation, is added to unite the basic principles and guidelines of this topic.
- The Assessing Young Children chapter revises and expands the former Portfolios

Kingore, B. (2005). *Assessment,* 3rd ed. Austin: Professional Associates Publishing.

for Young Children chapter to simplify authentic assessment procedures in pre-kindergarten through first-grade classrooms. A pictorial rubric generator is added in response to requests from primary teachers for rubrics appropriate for young learners and ESL students.

- The chapter, Open-Ended Techniques, incorporates observation, checklists, interviews, inventories, self-assessment forms, and numerous simple assessment procedures.

- A new chapter, Products, discusses products as assessment tools and shares multiple examples that customize product options to learning profiles.

- Another new chapter, Integration of Standards, responds to assessment needs resulting from national, state, and district academic standards.

- New forms are included, and all forms, including the Rubric Generator, are refined, updated, and/or greatly expanded to increase application ease.

- More examples are included to increase clarity.

The goal of this book is to provide teacher-useful and student-friendly procedures for implementing authentic assessment. This book contains many of the best answers we have worked out in this collaborative effort. Three icons appear throughout the book to call attention to tips and applications.

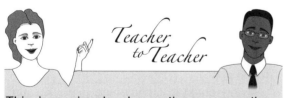

This icon signals observations, suggestions, opinions, and insights that teachers have shared regarding assessment concerns. Discussing them with other educators helps you make decisions about the best assessment practices for your classroom.

This alerts the reader to tips that especially relate to the content being addressed. These tips are simple suggestions to more efficiently and successfully implement assessments.

This signals a technique or learning experience valuable in preassessment. Applications are woven throughout the book inasmuch as pre-assessment requires ongoing applications.

Many of the strategies and procedures in this book use special forms. While I continue to believe that higher-level student responses are often prompted by blank paper, many teachers expressed a need for more ready-to-go forms and graphic organizers to make the assessment process more efficient and effective. This edition includes well over 100 reproducible forms, posters, and student examples for photocopying. In response to numerous requests, these reproducibles are also available on a CD-ROM that enables teachers and students to customize assessment procedures.

Warm regards and thanks to the hundreds of teachers, administrators, and the thousands of students in Canada, Alabama, Arkansas, California, Colorado, Florida, Georgia, Idaho, Illinois, Indiana, Iowa, Kansas, Kentucky, Maryland, Michigan, Minnesota, Missouri, Montana, Nebraska, New Jersey, New York, North Dakota, Ohio, Oklahoma, Oregon, Tennessee, Texas, Virginia, Washington, and Wisconsin. Their cooperation, suggestions, questions, feedback, and candor proved invaluable in refining this process.

Kingore, B. (2005). *Assessment,* 3rd ed. Austin: Professional Associates Publishing.

· CHAPTER 1 ·
Developing a
Background in Assessment

We have a wide range of complex achievement targets to assess.
We need all the tools we have at our disposal to do this job.
Our challenge is to find ways to use all these tools well and
to use them in balance.
—*Richard Stiggins*

Assessment and instruction work in tandem and are woven together so imperceptibly in successful classrooms that they seem one continuous whole. Assessment results guide initial instruction which is then continually assessed to determine needed adjustments in the instructional pace and level as well as to substantiate the degree of success in terms of students' achievements. The focus of this book explores classroom instruments and applications that make assessment efficient and integrated with instruction. The intent is to help teachers implement assessments that are practical and produce useful, high quality information.

DEFINITIONS

The terms *test, assessment,* and *evaluation* are frequently used interchangeably. Analyzing similarities and differences in their attributes and intents, however, clarifies their applications (see Figure 1.1).

Test is the narrowest of the terms and refers to using a set of questions or tasks to measure a sample of learning behavior at one point in time. It is structured to be administered and scored consistently to gather data, form comparisons, and record achievement. A test is an application of both assessment and evaluation because it involves the gathering and grading of data. A related term, *high-stakes test,* is frequently used with standards-based programs. It signals that the results of a test significantly impact a school as well as its teachers and students in terms of ratings and public recognition.

Assessment is more encompassing, incorporating multiple formats and sources. It is the continuous gathering of data to determine students' needs and accomplishments. It is intended to inform administrators, teachers, and students; it is used to drive instruction, analyze curricula, and enable students to continue progressing in their learning. Assessment includes varied procedures such

Kingore, B. (2005). *Assessment,* 3rd ed. Austin: Professional Associates Publishing.

Figure 1.1: BALANCED ASSESSMENT

Assessment Applications

- Objective or subjective
- Multiple formats and procedures
- Diagnose strengths and needs
- Determine the pace of the instruction
- Provide instructional feedback
- Gauge progress
- Promote continuous learning
- Determine flexible grouping decisions

- Assess and evaluate achievement
- Monitor curriculum effectiveness
- Periodic or ongoing

BALANCED ASSESSMENT
Collecting and interpreting
Objective and subjective data

Similar

- Assess and evaluate achievement
- Ongoing or periodic

Test Applications

- Objective
- Forced-choice
- Diagnose achievement levels
- Determine the success of the instruction
- Track students
- Grade achievement skills
- Promote comparisons
- Determine success or failure

Evaluation Applications

- Objective
- Forced-choice or performance-based
- Establish grades and ratings
- Determine accountability
- Evaluate learning standards
- Grade progress
- Formulate education policies
- Determine placements in programs

Similar

- Evaluate achievement
- Measure the program effectiveness
- Periodic

Kingore, B. (2005). *Assessment,* 3rd ed. Austin: Professional Associates Publishing.

as observations, checklists, interviews, port-folios, rubrics, and conferences. A related term, *Authentic assessment,* is used to distinguish that the assessment represents real work in classrooms rather than the proxy of learning sampled on a test or commercial assessment. Authentic assessment occurs in learning environments as instruction and learning intersect. It is continuous and diagnostic as it enables teachers to respond to students' needs and enables learners to develop and refine their skills.

Evaluation is the interpretation and judgment of assessment information and students' accomplishments. Its function is to interpret data and reach decisions of quality; it is used to grade the degree of students' learning and their level of performance. Grading products, rubrics, and tests are typical examples of evaluative procedures. When used to grade the level of school-wide performance, related terms emerge, such as *adequate yearly progress* and *school improvement.* While both classroom and school-wide evaluation are related, the focus of this book is in the classroom rather than particularly address school-wide performance.

In summary, testing provides a photograph of learning achievement. It may be clear or out of focus inasmuch as it samples specific knowledge and skills at one specific time. Assessment provides a video tape or portfolio of learning. It encompasses a view over time with more comprehensive data from multiple perspectives and procedures. Evaluation produces a judgment of assessment results. The three are decidedly interdependent: the efficacy of one affects the efficacy of all. Thus, the objective is to seek a balance of data from authentic assessments and standardized tools. A combination of tests, assessments, and evaluations ensures a more accurate consideration of the multiple facets of students' talents and learning needs.

ELEMENTS OF QUALITY ASSESSMENTS AND EVALUATIONS

Well-designed assessments are:

- **Clear, complete, and compelling.**[1]
  Assessments must clearly define the levels of quality and include the key facets of performance that are considered the best thinking by experts in the field.

- **Practical.**
  The process must efficiently balance the time and effort expended by students and teachers with the quality of the feedback procured. The information must be useful to improve students' performance and knowledge. An assessment is practical for student use when the language is student-friendly.

- **Diagnostic and aligned with standards.**
  The information must be meaningful and guide instruction. The assessment must be aligned with learning standards to dependably progress students toward important learning targets. It includes a range from low baseline to high ceiling to measure all students' learning.

- **Valid and reliable.**
  The assessments must measure what they purport to measure. They must provide a consistent measurement of the quality of knowledge and skills from one occasion to the next and from one evaluator to the next.

- **Equitable.**
  Quality assessments must provide a more objective standard in scoring and feedback so they are less subject to rater bias and inconsistent expectations.

- **Varied.**
  Variety is important to maintain interest in the assessment process but, more importantly, to access the different ways students learn.

[1] See Stiggins, R., 2001.

Kingore, B. (2005). *Assessment,* 3rd ed. Austin: Professional Associates Publishing.

CHANGING ROLES

Authentic assessment influences the traditional roles of a teacher and students. More integrated and authentic assessment procedures invite more collaboration among students, teachers, and parents. Teachers experience a shift away from what George Betts refers to as a *D.O.K. (Dispenser of Knowledge)* toward being a *guide on the side.*

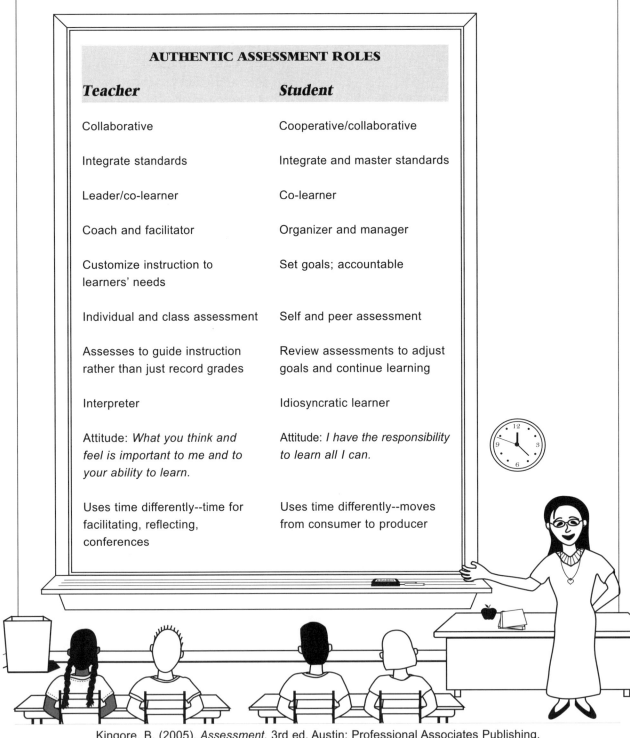

AUTHENTIC ASSESSMENT ROLES

Teacher	*Student*
Collaborative	Cooperative/collaborative
Integrate standards	Integrate and master standards
Leader/co-learner	Co-learner
Coach and facilitator	Organizer and manager
Customize instruction to learners' needs	Set goals; accountable
Individual and class assessment	Self and peer assessment
Assesses to guide instruction rather than just record grades	Review assessments to adjust goals and continue learning
Interpreter	Idiosyncratic learner
Attitude: *What you think and feel is important to me and to your ability to learn.*	Attitude: *I have the responsibility to learn all I can.*
Uses time differently--time for facilitating, reflecting, conferences	Uses time differently--moves from consumer to producer

Kingore, B. (2005). *Assessment,* 3rd ed. Austin: Professional Associates Publishing.

ASSESSMENT AND EVALUATION PROCEDURES

In the classroom, a variety of assessment procedures can be used to provide tangible evidence of students' understanding and achievement throughout the learning process--before instruction begins (preassessment), as instruction progresses (continuing or formative assessment), and at the end of a segment of instruction (culminating or summative assessment).[2] Preassessment clarifies students' interests and levels of readiness; it signals at which level and pace to initiate instruction for different students' needs. Continuing assessment supports instruction by substantiating the learning in progress. These assessments occur throughout an instructional segment to guide a teacher's instructional decisions regarding students who would benefit from reteaching, additional practice, or acceleration of skill levels. Culminating assessment is typically evaluative to document students' levels of achievement following instruction. In addition to determining grades, culminating evaluation guides regrouping decisions for reteaching or advancing to the next instructional segment.

Both assessments and students' self-assessments are applicable at each of these

[2] See Stiggins, 2001 and Tomlinson et al., 2002.

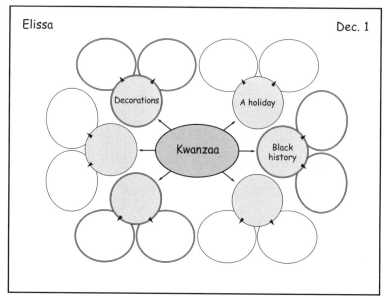

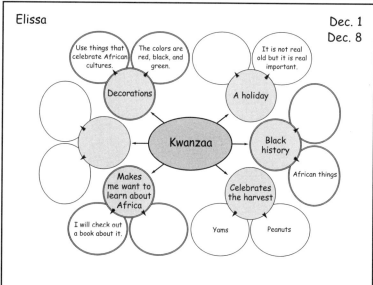

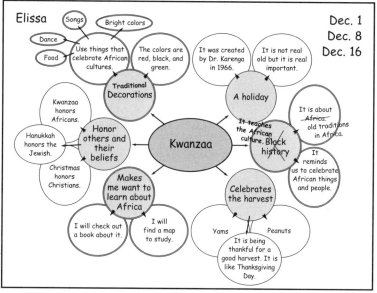

Kingore, B. (2005). *Assessment,* 3rd ed. Austin: Professional Associates Publishing.

Developing a Background

ANALYSIS GRID

NAME **Bert**
DATE **Sept. 9**
TOPIC **Organelles**

A = always   S = sometimes
          N = never

	Nucleus	Chloroplast	Cell wall
Animalia	A	N	N
Fungi	A		A
Monera	A		
Plantae	A	A	A
Protista	A		

Kingore, B. (1999). Teaching without Nonsense. Austin, TX: Professional Associates Publishing.

ANALYSIS GRID

NAME **Bert**
DATE **Sept. 9/Jan. 18**
TOPIC **Organelles**

A = always   S = sometimes
          N = never

	Nucleus	Chloroplast	Cell wall	Mitichondria	Ribosome	Endoplasmic reticulum	Golgi apparatus	Vacuole
Animalia	A	N	N	A	A	A	A	A
Fungi	A	N	A		A	A	A	N
Monera	A		S	N			N	A
Plantae	A	A	A	A	A	A	A	A
Protista	A		S	A	A	A	A	S

Kingore, B. (1999). Teaching without Nonsense. Austin, TX: Professional Associates Publishing.

ANALYSIS GRID

NAME **Bert**
DATE **Sept. 9/Jan. 18/May 27**
TOPIC **Organelles**

A = always   S = sometimes
          N = never

	Nucleus	Chloroplast	Cell wall	Mitochondria	Ribosome	Smooth Endoplasmic reticulum	Golgi apparatus	Vacuole	Plasma membrane	Rough Endoplasmic reticulum
Animalia	A	N	N	A	A	A	A	A	A	A
Fungi	A	N	A	A	A	A	A	N	A	A
Monera	N/A	S	S	N	A	N	N	N/A	A	N
Plantae	A	A	A	A	A	A	A	A	A	A
Protista	A	S	N/S	A	A	A	A	S	A	A

Kingore, B. (1999). Teaching without Nonsense. Austin, TX: Professional Associates Publishing.

learning junctures. Involving students in self-assessment for any of these assessment occasions increases students' responsibility for learning and motivation to work toward a higher level of quality.

Rather than label students, assessment results should motivate future learning by providing baseline data to measure growth. *This is your beginning or current level. Let's see how far we can help you can go.* Both preassessment and continuing assessment can motivate students' aspirations for higher levels of achievement when used as an indicator by which to compare future learning and concretely show learning growth.

Assessment techniques that are used for preassessment, continuing assessment, and culminating assessment are not mutually exclusive; indeed, many of the same techniques or learning experiences can be used as assessments at any or all of these three junctures in learning. The examples shared here use a concept map with a younger student and an analysis grid with a secondary student to clarify this process. For these examples, three separate samples are used to simulate each assessment juncture over time. In reality, students produce only one product on which they use different colors to show the changes in their knowledge at each assessment occasion.

Kingore, B. (2005). *Assessment,* 3rd ed. Austin: Professional Associates Publishing.

The following sequence delineates the achievement process that a combined application of preassessment, continued assessment, and culminating assessment allows.

1. *Preassessment*
Each student completes a preassessment. Students document their work by writing on the assessment their name, date, and a score--the number of correct answers or the degree of mastery according to a rubric. Students should set goals regarding the changes in their achievement that they intend to accomplish by the next assessment. The teacher or students store the preassessment for comparison at a later date.

2. *Continuing assessment*
At teacher-designated times during instruction, students retrieve their preassessments and use a different colored pen to embellish, delete, or correct items on the originals. The use of a different color helps students concretely validate their increased accuracy and quantity of information. Students add a legend to the top of the assessment with the beginning date written in the first color and the review dates written in other colors to clarify changes in their knowledge and understanding over time. Students should revisit and adjust their goals for continued learning.

3. *Culminating assessment*
After instruction is completed, students retrieve their previous assessments and use a different colored pen to embellish, delete, or correct items on those assessments. Culminating assessment grades are typically recorded in a grade book. The teacher, often with a student, reviews the culminating assessment to determine any reteaching needs before advancing to the next instructional segment.

When aligned with learning standards and accompanied with clear quality targets shared with students prior to the task, this assessment process is clear, diagnostic, valid, equitable, and easily varied. This procedure is practical as the class time invested produces learning changes. It is useful as it results in products that document growth and serve as discussion prompts among teachers, children, and parents. It also demystifies the assessment process and makes it shared information for reaching learning targets. Students and parents benefit from these concrete demonstrations of changes in students' levels of knowledge and understanding.

ASSESSMENT AND EVALUATION FORMATS

Review the formats in Figure 1.2 to guide decisions regarding assessment and evaluation options. Select formats that match your instructional priorities and students' needs. Balance the selection of test data and forced-choice responses with assessment tools and techniques that can be ongoing, occur in natural learning situations, matched to students' learning profiles, and require students to generate responses. Consider expanding traditional applications so that many formats become useful for preassessment (P), continuing assessment (CON), culminating assessment (CA), and/or students' self-assessment (SA).

A combination of tests, assessments, and evaluations ensures a more accurate consideration of the multiple facets of students' talents and learning needs.

Kingore, B. (2005). *Assessment,* 3rd ed. Austin: Professional Associates Publishing.

Figure 1.2: ASSESSMENT AND EVALUATION FORMATS

FORMAT	EXPLANATION--*This assessment tool is:*
Anecdotal record	An informal record of an observed event or behavior
Assessment accompanying curricula materials	A district or commercial device to assess specific content, topic, or skills
Audition	An assessment of a student performing authentic tasks
Checklist	A list of standards, skills, or behaviors applicable to achievement
Conference--informal or formal	An informal or formal achievement conversation involving teacher, student, peer, or family members
Demonstration	An assessment of a student performing authentic tasks associated with standards
Discussion	An informal interactive, inquiry-based conversation among teachers and students
Graphic organizer	A spatial device assessing the relationships among content and concepts
Interest inventory	An informal assessment of interests and experiences
Lab report	A record of learning responses and reflections
Learning Log	A record of learning responses and reflections
Math problem solving	An assessment of a student's application of concepts and skills in math
Observations of behavior	A teacher informally watching students during a classroom learning situation
Peer collaboration	An assessment guiding students' understanding of learning expectations among peers
Performance or performance task	An assessment of a student performing authentic tasks associated with standards
Portfolio and products	A collection over time of samples of students' learning achievements
Project	A learning task associated with standards; completed by a student or small group
Question	An informal, interactive, inquiry-based assessment--usually oral
Record--independent reading of fiction and nonfiction	A record to assess the level and pace of a student's literacy activities
Rubric	An evaluative device specifying criteria and levels of quality for a learning task
Standardized test	A commercial, formal, norm-referenced or criterion-referenced test of specific content
Student self-assessment	An assessment format used by students to assess their skills and achievement
Test accompanying adopted materials	A commercial, formal test of specific content and skills
Unit test--teacher developed	A teacher-prepared test of a segment of instruction
Writing sample	An assessment of a student's application of concepts and skills in written work

Kingore, B. (2005). *Assessment,* 3rd ed. Austin: Professional Associates Publishing.

APPLICATION--*This assessment tool is used to:*

Application	PREASSESSMENT	CONTINUING ASSESSMENT	CULMINATING ASSESSMENT	SELF-ASSESSMENT
Allow teachers to document insights and observations during classroom activities	•	•	•	•
Diagnose and compare summary information regarding achievement	•	•	•	•
Allow for the assessment of processes and achievement level in an authentic learning situation	•		•	•
Guide and record observations of standards and skills applications	•	•	•	•
Facilitate one-on-one exchanges, elicit a student's perception of achievement, and goal set	•	•	•	•
Allow for the assessment of processes in an authentic learning situation	•	•	•	•
Assess content integration and a student's perception of achievement; document with a rubric or checklist	•	•	•	•
Allow for the assessment of concept complexity, depth, and relationships	•		•	•
Provide information about experiences to customize a student's learning opportunities	•			•
Provide information about a student's responses to learning	•	•		•
Provide information about a student's responses to learning	•	•		•
Provide an authentic measure of a student's problem solving skill	•	•		•
Analyze productive or nonproductive learning behaviors and skills integration	•	•		•
Motivate students to recognize and aim for high standards of quality through cooperative efforts	•	•		•
Allow for the assessment of processes in an authentic learning situation	•	•		•
Allow for the analysis of complexity, depth, achievement, and growth over time	•	•		•
Assess content integration through product, process, communication, and cooperative group efforts	•			•
Assess content integration and a student's perception of achievement; document with a rubric or checklist	•			•
Identify a student's reading levels, use of reading strategies, and instructional needs	•			•
Provide a standard of quality for achievement and grading	•		•	•
Allow for district-wide or nationwide comparisons of achievement			•	
Help a student recognize levels of expectations and standards of quality	•		•	•
Diagnose and compare summary information regarding achievement	•		•	
Diagnose and compare summary information regarding achievement	•		•	
Provide an authentic measure of a student's composition skill	•	•	•	•

Kingore, B. (2005). *Assessment,* 3rd ed. Austin: Professional Associates Publishing.

YEARLONG ASSESSMENT PLAN

After reviewing formats, outline which ongoing assessment and evaluation options will provide comprehensive information throughout the year for your classroom needs. At the beginning of the year, the emphasis is preassessing to diagnose students' readiness and needs. During the year, preassessment, continuing assessment and culminating assessment are each emphasized to monitor progress. At the end of the year, culminating assessment provides documentation of the placement decisions and learning plans for each learner. Districtwide or statewide testing is culminating evaluation when scheduled at the end of the year. When scheduled during the school year, its diagnostic value is an asset to use as continuing data that guides and redirects instruction.

Determine which records will best organize and document the results of your assessment process. Then, analyze who needs to know this information, such as current and future teachers (T), students (S), family members (F), and administrators or specialists (A). Strive to keep students and their families very involved as the more everyone understands achievement the more children can learn. Use the following example of one grade level's assessment plan to prompt the yearlong decisions that integrate assessment and instruction.

Yearlong Assessment Plan

SCHEDULE	ASSESSMENT FORMATS	DOCUMENTATION RECORDS	AUDIENCE
Beginning of the Year	Content-area preassessments Interest inventory Parent information	Pre-tests; standards analysis Completed inventories/interviews From Parent to School forms	*T S F A* *T S F* *T S*
During the Year	Each unit: • Preassess, • Continuing, and • Culminating assessments Testing Conference and goal setting	Portfolios, students' self-assessments, learning logs, anecdotal records, rubrics, unit tests, and report cards Learning standards state test Conference notes; goal setting plans	*T S F* *T S F A* *T S F*
End of the Year	Tests Student products Conferences	District achievement test School Career Portfolio Conference notes	*T S F A* *T S F A* *T S F*

Kingore, B. (2005). *Assessment,* 3rd ed. Austin: Professional Associates Publishing.

• CHAPTER 2 •
Student-Managed Portfolios

Never do for students what they should do for themselves.
—Anonymous

Portfolios are the compass of authentic assessment. Begin your assessment process, or refine your process, by focusing on portfolios. Determine the portfolio definition and guidelines that are most applicable to your instructional objectives, and then develop organization and management procedures that promote a student-managed portfolio system. Figure 2.1 elaborates potential objectives.

PORTFOLIO DEFINITION AND GUIDELINES

DEFINITION: A portfolio is a systematic collection of student work selected largely by that student to provide information about the student's attitudes, motivations, levels of achievement, and growth over time.

A significant word in this definition is *systematic.* The portfolio process must have a system or it will not develop purposefully nor perpetuate itself. The portfolio system determines how and which products get into a portfolio, how it is managed, and what its assessment and evaluation applications are.

It does not need to be the same as what is described in this book, but you do need to develop a system. Appendix A presents an outline for successfully implementing a portfolio system.*

One predominant concept in this definition is the importance of student-selected products. To document learning standards and achievement, teachers must determine which items are required portfolio pieces for all students. Then, the remainder of the products must be student-selected to individualize the portfolio and motivate students to excel. Set specific guidelines for determining the number of products in a portfolio, how many items students select, and how many pieces teachers select.

A second vital concept in this definition is the use of the portfolio to document a student's growth over time. Students and other invested individuals should review the portflio to determine how each student is developing as a learner. Indeed, many students are more motivated to excel when they

Figure 2.1: PORTFOLIO OBJECTIVES

1. **Develop students' feelings of self-worth.**
   Students develop feelings of self worth as they review their portfolios over time and concretely observe their growth and changes as learners. They substantiate to themselves that their efforts result in achievement.

2. **Increase students' responsibility for learning.**
   The portfolio process enables students to increase their responsibility for learning when they analyze several examples of their work to select portfolio products and reflect upon their achievements and needs.

3. **Refine students' organization and management.**
   Organization and management are valued life skills. Inasmuch as most students are not well organized, a clearly structured portfolio system models for students how to organize and manage their products over time.

4. **Implement effective self-assessment and collaborative evaluation.**
   Many students talk about grades as something *given* to them by teachers. However, the objective is for students to reflect upon what they have *earned* by their effort. Clearly develop criteria, often shared in the form of holistic or analytical rubrics, promote students' self assessments and lead to collaborative evaluations between teachers and students as they consider the merits and demerits of a product or process.

5. **Document learning needs.**
   The work students produce exemplifies their learning needs. Portfolio products are useful as authentic examples of class work to compare with standardized evaluations. Open-ended portfolio products substantiate the concepts and skill levels attained by students with fewer skills, students on grade level, students with learning differences, and students who would benefit from extended learning opportunities.

6. **Document district and state learning standards.**
   Portfolios document learning standards by substantiating students' application of concepts and skills. Students' reflections can specifically address the standards inherent in the product.[3]

7. **Document abilities for special classes, college, or employment.**
   The portfolio is a concrete means of demonstrating achievements related to placement in special classes, employability, or interviews for college admission.

8. **Celebrate learning.**
   Portfolios should be as unique and varied as the individuals they reflect. When viewed across several months or years, they promote students' celebrations of learning.

[3] Chapter 9 includes examples of procedures that directly relate learning standards to student reflections.

Kingore, B. (2005). *Assessment,* 3rd ed. Austin: Professional Associates Publishing.

see for themselves that they are making progress. Repeated tasks and triplets are two techniques that specifically document student growth; they are discussed at the end of this chapter.

The goal is for portfolios to be educationally effective for educators and students. Portfolios need to emphasize product and process, effort and achievement, student ownership, and self-evaluation. Figure 2.2, the two-column analysis below, offers guidelines that compare effective portfolios with ineffective portfolios.

Several tools are shared to assist your portfolio implementation. Figure 2.3 discusses the types of potential portfolios; figure 2.4 alerts you to needed materials; figure 2.5 outlines a plan for a portfolio system.

Figure 2.2: GUIDELINES

EFFECTIVE PORTFOLIOS:	INEFFECTIVE PORTFOLIOS:
• Are a natural part of daily classroom activities. They are thoroughly integrated into the instructional program. *This is one of the ways we demonstrate learning.*	• Are contrived, having only a few products stuck in during the last week of school. *We do this because we are told to have portfolios.*
• Evolve from a systematic process.	• Have a random, spontaneous collection.
• Encourage student responsibility, pride, and accountability for learning.	• Increase teachers' filing and paper management time.
• Allow students to polish and refine what they are learning to do well.	• Accent students' deficiencies and weaknesses.
• Encourage students' metacognition and increase their capacity for self-evaluations.	• Exclude students from the assessment and evaluation process. Evaluation continues to be something done *to* students.
• Invite challenge and complexity in students' thinking and in the works they produce.	• Rely on products with single correct answers and simplistic fill-in-the-blank tasks.
• Focus discussions about learning and development among students, teachers, and parents.	• Are only used for conferences between parents and teachers.
• Are student centered and motivate students to be autonomous learners.	• Are controlled by teachers but kept by students because teachers require them to do so.
• Enable students to set learning goals and celebrate their learning accomplishments.	• Fail to integrate cognitive and affective domains in learning.

Kingore, B. (2005). *Assessment,* 3rd ed. Austin: Professional Associates Publishing.

Student-Managed Portfolios

Figure 2.3: KINDS OF STUDENT PORTFOLIOS

Yearly Portfolio

This portfolio is a large and varied collection of products mainly selected by the student to represent ability, interests, attitudes, growth, and achievements. This portfolio is actively used throughout the school year. At the end of the year, the majority of the portfolio is bound and taken home as a keepsake.

School Career Portfolio: A Showcase Portfolio

This portfolio solves the dilemma of how to share work with next year's teacher without the portfolio becoming unwieldy and bulky. At the end of each year, a limited number of items from the Yearly Portfolio, typically less than six products, are collaboratively selected by the student and teacher to demonstrate the student's significant accomplishments and levels of achievement. These products are placed in the School Career Portfolio and go on to next year's teacher. The School Career Portfolio is added to each year and then bound and presented to the student after several years or with the diploma at graduation.

Professional Portfolio

This portfolio is typically developed during the high school years. A small number of items are carefully selected to present the details of the individual's experience and talents related to specific employability or interviews for college admission. Students are encouraged to focus on the skills required in the field in which they intend to work or the college they wish to attend rather than attempt to develop a generic or global view of talents. This portfolio should reflect the individual.

Class Portfolio

The class portfolio is typically a photo album in which weekly entries are made to herald the content and experiences of the class. Students usually take turns serving as the class historian who makes choices about what to include that represent the events of that week in class. Students and the teacher collaboratively assemble works that reflect the achievements and projects of the class as a whole. The class portfolio becomes a collective scrapbook or data base in which all of the students evaluate class work and gain ownership in the learning process as they celebrate completed tasks and occasions.

Kingore, B. (2005). *Assessment,* 3rd ed. Austin: Professional Associates Publishing.

Figure 2.4: MATERIALS CHECKLIST

As you read this chapter and refine your current use of portfolios, use this checklist to record a list of needed materials and forms to copy. Continue to keep the list short and inexpensive so cost does not prevent you from a great portfolio experience.

❑ **Audiotapes and tape recorder**

❑ **Camera and film or digital camera**

❑ **Collection folders**

❑ **Colored paper**

❑ **Computers, computer generated products, disks for digital portfolios**

❑ **Crate, box, or file drawer to store class portfolios**

❑ **Date stamp**

❑ **Filing system**

❑ **Forms:**   **PAGE/FIGURE:**

   ❑ _____   _____

   ❑ _____   _____

   ❑ _____   _____

   ❑ _____   _____

   ❑ _____   _____

❑ **Hanging Files**

❑ **Paper of various colors and sizes**

❑ **Portfolio containers--Folders, envelopes, three-ring binders, computer disks**

❑ **Post-it™ notes**

❑ **Stapler**

❑ **Timer**

❑ **Videotapes and access to a video camera**

❑ _____

❑ _____

❑ _____

Student-Managed Portfolios

Kingore, B. (2005). *Assessment,* 3rd ed. Austin: Professional Associates Publishing.

Figure 2.5: PLANNING A PORTFOLIO SYSTEM

Effective portfolios are not a lucky accident. Do not rely on spontaneous moments when wonderful products develop and students rush to their portfolios to include the new treasure. Instead, plan a system so the portfolio process develops purposefully and continuously. Use the following guided outline to create the system that will work best in your situation. As you read this chapter and/or refine your current use of portfolios, return to this outline to review your plan. Analyze the questions, make your own decisions, and implement your plan.

Purposes and audiences	• How will the portfolio help a student review past learning experiences to guide future learning goals? • How does this correlate to school, district, or state learning standards and assessment requirements? • Who will want or need to view the portfolio? DECISIONS: _____ _____ _____
What to include	• On which curriculum areas should portfolios focus? • What kinds of products will best document learning? • How can very large or three-dimensional items be managed without excessive storage space? DECISIONS: _____ _____ _____
Selection criteria	• Who selects the different portfolio pieces and decides how many to include? • When and how often should pieces be selected? DECISIONS: _____ _____ _____

How to organize and manage	• How can the organization remain simple enough to enable students to manage portfolios? • Which containers are most appropriate? • Which filing system works best to keep the products organized? DECISIONS:
Use	• How can a portfolio document state learning standards? • How can a portfolio help students gauge growth and achievements? • How can a portfolio help promote a positive statement for each student? • How can my students and I use a portfolio to assist conferencing or sharing instructional information with students, parents, and colleagues? • How can a portfolio substantiate the grades on a grade card? • How can I use portfolios to provide instructional feedback to me and increase my instructional effectiveness? DECISIONS:
Assessment and evaluation	• How can I use portfolios to provide clear documentation of what students have learned and thus provide assessment information to administrators? • How can I involve students in interpreting the information in their portfolios and making judgments about their own learning instead of just collecting products? • Which metacognitive techniques most effectively enable my students to self-assess their motivation and learning processes while reflecting on what went well and what to change? • Which self-evaluation techniques promote student ownership in evaluation results? DECISIONS:

Student-Managed Portfolios

Kingore, B. (2005). *Assessment,* 3rd ed. Austin: Professional Associates Publishing.

Determine which areas of the curriculum are the intended focus of your portfolios. Single subject portfolios are possible but may end up accenting the weakest skill area for some students. An integrated curriculum portfolio has the advantage of increasing the opportunity for each student to excel in one or more areas. In self-contained classrooms, educators determine three or four content areas to include. In departmentalized classrooms, form a team approach with a core of three or four teachers so students produce an integrated portfolio instead of developing separate portfolios in each subject.

ORGANIZATION AND MANAGEMENT

> *I used to collect work from my students, but the piles just got higher and higher. **I never had time to file them.** It didn't work as well as I had hoped.*
>
> *I can't keep portfolios for all of my students. **My classes are too big!***
>
> *I know portfolios are important, but **I just don't want the mess.***

These comments from teachers are typical of the concerns associated with the portfolio process. Most teachers appreciate the idea of portfolios but feel overwhelmed by the organization and management. One aspect of the problem is teachers using the pronoun *I*

when they discuss together the management of portfolios. Portfolios are too much to manage when teachers attempt to do most of the work for the students. The key is to organize the process in such a way that the students are able to manage their own portfolios. With student-managed portfolios, students make most of the decisions about what goes in the portfolio and analyze the results over time to assess how they change as learners. Students are responsible for managing and filing their own work, and the emphasis is on self-reflection.

In thousands of classrooms, students, age four through adults, are successfully managing their own portfolios by using the procedures discussed in this chapter. Student-managed portfolios evolve from teachers' artful planning. Teachers determine a filing system, appropriate containers, collection files, and the organization method of the portfolio contents that enables students to proceed toward independence.

FILING SYSTEM

A filing system keeps the containers organized. When portfolio containers are just stored in a box, the containers tend to get mixed-up every time one is in use. For example, a student takes her portfolio container to her desk to share it with a peer; when he or she finishes, it is not likely to be returned to the same location within the box. A filing system is needed to solve this potential disarray.

An effective yet simple filing system uses hanging files in a box, crate, or file drawer. The hanging file is the place holder; it is not the portfolio container. The portfolio container goes in and out of that file while the hanging file always stays in place and keeps the system organized. Each student has a hanging file; each hanging file has a tab with a student's name or photo on it. The files may be arranged alphabetically by students' names or numbered and filed in sequence.

Some teachers use several different colors of hanging files in the same crate. The colored sections help students find their own portfolios quickly.

CONTAINERS

The significance of portfolios is determined by the contents of the portfolio rather than the style of the container. However, most teachers are apprehensive about the containers and how much classroom space will be consumed by this process. Address this concern directly and early in your planning to avoid confusion and disarray later in the school year.

A wide variety of containers are successfully being used in classrooms across the nation. The secret to the *perfect* container is not to worry about what others are using and just choose the container that best fits your teaching style and classroom needs. If you work with a large number of students, you may want containers that use little space. If you frequently use three-dimensional products in your teaching, then your containers need to accommodate those products or allow for the use of photographs and videotapes of those large items.

Many containers are available. Consider the following factors when determining the best choice of container for your class.

1. *Sturdy*. The containers should be strong enough to withstand frequent use throughout a whole year.
2. *Product appropriate.* The container needs to be appropriate to the type of products that will be collected.
3. *Storage appropriate.* Choose containers that will not occupy more classroom space than is comfortably available in your room.
4. *Economical.* Limiting the cost of supplies makes the project more feasible.
5. *Accessible.* Plan containers that are readily accessible to students. Then, they can manage their own paperwork, and the process is incorporated naturally into daily learning activities.

A computer disk is the smallest and simplest answer to the question of what to use as a portfolio container. However, if you are interested in using computer disks for anything more than word processing, be sure students have ready access to a scanner. Pictures, photographs,

Student-Managed Portfolios

Containers	
• File folders	• Computer disks
• Pocket folders	• Shopping bags
• Expandable files	• Shoe boxes
• Three-ring binders	• Pizza boxes
• Photo albums	• Manila envelopes
• Scrapbooks	• Cardboard magazine storage boxes
• Zip-locking bags	• Boxes

Kingore, B. (2005). *Assessment,* 3rd ed. Austin: Professional Associates Publishing.

and other graphic products need to be scanned onto the disk. If students do not have access to a scanner, a digital camera can capture the details of drawn and written products. Avoid setting up such time-intensive extra tasks for yourself by including students in the process.

DECISION

List the potential containers and filing systems that will work best in your setting.

_____

_____

_____

_____

Formats for students to use to customize their portfolio container

- Portrait of self or family
- Drawing of home
- Collage of favorites, such as words, animals, represented ideas, or symbols
- A picture or collage of interests, favorite things, places, or books
- *Things I Like to Do*
- *Things I Want to Learn*
- *Things that Are Important About Me*
- Patterns or designs
- Tangram illustrations
- Tessellations
- A bio poem for self
- Quarterly images--divide the cover into quadrants; students illustrate a different idea each quarter of the school year

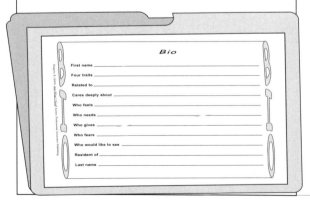

After you determine which containers you want to use, make them available to the students to design or decorate. Personalizing the containers adds to their individuality and sets the tone that each portfolio is unique.

Encourage students to be creative and fold large paper items to fit in smaller containers. Then, small containers don't have to limit students to only notebook paper. The portfolios resemble pop-up books as students unfold pages to show their work.

COLLECTION FILES

The collection file is the storage place of work being held for later consideration or before work is taken home. Students need access to several products in order to evaluate which ones to include in their portfolio. Collect and temporarily store work produced in the subject areas represented in the portfolio. These products are saved and evaluated for possible selection at the next regularly scheduled portfolio selection session.

Many classes already use work folders to store completed papers so they have this collection file process in place. Another simple solution that works well is a plain manila folder stored in front of the portfolio container in each hanging file. Use this plain folder to hold all completed work until portfolio selections occur. While other options are possible, this method takes up little space, is easy to maintain, and requires no additional materials except manila folders.

Kingore, B. (2005). *Assessment,* 3rd ed. Austin: Professional Associates Publishing.

Work that is to be graded is first completed by the student, then graded by the teacher, and finally placed in the collection folder by the student when it is returned with a grade. Work that is not to be graded is placed directly in the collection file as the student completes that assignment. The collection file is retrieved for portfolio selection sessions when the products are reviewed to select the entry piece. The remaining work not selected for the portfolio is then taken home by the student so parents continue to see school work on a regular basis.

Create a small picture symbol for your portfolios, such the ones below. Tape that symbol on your class calendar on the day that portfolio selection is scheduled so students are more concretely aware of the schedule. Then, move the symbol ahead to the next selection date each time you complete portfolio selection.

ORGANIZING PORTFOLIO CONTENTS

Several options help students organize their products within their portfolio. Choose from the following options or develop one more suited to your class.

 ### *Chronological order*
The products are sequenced from the beginning to the end of the year. This arrangement is easily managed by having students consistently file new products in the back of other work in their portfolios.

 ### *Subject area*
The portfolio contains separate colored files, dividers, or pockets for each curriculum area, e.g., writing, science, math. The products are then organized in each subject area of the portfolio.

 ### *Themes*
The portfolio is organized around the themes of the school or class, e.g., Challenges or Patterns.

 ### *Topics*
The portfolio is divided for specific topics of the class and/or interests of each student, e.g., dinosaurs, medicine, or oceanography.

 ### *Genres*
The portfolio is divided into types of products or genres of particular curriculum subjects, e.g., reading genres.

 ### *Talents*
Especially when completing professional portfolios, high school students might organize their portfolio products according to the talents they wish to accent to prospective employers, e.g., communication skills, technology, systems comprehension, or interpersonal skills.

 ### *Combinations of the above*
The organization types may be combined to better accommodate students needs, e.g., the products may be chronologically arranged within separate subject areas.

Young students and students who are inexperienced in portfolio management best succeed if their portfolios are initially organized chronologically. It is the simplest organizational

Student-Managed Portfolios

Kingore, B. (2005). *Assessment,* 3rd ed. Austin: Professional Associates Publishing.

method to organize, instruct, and maintain. Even four year old students can successfully file their work when portfolios are organized chronologically.

Older students are capable of choosing from several organizational formats presented to them. After a class discussion of options, students can determine the portfolio organizational format they think will work best for them and then exchange ideas among themselves. This process has the advantage of customizing organizational choice to the students and reinforcing that the portfolio is student owned and managed.

A self-esteem boost often results when students file each new entry in the back of their portfolio. The added benefit is that students constantly see their earlier work each time they add to their portfolios. This concretely reminds them of their own growth. Young students and students with special learning needs benefit greatly from being able to clearly view their progress over time.

PRODUCT EXAMPLES TO INCLUDE

Teachers often wonder what kinds of products are effective choices for portfolios. There are certainly no absolutes, as the portfolio should reflect the instructional climate of the classroom. However, the list in Figure 2.6 is a compilation of products teachers reported as most helpful in providing assessment and evaluation information about their students. The list is not intended to dictate what products to include but rather to suggest options to consider. Skim the list, and check any products that match your instructional priorities. At the bottom of the form, write additional significant products.

In general, teachers report that having more open-ended tasks results in products that better document the different thinking levels and learning achievements of students. Open-ended tasks encourage students to produce various levels of complexity and depth that reflect their abilities rather than recall a more simple, single-correct answer.

In classrooms using cooperative learning, group products are often produced. Teachers conclude that group products may be included in individual portfolios if the name of every group member is listed on the product. Furthermore, the product should be one that can be photocopied so more than one group member can select that product for their portfolios.

Use a camera to photograph items that would be too large to comfortably store in portfolio containers. A photograph will never be as good as the real item, but it helps solve the problem of how to represent large projects in small containers. Have students attach a narrative to the photograph describing the main points of the process and product.

Portfolios should be as individual as the teachers and students involved. It is not always necessary for all students to select the same type of product. Determine which benchmark items should be included in every portfolio for documentation of achievement; and then, let the students select their products according to their unique talents, interests, needs, and feelings of accomplishment.

Kingore, B. (2005). *Assessment,* 3rd ed. Austin: Professional Associates Publishing.

Figure 2.6: PORTFOLIO PRODUCT EXAMPLES

❑   Products and captions documenting learning standards achievement

❑   Art, symbols, graphic connections to content

❑   Attitude or interest surveys

❑   Photographs, sketches, or videotapes of three dimensional products or demonstrations accompanied by a written explanation

❑   Photocopies of products, awards, or honors

❑   Dictations or originally written reports, literature extensions, or stories

❑   First drafts and revisions--a biography of a product

❑   Math products which provide evidence of problem solving and higher-level thinking

❑   Goals set by students (and parents or teachers)--academic, behavioral, social, study skill, or research goals

❑   Lab reports and observations

❑   Learning logs and/or journal responses

❑   Integration or transfer of skills across subject areas

❑   Charts, graphs, and other graphic organizations of content (especially those designed by the individual student)

❑   Personal response to a current event, issue, or problem

❑   Self-evaluations and reflections

❑   Audiotapes of oral reading, math process explanations, reports, or story retellings

❑   Computer-generated student products

❑   Tests or quizzes

❑   Cooperative investigations; group reports or projects

❑   Repeated tasks

❑   Triplets

❑   _____

❑   _____

❑   _____

❑   _____

Kingore, B. (2005). *Assessment,* 3rd ed. Austin: Professional Associates Publishing.

PRODUCT SELECTION

A PORTFOLIO IS A FILE, NOT A PILE.

Avoid the scrapbook syndrome: *I'll just put all this stuff in it.* Effective portfolios involve students in discussing and analyzing their work. Students must make decisions about what items are the most significant representations of their learning. Thus, the procedure involves more than just saving papers. Effective portfolios involve the following processes.

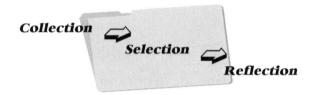

Collection

Selection

Reflection

There is a difference between collection (merely saving items) and selection (the decision-making process of prioritizing which items to include). Selection requires students to analyze the *what and why* of their work. The high-level thinking required of students in the selection process results in more potential life-value for those students and portfolios that have greater assessment and evaluation validity. Much of students' success in future working environments depends upon the strength of their ability to analyze alternatives and problem solve. Thus, the class time devoted to this selection and reflection process serves as a guide and motivation for students' future achievements.

After students collect their work over a short period of time, they review those products and use specific criteria to select one for their portfolio. Before they file it in the portfolio, they reflect about their decision and write a reflection statement or caption to attach to the product. This metacognitive process is a significant part of the educational value of portfolios.[4]

To make portfolio selection a regular part of the class schedule, establish a specific day and time when selection always occurs. In busy classes, what is not scheduled just does not get done! (Refer to the bulletin board illustration later in this chapter that features students' selections for their portfolio.)

DETERMINING YOUR PREFERRED NUMBER OF PRODUCTS

Control the size of a portfolio by reasoning in reverse. Determine the number of products ultimately desired to be in the portfolio at the end of the year. The number of items should be small enough to manage and store, but it should be large enough to concretely demonstrate students' growth, document levels of achievement, and reflect individuality. Also, plan the ratio of student-to-teacher selections so the majority of the portfolio is determined by the individual student.

When the teacher chooses most of the products, the portfolio becomes something else students do because they are required to rather than the portfolio being personally important and satisfying to the student.

In self-contained classes, control the total size of each portfolio by thinking in terms of approximately an inch or an inch-and-a-half thickness. To attain this size, have students select one product each week, resulting in approximately thirty-six products selected by the student. The teacher might select ten to twelve additional pieces making the yearly portfolio total almost fifty products. Depending upon the size of the products, that usually results in a portfolio that is one to two inches thick. Teachers find that amount to be an

---

[4] Chapter 4 has several examples of metacognitive forms and responses for students to use.

Kingore, B. (2005). *Assessment,* 3rd ed. Austin: Professional Associates Publishing.

excellent representation of students' learning experiences while maintaining a manageable size.

In departmentalized classes, think approximately one-fourth to one-half inch thickness per portfolio. Departmentalized classes have less time per day in each class. Thus, one product selected every three weeks is suggested for a total of twelve products. These teachers typically choose an additional six to eight pieces so the total number of products in the portfolio is approximately twenty. If three or four departmentalized teachers work as a team, the products selected from each class are combined into an integrated portfolio about one inch to two inches thick.

In classes with younger children, think one-fourth to one-half inch thickness for each portfolio. Young children produce fewer paper products;[5] much of the learning completed with this age group is process-oriented. Therefore, one product selected every two or three weeks is sufficient for these classes. Most of the portfolio selections are determined by the teacher to validate the growth the children demonstrate in their learning.

THREE THINGS THAT ARE INCLUDED ON EVERY PORTFOLIO PRODUCT

For most elementary and secondary students, each portfolio product needs to have a **name, date, and reflective statement or caption** on it. The name obviously is needed to identify whose work it is. The date allows students to be aware of the changes in their own learning and their growth over time. The reflective statement or caption defines why that product was selected, what it means in relation to previous learning benchmarks, or what specific value it has to the learner.

Teachers sometimes wonder if it would be simpler to omit the reflective statements when the portfolio process is initiated. It seems easier to have one less thing to manage as you begin. If possible, however, incorporate the reflective statements from the very start. Products without captions have less significance over time. When parents, teachers, or even students look back on portfolio products without a caption, it is more difficult to understand and value the importance of each piece. The reward for incorporating reflective statements is that students, parents, and teachers gain an increased awareness of the student's patterns of learning strengths and attitudes toward their learning.

Very young students and students with special learning needs may require different considerations to be able to successfully complete the selection and reflection process. Chapter 3 presents helpful alternatives for these students.

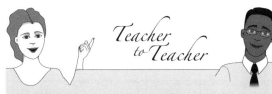

Teacher to Teacher

Ask students to use a pencil to lightly number the products in their portfolio in sequential order. Then, if items drop out, they are more easily returned to the correct place.

Portfolios offer a concrete record of the development of students' talents and achievements during a year or more. In classrooms where all students develop portfolios, the process enables each student to be noticed for the level of products he or she produces. In this mannner, portfolios increase inclusion instead of exclusion by providing multiple opportunities for children from every population to demonstrate talents and potential. Portfolios allow schools to honor the diversity of students and discover the strengths of each learner.

[5] See Chapter 3 for further discussion.

Kingore, B. (2005). *Assessment,* 3rd ed. Austin: Professional Associates Publishing.

Student-Managed Portfolios

TEACHER PRODUCT SELECTION

Who writes the reflection when teachers require a specific product to be included in every students' portfolio? It is not authentic for students to write the caption because they did not make the choice. What might students write for a caption? *I put this in my portfolio because my teacher said I had to.* An option most teachers find helpful is to use a teacher

portfolio caption form, such as Figure 2.7. A teacher fills in the date, product, and a statement explaining the significance of the portfolio item choice. The teacher's reflection is then photocopied so each student can staple a copy to his or her product. On the bottom of the form, the student them adds a response about the product or the selection. The teacher selection form clarifies the reason for the product being selected and clearly signals to parents and others who view the portfolio which items are teacher-selected.

SELECTION CRITERIA CHARTS

Criteria charts are lists of criteria for selecting portfolio products. Post it in the classroom for students and visitors to reference. As students review several pieces of their work and ponder which product to select for entry into their portfolio, the criteria chart

Figure 2.7: TEACHER PRODUCT SELECTION

STUDENT _Martha_   DATE _September 5_
PRODUCT _Math Repeated Tasks: Problem Solving_

Why I feel this product is significant: _It will document your growth in computational skills and problem solving over time. It also gives you the opportunity to demonstrate analytical skills in your reflection of each product._

STUDENT RESPONSE: _I liked choosing my own kind of math problems to work. I tried hard to complete a more complex problem._

Figure 2.7: TEACHER PRODUCT SELECTION

STUDENT _____ DATE _____

PRODUCT _____

Why I feel this product is significant: _____
_____
_____
_____

STUDENT RESPONSE: _____
_____
_____
_____

helps them focus on specific criteria. This process helps students develop their ability to monitor and evaluate their own achievements and goals.

To develop a criteria chart, post a large sheet of chart paper or poster board on the wall. Write a title and a leading sentence prompt on the chart. Then, while discussing selection criteria with students, record ideas on the chart in the vocabulary expressed by the students.

Do not attempt to complete the chart at one time. Higher levels of responses will emerge as students become aware of many ways to think about and evaluate their work. Within a few weeks, the class can have a criteria chart which has great value because of their ownership in the process.

The following criteria charts are examples to model the collection process in a kindergarten and a middle school class. Every

criteria chart should be unique to the specific classroom and reflect the vocabulary and priorities of the class.

Criteria charts are one way to guide students toward writing more thoughtful captions. When students too frequently use simple response traps such as *I like it* or *I got a 100 on it,* ask them to look over the criteria chart, choose another criterion, and add that idea to their caption.

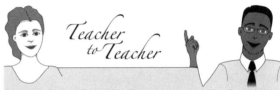

As you record a criteria statement on the chart, add the initials of the student who suggested that idea. Those initials serve to recognize the

Criteria Chart: *Kindergarten Class*

I will put in my portfolio:
- Important papers
- Things I learned
- Things I like doing
- Pictures I make
- My stories
- Hard problems I figure out
- Things I am proud of

Carrie   Matthew   Jenny   Courtney   Deborah
Jason   Sherri   Cody   Sarah   Josh
Jonathan   Aria   Jack   Wendy
Aaron   Hillary   Charles   Shannon   Tomás

I AM LEARNING SO MUCH!

Criteria Chart: *Middle School*

These are significant questions to think about as I select products for my portfolio.

- How I am changing as a learner
- How my work is improving
- What I did well; why it turned out so well
- What I like to do and why I like to do it
- What was hard for me; why it was hard
- What I want to keep working on
- Which product shows I have mastered a required skill
- What I'm proud of
- Which products are important for my future classes

J.S.   Z.T.   H.S.   J.B.   W.L.   A.M.   O.P.
P.B.   L.A.

Student-Managed Portfolios

Kingore, B. (2005). *Assessment,* 3rd ed. Austin: Professional Associates Publishing.

student for a strong idea and increases the motivation for others to add thoughtful responses.

PORTFOLIO SELECTION BULLETIN BOARD

A bulletin board is a useful component in the portfolio selection process. It can help organize the process as it provides a show-case for the products students select. By using the bulletin board, teachers do not have to wonder if everyone appropriately completed the selection process. One glance at the bul-letin board confirms that everyone is finished or indicates who may need assistance. In self-contained classes, this bulletin board changes every week and celebrates students' work. In departmentalized classes, alternate use of the board to highlight different class sections. Students enjoy seeing what peers in other class sections have done.

Preparation. Use a bulletin board that is available all year for portfolio products. Put a light colored backing on the board and add a border if you prefer. Then, use different colors of construction paper or yarn and a sta-pler to divide the board into boxes, enough for the number of students you have in your class or in one section. Put one student's name in each box. Add a caption, such as *Portfolio Parade*.

Application. After students have selected and captioned a product for their portfolio, they post it in their box on the board. Students use self-adhering plastic clips, push pins, clothes pins, or staples to post their work. When it is time to select new products, students take down and file the posted prod-uct in their portfolio before choosing the next product to display. In this manner, the bulletin board remains up all year yet changes every week. It is student-centered instead of teacher-decorated.

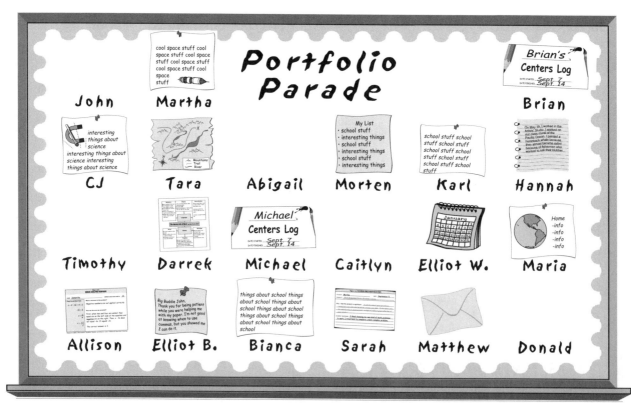

Kingore, B. (2005). *Assessment,* 3rd ed. Austin: Professional Associates Publishing.

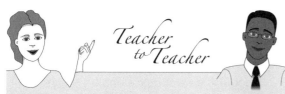

Organization is an issue with kindergarteners and special needs students. If it is too complicated at first for these students to take down and file their work, just staple the new selected product on top of last week's selection. Every reporting period, take them down for students to file as a packet in their portfolio.

Repeated tasks are an excellent preassessment tool when the tasks directly relate to the skills and concepts students are to know by the end of the year. Students complete the task the first time to provide information for the teacher regarding levels of readiness and learning needs. Prior knowledge and skill levels are particularly evident from these assessments. That beginning repeated task is filed in the portfolio. Later, the task is repeated one or more times and the results compared to document growth and continued learning needs.

ASSESSMENT TECHNIQUES THAT DOCUMENT STUDENT GROWTH

One value of portfolios is their potential to concretely demonstrate student growth over time. Many students are more motivated to excel or try harder when they see their improvements for themselves. Repeated tasks and triplets are two assessment techniques that specifically demonstrate student growth.

REPEATED TASKS

Repeated tasks simply make systematic a technique that great teachers have always

used. Repeated tasks are learning experiences that students complete at one point in time and then later complete again to note gains in skills or achievemennt. Pre-tests and post-tests are traditional examples of repeated tasks. In portfolio processes, incorporate several repeated tasks that enable students, parents, and teachers to clearly see growth.

Initially, survey your learning standards to determine the skills students must demonstrate by the end of the year. Then, plan and implement learning tasks for students to complete that incorporate those skills. Students complete these tasks early in the year and then two or more additional times to document growth and achievement gains over time. Any learning experience appropriate to your curriculum is a potential repeated task. Listed below are several examples of effective repeated tasks for a variety of grade levels and relating to diverse learning profiles.

Three-Minute Celebrations
After completing a repeated task for a second time, students get out both tasks to compare and contrast. In approximately a three-minute celebration of learning, students are encouraged to talk with a classmate about what they notice and how they feel they are changing as a learner.

Kindergarten-Grade One
Each child:
- Draws a picture of self, family, or where the child lives (not limited to a house) with dictation or the child's written explanation.
- Retells a folk tale or story on an audio or video tape.
- Produces a fine-motor sample by tracing one hand and cutting it out.

Kingore, B. (2005). *Assessment,* 3rd ed. Austin: Professional Associates Publishing.

Student-Managed Portfolios

- Completes a *Look What I Can Do* book-- half-page books in which students demon- strate their levels of skills applications relating to learning standards. Each half page provides a required learning stan- dard, such as writing an original math story problem, the letters of the alphabet, or all of the geometric shapes they can draw.[6]

Elementary Grades

Each student:

- Draws a picture of family with sentences written by the child about the family.
- Produces a handwriting sample by writing content that includes every letter of the alphabet. For example, Figure 2.8 shares a brief response spaced for primary hand- writing, and Figure 2.9 provides a longer response spaced for intermediate hand- writing. Linda Coffman and Jo Hackenbracht, teachers in Urbana, Ohio, shared a third example sentence: *If you just mix apples, berries, and grapes with poppy seeds, you can have a quick, zippy salad.*
- Writes and completes the hardest math story problem the student knows how to solve that applies current math operations and concepts currently being studied.
- Completes a literacy and vocabulary task by writing the most important words the student knows in five minutes.
- Assesses spelling mastery based upon a list of 100 to 500 high-frequency words.
- Composes writing samples, possibly focusing on different types of writing, such as narrative, persuasive, or expository. The writing prompt or writing topic does not need to be the same each time.
- Draws a map of where the student lives. The student is encouraged to include as many details and as much specific infor- mation as possible.
- Writes the five most significant facts the student knows about a science, math, or social studies topic.

- Duplicates reading samples of fiction and nonfiction showing the student's independ- ent reading level.
- Records a reading sample documenting the student's independent reading level.

Older students initially date and complete a repeated task using one color ink. Later, the second task is dated and completed on the same paper using a second color ink as the student embellishes, deletes, and corrects any items on the initial work. The change in color accents growth. Additional colors can be used over time expanding the original response.

At the beginning of the year, have students design the front of their portfolio container and date their work. At the end of the year, they design the back of their container and date it. Now the portfolio design becomes one more repeated task without extra materials.

Middle School and High School

Each student:

- Draws a map for geography or social studies before and after studying that location or fills in details on an appropriate blank map.
- Completes a literacy and vocabulary task by writing for five minutes the most impor- tant words the student knows related to the course or topic.
- Assesses spelling based upon a list of 100 to 500 high-frequency words or words spe- cific to this course or topic.
- Creates a concept map organizing the

---

[6] See Chapter 3 for a sample *Look What I Can Do* book and additional repeated tasks for young children.

Kingore, B. (2005). *Assessment,* 3rd ed. Austin: Professional Associates Publishing.

Figure 2.8: HANDWRITING

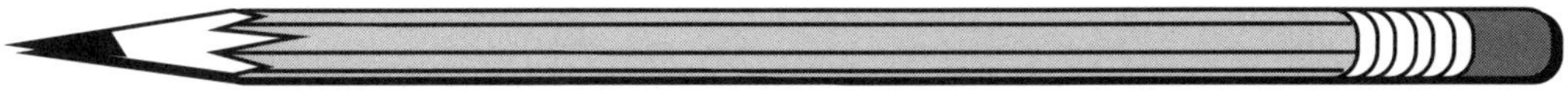

The quick, brown fox jumps over the lazy dog.

NAME _____ DATE _____

NAME _____ DATE _____

Kingore, B. (2005). *Assessment,* 3rd ed. Austin: Professional Associates Publishing.

Figure 2.9: HANDWRITING

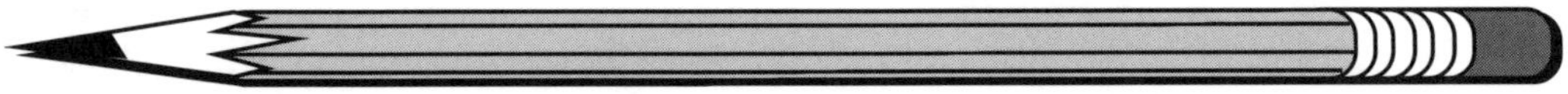

This is just one example of how my writing is very neat and legible. I am quickly developing into an amazing writer!

NAME _____ DATE _____

NAME _____ DATE _____

concepts and relationships known at the beginning and the end of a topic or a reporting period.

- Writes and completes the hardest math story problem the student knows that applies current math concepts and processes.
- Composes writing samples, possibly focusing on different types of writing, such as narrative, persuasive, or expository. Periodically, each student rereads the samples and writes a compare/contrast essay reflecting upon the changes in the student's writing and which class experiences or personal efforts have been the greatest influence on the student's writing.
- Poses definitions of vocabulary or key terms related to a specific topic.
- Develops written explanations of how to complete a process, such as a science experiment or math problem.
- Incorporates learning logs in math, science, and history.
- Draws a flow chart of a process or sequence.
- Records a video tape showing and explaining a history fair or science fair entry.

Teacher to Teacher

Here are two suggestions for simplifying the use of repeated tasks.

1. Put repeated tasks in a plain manila folder. Store it in front of the portfolio container so these tasks are easier to find for repeated completions.
2. Use colored paper to accent repeated tasks. Have the second completion of that task done on the back of the same page to make the comparisons of growth more obvious.

AUDIO AND VIDEO TAPING

ORAL READING

Audio or video tapes are useful for repeated tasks with fiction or nonfiction text to concretely demonstrate students' oral reading progress over time. Reading samples are periodically recorded by students and then compared to determine students' progress. Each student uses the Taping Log to keep a record of the recordings. This process enables the teacher and student to analyze the patterns of the student's response to text in decoding, construction of meaning, fluency, vocabulary, and the complexity of the reading material.

> ### TAPING LOG
>
> NAME _____
>
> DATE _____ TAPE # _____
> TITLE _____
> Content:
>
>
>
>
> DATE _____ TAPE # _____
> TITLE _____
> Content:
>
>
>
>
>
> Kingore, B & Kingore, J. (2004). *Centers in Minutes, Volume 1.* Austin: Professional Associates Publishing.

Time

- Allow approximately three minutes for each recording.
- An egg timer works well for simple time management.

Kingore, B. (2005). *Assessment,* 3rd ed. Austin: Professional Associates Publishing.

Prompts

> **FICTION TEXT**
> - *Read the whole book if it can be read in three minutes.*
> - *Choose a significant event or key part of the story you will read to read to a classmate.*
> - *Choose a favorite part of the story to read.*
> - *Read the turning point of the book.*
>
> **NONFICTION**
> - *Prepare and record several excerpts which reveal the most significant concepts.*
> - *Read excerpts that denote the main ideas of this material.*
> - *Focus on reading excerpts from the beginning, middle, and end of the text to organize a summary of the topic.*

MATH STORY PROBLEMS

Many students have difficulty understanding and computing story problems from a math book. To apply the process, students use audio or video tapes for repeated tasks with math manipulatives. Periodically, ask students to create and record story problems related to the concepts or operations currently being studied. The student uses the a taping log to keep a record of the recordings. This process enables students to approach story problems as an author instead of a consumer so they better understand the structure of the problems. Many students benefit from creating their own story problems as a guide that transfers to other published story problems.

Time
- Encourage extensive thinking by not timing students' planning.

- Allow approximately three minutes to record each story problem.
- An egg timer works well for simple time management.

Prompts

> - *Using these plastic dinosaurs, create three different story problems that result in the number nine.*
> - *Use these circle fraction tiles to create two different story problems about groups of people trying to share one pizza.*
> - *Use this button collection to create three different story problems that discuss the ratio of one kind of button to other kinds of buttons.*

A videotape is an excellent way to record large displays. After the science fair or history fair, for example, allow students to videotape their display as they briefly explain their main ideas. A timer can be used to encourage students to carefully plan what they want to include on the recording.

Ask students to bring a videotape from home for school recordings. The same tape becomes a School Life Video and can be used for several years if recorded segments are kept to a brief recording time. Parents are very excited about the school life videos!

Kingore, B. (2005). *Assessment,* 3rd ed. Austin: Professional Associates Publishing.

TRIPLETS

The triplet technique developed in response to a problem experienced by many teachers and students when using the portfolio to conference with parents. Often, the parents became so interested in the portfolio that they wanted to discuss every product. That process took more time than typically planned for parent conferences or student-involved conferences. Thus, the teacher and/or student needs to preplan which products to accent in a parent conference rather than attempt to review the entire portfolio.

A triplet is three products that the student or teacher selects from the student's portfolio in advance of the conference. The purpose of the triplet is to demonstrate the main instructional point that the parent needs to understand. For example, a product from the beginning, middle, and end of the year are selected to substantiate the student's growth throughout the year. Or, three products typical of the special needs or behaviors that the student is demonstrating are selected. During the conference, the teacher or student uses the triplet to focus the interactive discussion. They should also inform the parent about other scheduled times when students can share their portfolios with their family so the portfolio can be reviewed more often than just during a conference

Triplet Examples

PRIMARY AND ELEMENTARY
Three products are selected by the teacher to focus on a significant instructional point about a student's achievements.

UPPER ELEMENTARY, MIDDLE SCHOOL, AND HIGH SCHOOL
Each student chooses three products to respond to the questions: *What should your portfolio tell me about your achievements?*

What products can you use to show an employer your special talents and skills?

When products are taken out of the portfolio, someone has to refile them, and it is often difficult to get them back in exactly the same place. Before conferencing with a particular item, avoid the refiling problem by using a sticky note as a flag on the edge of that selected product. Now the teacher or student can quickly turn to each product when ready to discuss it and never take it out of the storage sequence.

Portfolios are not collections of best works. They are documentations of learning.

FROM TEACHER TO TEACHER: WORDS OF EXPERIENCE

Teachers across the nation shared advice, support, and ideas for simplicity. This section presents a composite of some of the most frequent suggestions from teachers in elementary through high school who implemented portfolios and authentic assessment.

One surprise for me is how few discipline problems I have encountered. In each of the three years I have used portfolios, I believe my

Student-Managed Portfolios

Kingore, B. (2005). *Assessment,* 3rd ed. Austin: Professional Associates Publishing.

students felt more successful because they were able to see the changes in their own learning. That truly motivates them to try harder, and they spend less time off-task in class.

Portfolios are a self-esteem boost for the special-needs students in my inclusion class. They see they are doing better each time we review the portfolio products.

I assess portfolio products to assure that a level of depth and complexity is reached that is appropriate for my advanced-level students. Their products can demonstrate and document all their areas of giftedness.

We began by collecting work for seven weeks before we stopped to have students select items for their portfolios. We were avoiding the selection process because we were not sure what we were doing. But waiting that long produced a gigantic mess! Our message to teachers is to plan your portfolio system and put your whole organization system to work from the start.

Rather than feel as if you have to do it all, plan for the year and set realistic goals for yourself according to your level of experience with portfolios (beginner, intermediate, or advanced).

I've learned that students inevitably achieve at higher levels when they are aware of the assessment criteria before they begin the assignment.

Conferences are more successful when students are prepared for the questions to be discussed during the conference. Give students a sample of questions to think about prior to conference time so they have time to reflect.

Our team found out that goal setting, product selection, and reflection did not get done by the students or teachers if we did not schedule

it. We had to set aside specific times to address those issues.

Use rolling files for students' accessibility to portfolios in your classroom. They can be moved easily about the room as needed.

Authentic assessment has significantly influenced the way I teach. I find myself watching more intently and informally questioning students more about their process.

When students survey their collection of work to select a piece for their portfolio, you get a clear view of your teaching priorities and the kinds of learning tasks you've been providing. I'm a better teacher because I am using the portfolio for my assessment, too.

Authentic assessment has taught me to trust students more. They really do care about succeeding when the learning experiences are relevant and when they understand how to be successful.

Keep all of the supplies most often needed for portfolios, such as a stapler, date stamp, scissors, and forms, in a central area or with your portfolio filing system.

I think one of the most amazing things to me was how supportive the parents have been. They seem really impressed with what their kids know about their own learning.

Most of our first year, we just kept worrying if we were doing it all right. Our advice is to relax and learn along with the students what parts work best in your classes.

Kingore, B. (2005). *Assessment,* 3rd ed. Austin: Professional Associates Publishing.

• CHAPTER 3 •

Assessing Young Children

There is always one moment in childhood when the door opens and lets the future in.

—Graham Greene

Assessment of young children is most valid in learning environments where they are actively engaged in authentic learning tasks. Assessment techniques must be customized to developmentally appropriate options. Effective and efficient methods of assessment and evaluation of young learners include analytical observation, student-managed portfolios, and rubrics that simplify the required level of reading and writing.

ANALYTICAL OBSERVATION

Primary teachers understand the importance of classroom observation. Since young children are more limited in their verbal ability to explain their learning and in their written ability to express themselves, teachers continually analyze children's behaviors to interpret what they see occurring in learning situations. Observations during authentic learning experiences enable primary teachers to formulate and substantiate students' strengths and needs. Analytical observation helps define children's prior knowledge, levels of

development, acquired proficiencies, learning needs, and the multiple facets of their talents and potential.

Observation is a valued preassessment tool. It helps guide teachers' decisions regarding the most appropriate instructional pace for specific children and at which levels to initiate instruction.

Analytical observation enables teachers to assess the *process* of children's learning as well as the products they produce. Particularly with young children, the process of learning reveals much about their level of understanding. In fact, there are times when the process is as important as the product in assessing children's achievements and learning needs.

As teachers observe, they verbally interact with their children to elicit the children's

Kingore, B. (2005). *Assessment,* 3rd ed. Austin: Professional Associates Publishing.

perceptions of learning. Numerous inquiry probes, such as *Tell me about your picture*, enable teachers to gain information as children are engaged in learning situations. Examples of inquiry probes effective with young children are included in Chapter 7, *Open-ended Techniques*. The values of analytical observation, what teachers attempt to observe, and how to document observations to share with others are additional aspects of observation explored in Chapter 7.

STUDENT-MANAGED PORTFOLIOS

The objective with prekindergarten, kindergarten, and first-grade students is to initiate the portfolio process by having students save and file work to celebrate their learning achievements.

Portfolios for this age group can be relatively small and yet provide a tremendous source of pride for children and families. Plan about a one-fourth to one-half inch thickness as the total size per portfolio for the year. Young children produce fewer paper products since much of the learning completed by this age group is process oriented. Thus, the teacher simply plans to select one product every two or three weeks to have children file in their portfolios as documentation of the fantastic growth and changes in the abilities of these children.

INTRODUCING THE PROCESS TO YOUNG CHILDREN

Make portfolios as concrete as possible to enable the children to understand what portfolios are and become excited about creating their own. Show them a portfolio book from last year's class or put together a collection of children's work to create a mock-up of how their portfolios may look. Explain to them that they will take many papers home to show

PORTFOLIO OBJECTIVES

1. **Develop students' feelings of self-worth.**
   When young children review their portfolios, they see products to compare over time and they realize that their skills have increased. They feel important and successful.

2. **Teach young children to file their portfolio products.**
   Typically, young children are not organized. Organization and management are valued life skills they have to learn over time. A simple but clearly structured portfolio system models for students how to organize, manage, and maintain their work.

3. **Use repeated tasks to document learning standards, growth, and achievements of each student.**
   Repeated tasks document learning standards by substantiating children's increased integration of concepts and skills over time.[7]

4. **Document special learning needs.**
   The work students produce exemplifies their learning needs and is useful to compare with standardized evaluations. Open-ended portfolio products substantiate the level of concepts and skills attained by young students with fewer skills, students on grade level, students with learning differences, and students who would benefit from extended learning opportunities.

Objectives

---

[7] Chapter 9 includes examples of procedures that directly relate learning standards to student reflections.

Kingore, B. (2005). *Assessment,* 3rd ed. Austin: Professional Associates Publishing.

their family but keep a few papers at school to combine into a wonderful book to amaze their family at the end of the year.

Have an adult visitor such as a parent or the principal talk with the class about how wonderful it will be to have this portfolio book at the end of the year. Discuss together how the children can look back through their portfolios when they are older and remember this year of school and the great things they learned.

While some teachers successfully involved young children in the selection process from the start, other teachers reported that prekindergarten and kindergarten children had difficulty making selections and dictating

captions early in the year. They also noted that, because of the age of the children, the time it took to complete the selection and reflection process was excessive. Thus, many teachers experienced in the portfolio process with very young children suggest that the teacher instead of the children initially determines which products go in the portfolios.

Teachers also reported that many parents did not initially understand the instructional objectives inherent in the products young students complete. To compensate for this

Figure 3.1: TEACHER PRODUCT SELECTION

NAME: Joan _____   DATE: _____

The task was _to draw a picture of your family and tell me about the picture._

The skills demonstrated by this task were:
- _Fine motor coordination_   · _Awareness of features_
- _Vocabulary_   · _____
- _Sentence structure_   · _____

Kingore, B. (2005). *Assessment*, 3rd ed. Austin: Professional Associates Publishing.

Figure 3.1: TEACHER PRODUCT SELECTION

NAME: _____   DATE: _____

The task was _____

_____

_____

_____

_____

The skills demonstrated by this task were:

- _____   · _____

- _____   · _____

- _____   · _____

Kingore, B. (2005). *Assessment,* 3rd ed. Austin: Professional Associates Publishing.

lack of understanding, it is recommended that teachers complete a Teacher Product Selection caption, such as Figure 3.1, and duplicate it for students to staple on their product. This process enables parents to understand the learning task and skills represented within that product.

After the teacher has selected a product to save in the portfolio, the children write their names on the caption strips. Any stage of scribbling or creative spelling can communicate that child's name as long as it is recognizable to the child! The children's ability to write their names on the teacher selection caption serves as another repeated task since their writing growth will be obvious as the year progresses. If not already on the product, children also need to write the date to record when the product was completed. A date stamp is easily used, or most children can copy the number for the date if it is provided for them on the chalkboard.

WHICH PRODUCTS BEST DOCUMENT YOUNG STUDENTS' ABILITIES?

A portfolio is an integral reflection of what children learn rather than artificial activities and isolated skills. Attention to meaningful learning tasks is a crucial consideration in selecting products. Many preschool and primary teachers voice concern about what to put in portfolios because so much of their children's learning does not result in a paper and pencil product. Figure 3.2: Examples of Portfolio Products is meant to prompt ideas of the wide range of products appropriate for young children's portfolios. It is not inclusive of all kinds of work which could be selected.

REPEATED TASKS THAT ACCENT STUDENT GROWTH

Preschool and primary teachers need specific products in portfolios that concretely demonstrate students' growth or change in skills and achievements over time. Several repeated tasks are discussed in this chapter as elaborations of tasks listed in Chapter 2. To maximize the value of a repeated task, the task must first be completed early in the year and then repeated later. The contrast of the two or three repetitions demonstrates the students' growth to the children, parents, and other educators.

Repeated tasks are an excellent preassessment tool. Students complete tasks the first time to provide information to the teacher regarding levels of readiness and learning needs. Background knowledge, beginning literacy, and fine motor coordination are particularly evident from these assessments. These beginning repeated tasks are filed in the portfolio. Later, each task is repeated one or more times and the results compared to document growth and continued learning needs.

THREE-MINUTE CELEBRATIONS
After completing a repeated task, children get out both tasks to compare. In approximately a three-minute celebration, students are encouraged to tell one other person what they notice and how they feel about the two products.

Child's self portrait
Each child draws a picture of self. In classrooms with a wide range of readiness levels, these portraits run from scribbles to fairly refined human figures. When completed at the beginning and the end of the year, this product illustrates the child's development of fine motor skills and self-image.

Kingore, B. (2005). *Assessment,* 3rd ed. Austin: Professional Associates Publishing.

Figure 3.2: EXAMPLES OF PORTFOLIO PRODUCTS

PRODUCT	EXPLANATION	PURPOSE
Art	Art pieces should include the child's natural, creative explorations and interpretations (rather than crafts).	Art reflects developmental levels, interests, graphic talents, abstract thinking, and creativity.
Audio tapes	A child tapes story retellings, explanations of concepts, philosophical viewpoints, musical creations, problem solutions, and ideas.	Audio tapes verify vocabulary, fluency, creativity, high-order thinking, and concept depth.
Computer products	Document computer skills through applications of software, word processing products, and programs created by the child.	Computer-generated products indicate computer literacy, analysis, content-related academic skills, and applied concepts.
Dictations	Write a child's dictated explanation of a product or process. Prompt these dictations with statements such as: *Tell me about your work,* or *Tell me how you did that.*	Dictations increase adults' understanding of the why and how of what children do. It may indicate vocabulary levels, high-level thinking, fluency, and content depth.
Graphs or charts	Some children produce graphs or charts to represent relationships, formulate problems, illustrate math solutions, and demonstrate the results of independent investigations.	Graphs or charts demonstrate specific skills or concepts applied in the task, high-level thinking, data recording strategies, and organizational skills.
Photographs	Photograph the child's math patterns, creative projects, dioramas, sculptures, constructions, experiments, models, or organizational systems.	Photographs represent three-dimensional products. They provide a record when no paper product is feasible.
Reading level	Duplicate one or two examples of text that a child reads independently. Include the child's reflection of the book to demonstrate analysis skills.	Text samples help document reading level and a child's sophistication when interpreting written material.
Research	Students' interests often result in information and expertise in one or more areas. Share examples of the independent studies pursued by the child.	Research products reveal specific interests, synthesis, content depth, and complexity of a learner's thinking.
Video tape	Video tapes are wonderful ways to document performing arts, a child's learning process, and oversized products. Limit tape entries to three to five minutes to encourage the child to plan the presentation.	A video presents a significant visual record and integration of skills and behaviors. When recording group interactions, a video can demonstrate interpersonal and leadership skills.
Written products	Provide examples of original works written by a child, including stories, reports, scientific observations, poems, or reflections.	Written products can demonstrate language skills, thinking, organization, meaning construction, concept depth, and complexity.

Adapted from: Kingore, B., Ed. (2002). *Reading Strategies for Advanced Primary Readers.*
Austin: Texas Education Agency.

Assessing Young Children

Kingore, B. (2005). *Assessment,* 3rd ed. Austin: Professional Associates Publishing.

Family portrait

Each child illustrates a picture portraying the members of his or her family. These pictures indicate the children's awareness of their surrounding environment and knowledge of their family member's individual identity. It also helps teachers to understand more about each child's home environment and who they consider to be a member of their family, even when it includes a favorite pet!

Picture interest inventory

Fold large pieces of paper in half in order to create two drawing areas on each sheet. On one half, ask students to draw pictures of their favorite things; on the second half, they illustrate what they are interested in learning at school. Write their dictation for each of their drawings, and incorporate the information in instructional planning, e.g., extend the unit on zoo animals to include bones and fossils because several children are interested in bones. (For very young children or those with shorter attention spans, each half may be completed at a different time. Simply fold the paper so only the half they are to draw on is exposed.)

Audio tape the retelling of a folk tale

Individually, using each student's personal audio tape, record the child retelling a well-known folk tale such as *The Three Little Pigs*. This process takes only a couple of minutes for each child, and the product is a fascinating measurement of oral language development when the same folk tale is recorded at the beginning and then again at the end of the year. Begin each entry on the tape by stating the date and the task: *Today is September 27, and Jasmine is going to tell the story of 'The Three Little Pigs'.*

Drawing of geometric shapes

Provide paper folded into fourths. Dictate a different shape for each child to draw in each of the four boxes to measure fine motor skills, awareness of shapes, and readiness for writing between lines. Including geometric shapes incorporates the same fine motor skills and directionality that is needed to print letters and numerals.

Look What I Can Do books

Using copies of the blank bottom half of Figure 3.3, list on each page a different skill that you want children to demonstrate. Review your learning standards and focus on the skills students are to learn by the end of the year, such as alphabet letters, words, numerals, math story problems, and geometric shapes. The top half of Figure 3.3 becomes the title page when the book is stapled together. Children enjoy making these books and look forward to repeating the task. Plan for children to complete the book at the beginning, middle, and end of the year to document skills and achievements.

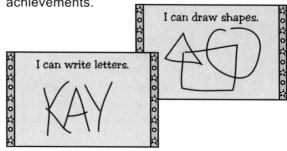

TEACHING YOUNG STUDENTS TO FILE AND MANAGE PORTFOLIOS

Even four-year olds can successfully file their own products when teachers organize portfolios in a developmentally-appropriate manner. A plastic crate with hanging files is a great choice for portfolios that young children manage. On each hanging file, write a child's name and staple that child's photograph to the portfolio so it extends above the top of the file and is easily seen. Using photographs on each file allows young children to file their own work in their portfolio even if they can not recognize their written names. It is fascinating how much children enjoy completing their own filing; apparently it makes them feel important and grown up.

Figure 3.3: LOOK WHAT I CAN DO

Look what I can do!

by

_____

Date _____

Kingore, B. (2005). *Assessment,* 3rd ed. Austin: Professional Associates Publishing.

Assessing Young Children

If student photographs are needed, a digital camera is the easiest means of develping these photos. However, if one is not available, limit the expense of the photographs by using a panoramic camera with film that allows you to include three to five children in one close-up photograph. After the film is developed, create a template pattern so the cut-out size of each child's head will be the same on each portfolio.

Small photographs are more durable when glued or stapled to a popsicle stick and each stick stapled to a hanging file so the photo extends above the top of the file.

Young students' manage their own filing best when the products in the portfolios are organized chronologically. Teach children to slide the products forward in their portfolio file forward each time and then place their newest selections in the back of their portfolio. By filing in the back, the portfolio remains generally in chronological order. Furthermore, each time students file a product, they see their earlier work. This becomes a concrete reminder of the students' learning. (Young children especially benefit from being able to clearly view their progress over time.)

Role play filing papers into a portfolio so young children can see how it is done. Model sliding the products forward in the file to make room to place the newest work in the back of the folder. Ham up how important filing is. Accent that the children will be filing papers just as older students and adults file their work.

 -

Figure 3.4: PORTFOLIO CAPTION STRIP

Dear Family,

We are making a portfolio of my work. We will add new things to it all year. Today, I filed my first paper in my portfolio. This is how I feel.

Love,

Kingore, B. (2005). *Assessment,* 3rd ed. Austin: Professional Associates Publishing.

Create an atmosphere of celebration when it is time to file the first products for the portfolios. It is fun to shake hands and congratulate children as they file their first papers. Prepare simple notes such as Figure 3.4 to send home and demonstrate to students' families this important beginning. Provide a copy of the note for each child; students draw their faces to show how they feel and then write their names at the bottom of the note.

INCREASING YOUNG STUDENTS' ROLE IN PORTFOLIO MANAGEMENT

When appropriate in the kindergarten or first grade year, increase children's thinking and ownership in the portfolio process by introducing choice and reflection. One approach is to collect two products for each child. Meet with the children, usually in small groups but individually if preferred, and state a simple criterion, e.g., *something you liked doing.* Ask each child to choose one of the products to file in their portfolio. Provide a simple caption card, such as one of the four samples on Figure 3.6, that states the criterion. Encourage children to write their names on the duplicated caption card and staple it to their product while they wait turns filing products.

The four sample caption cards should be duplicated, cut apart, and used one at a time. The cards allow a comfortable space for children to write their names or a sentence reflection without worrying about exact letter formation between the handwriting lines. The picture prompts on each card help children comprehend and remember what the criterion states.

A second version of caption cards combines cutting and pasting skills with students' reflections (Figure 3.7). Students are given one strip of faces and asked to cut out the face that shows how they feel about their work. Students then paste that face on a caption card.

Teacher to Teacher

Avoid using *best work* as a criterion for prekindergarten through first grade students. It is very value-laden; and young children are generally not ready to compare or contrast to determine what is best. The term *best work* leads children to ask adults what *they* think is best or to only select products with high grades on them. Children react more comfortably to criteria such as those listed in the captions in this chapter.

In kindergarten and first-grade, captioning can be used as a language arts activity during the week when selection occurs. At a teacher-directed center, the teacher works with one group each day and writes those children's dictations. The teacher prompts children's thinking with inquiry probes and statements.[8]

Tell me about your work.
Tell me more so I understand your ideas.
What was your favorite part?
What did you think was easy to do?
What was the hardest thing to do?

As the teacher takes dictations from one student, the others can complete an indepenent task or work with manipulatives. Thus, the teacher is able to individualize instruction and complete four to six reflections each day instead of trying to work with a whole class at one time.

Some children are certainly capable of using temporary or inventive spelling to write their own captions. Use the caption strips in Figures 3.5 and 3.6 and encourage those children to write their reason for selecting

---

[8] Additional inquiry prompts for young children are included in Chapter 6.

Kingore, B. (2005). *Assessment,* 3rd ed. Austin: Professional Associates Publishing.

Figure 3.5: CAPTIONS: FOUR CAPTION CARDS

NAME _____

DATE _____

I am proud of this!

NAME _____

DATE _____

Aha!

I learned
something new!

NAME _____

DATE _____

I used my brain!

NAME _____

DATE _____

I liked doing this!

Figure 3.6: CAPTIONS: THIS IS HOW I FEEL ABOUT MY WORK

NAME _____

DATE _____

This is how I feel
about my work.

NAME _____

DATE _____

This is how I feel
about my work.

Kingore, B. (2005). *Assessment,* 3rd ed. Austin: Professional Associates Publishing.

a product or what they think is important about their original product. Figures 3.7A and 3.7B are designed flexibly so students can check a response and/or write a response using the handwriting lines or without the handwriting lines. The choice is important because many primary teachers report better success for children when they use caption strips without lines.[9]

Young children get excited about their portfolios and often ask if it is time yet to file more work in their portfolios! Create a small picture symbol for the portfolios, such as the ones shared in the Collection Files section of Chapter 2. Tape that picture on a date on your class calendar to show children when it is time for product selection and filing.

In the first grade, the primary objective is to continue and expand the portfolio process initiated in prekindergarten and kindergarten. Many teachers emphasize the importance of continuing to develop students' self-worth and management skills in organizing and filing their own work. Simultaneously, increase the frequency of students' selections and reflections. By the second half of the year, students should be selecting a portfolio piece every one or two weeks from two or more items they have collected. At this point, children are practicing analysis skills as they think about their work and increase their ownership in the product selection process. Most first graders use simple caption strips to complete a reflection about a product for their portfolios. The teacher can add elaborations dictated by those children not ready to write more than a word or two. Big Buddies can also be used to assist students' captioning.

A PORTFOLIO MANAGEMENT CENTER

Some teachers find it useful to incorporate a portfolio center into the room. The center consists of a small desk or table that stores the portfolios and all the supplies needed to complete additions to portfolios, such as blank caption strips, pencils, and a stapler. A portfolio chart, such as Figure 3.8, guides children so they can complete the process independently.

BIG BUDDIES: OLDER STUDENTS AS FACILITATORS

Big Buddies is the name for a project involving older students interacting in learning situations with younger children to provide the individual attention teachers so desire for their students.[10] Big Buddies can involve a whole classroom of older students or only a few older students at a time working in a classroom of younger students. This project affords useful assessment applications in primary classrooms.

OBSERVATION

As Big Buddies facilitate young students' learning experiences, the teacher is free to oversee the interactions and observe students' skill levels, skill integrations, advanced behaviors, and any special needs.

DOCUMENTATION

As Big Buddies facilitate young students' learning experiences, the teacher writes notes or completes skills checklists to document students' achievements and needs.

PORTFOLIO APPLICATIONS

Modeling
• Big Buddies can show their portfolios to the younger children to make the portfolio

---

[9] The caption forms in Chapter 4 provide additional options to use.
[10] An elaborated discussion of the Big Buddies process is found in Kingore, 2004.

Figure 3.7A: CAPTIONS: CHECK BOXES

NAME _____   DATE _____

I wanted to put this in my portfolio because:
- ❑ I am proud of my work.
- ❑ I took time and thought hard.

Kingore, B. (2005). *Assessment,* 3rd ed. Austin: Professional Associates Publishing.

Figure 3.7B: CAPTIONS: CHECK BOXES

NAME _____   DATE _____

I wanted to put this in my portfolio because:
- ❑ I am proud of my work.
- ❑ I took time and thought hard.

Kingore, B. (2005). *Assessment,* 3rd ed. Austin: Professional Associates Publishing.

Assessing Young Children

Figure 3.8: PORTFOLIO CHART

Portfolio Chart

Remember to:

FILL OUT
- Name
- Date
- Why you chose this product

NAME Michael   DATE Feb. 26
I wanted to put this in my portfolio because:
  ✓ I am proud of my work.
  ✓ I took time and thought hard.
I wrote a funny story.
I used a lot of words.

Kingore, B. (2005). Assessment. 3rd ed. Austin: Professional Associates Publishing.

STAPLE
On the middle of the top of the page

FILE
In back of the other work in your portfolio

Kingore, B. (2005). *Assessment,* 3rd ed. Austin: Professional Associates Publishing.

process more concrete and excite those children about what a final portfolio can become.

- The Big Buddies, working one-on-one or with a small group of younger children, model how to select a product for a portfolio.

Reflection

- Particularly with four and five year olds, Big Buddies write the children's dictations for product captions so the younger children see their ideas expressed in print.

RUBRICS FOR YOUNG CHILDREN

Rubrics are guidelines to quality. They enable teachers to clarify to children what is expected in a learning experience and guide children to understand what to do to reach higher levels of achievement. Rubrics are also grading guides that describe the requirements for levels of proficiency as children respond to a learning task.

Many preschool, kindergarten, and primary teachers do not use rubrics. These teachers may believe that young children can not comprehend assessment and evaluation. However, young children obviously understand grading systems and quickly comprehend that a happy face, *A, 1,* or *Excellent* is what they want on their papers. Even for young children, rubrics take the *guess* work out of grades: *I guess she likes my paper,* or *I guess I didn't do very well.*

Young children benefit when they view the more specific information a rubric offers. With time and modeling, they learn to use rubrics and increase their responsibility for learning.

Effective rubrics are shared with children before they begin the task so they know the teacher's expectations and the characteristics of quality work. Well-constructed rubrics

provide children a clear target for which to aim. Additionally, rubrics are shared with parents and other adults to more clearly communicate achievement standards and the specific skills and growth children accomplish.

At our school, we found that using simple rubrics in kindergarten increased students' high expectations. Teachers in older grades began reporting that children entered their classes expecting to use rubrics and self-assess their work.

CHARACTERISTICS OF RUBRICS FOR YOUNG CHILDREN

Effective rubrics for young children:

- Are short; typically three or four criteria on just one page.
- Reflect the main ideas or most significant elements related to success in a learning task.
- Provide concrete information through pictures and simple language.
- Accompany both higher and lower product examples so children can interpret quality.
- Encourage students' goal-setting and self-evaluation. *I want to do well so I will...*
- Provide children with more information than just a checklist of skills or attributes.
- Enable students and teachers to accurately and consistently identify the level of competency or stage of development.
- Empower teachers with a standard by which to grade students' work more accurately and fairly.

A rubric increases student responsibility for learning as it increases teacher efficiency.

Assessing Young Children

Kingore, B. (2005). *Assessment,* 3rd ed. Austin: Professional Associates Publishing.

A RUBRIC FOR GROUP ASSESSMENT

The Group Assessment form, Figure 3.9, is an example of a simple rubric for children to use to score their effectiveness when completing a group task. The simple words and accompanying illustrations clearly communicate the expectations of group work and are easily used by children to self-evaluate the merits of their accomplishments. The teacher fills in the clock face to concretely show children at what time they are to finish. The criteria on the left signal students what is important as they work. After modeling and guided applications as a class, small groups of children are able to use this rubric independently.

When the task is completed, children check the level they earned--cloudy for a lower level, partly cloudy for a mid-range response, and full sun for a high degree of accomplishment. Letter or number grades can be substituted for the weather scores shown on the example. Then, teachers can use a different color to evaluate on the same form if a grade in the grade book is desired.

Teachers voice surprise at how ably and accurately most young children use rubrics.

THE PICTORIAL RUBRIC GENERATOR

The Pictorial Rubric Generator is a response to teachers' requests for a more concrete and simple way to communicate quality to young children and limited English students. While my original pictorial rubrics used four levels of proficiency, teachers determined during field testing that three levels are more effective when teaching young children to reach assessment decisions. Skim the Pictorial Rubric Generator and other rubrics you have developed to determine the specific criteria crucial to your most typical contents, processes, and products. Photocopy the applicable criteria and levels of proficiencies. Organize those criteria

and degrees of success on the blank rubric page, Figure 3.10, for ease in duplication. Then, rewrite and adapt the criteria as needed before pasting them in place. In this manner, you can readily construct developmentally appropriate rubrics for learning tasks without starting from scratch each time.[11]

Figure 3.11: PICTORIAL RUBRIC GENERATOR

NAME _____ DATE _____
TASK _____

Content	I wrote.	I wrote some things.	I wrote many interesting facts and details.
POINTS:			
Detailed			
POINTS:			
Punctuation and Capitalization	do you hear the dog he is very loud	Do you hear the dog he is very loud.	Do you hear the dog? He is very loud!
POINTS:			
Cooperation			
POINTS:			
TOTAL POINTS: _____			

Kingore, B. & J. (2005). *Assessment Interactive CD-ROM.* Austin: Professional Associates Publishing.

Children and/or teachers can also use a rubric before beginning a segment of instruction to assess their initial level. The same rubric is then used following instruction to evaluate growth and changes in achievements.

---

[11] Further procedures for using rubric generators are discussed in Chapter 6, Rubrics.

Kingore, B. (2005). *Assessment,* 3rd ed. Austin: Professional Associates Publishing.

Figure 3.9: GROUP ASSESSMENT

NAMES _____

_____

_____

_____

DATE _____

TASK:

Did your group?	 ☁	 🌤	 ☀
1. Listen well? 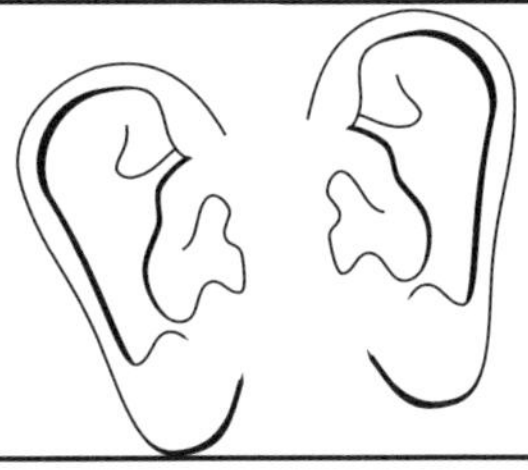			
2. Share? 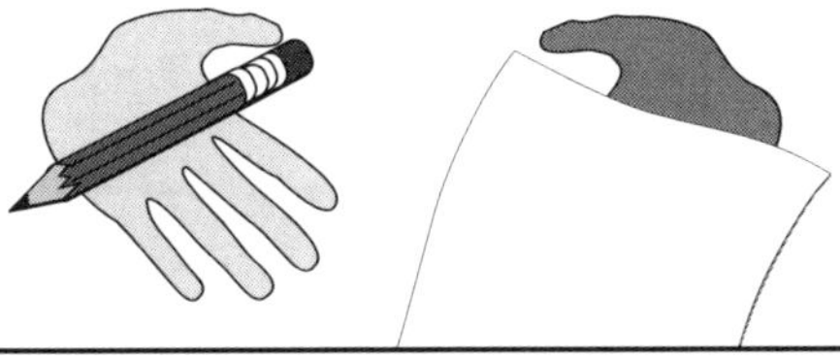			
3. Work together? 			
4. Think of your own ideas? 			
5. Finish on time? 			

Kingore, B. (2005). *Assessment,* 3rd ed. Austin: Professional Associates Publishing.

Figure 3.10: PICTORIAL RUBRIC GENERATOR

NAME _____ DATE _____

TASK _____

Content	I wrote.	I wrote some things.	I wrote many interesting facts and details.
POINTS:			
POINTS:			
POINTS:			
POINTS:			

TOTAL POINTS: _____

Kingore, B. (2005). *Assessment,* 3rd ed. Austin: Professional Associates Publishing.

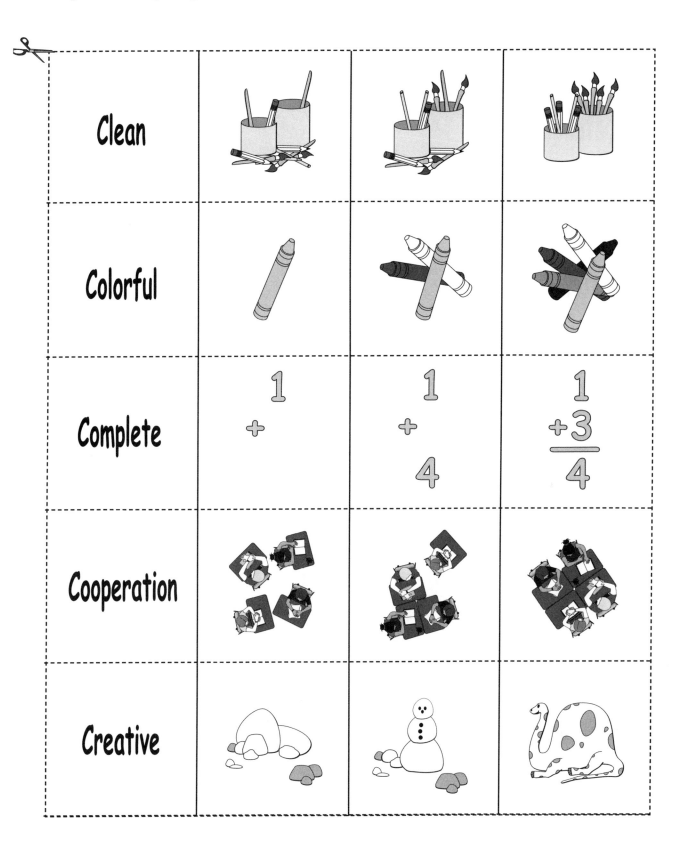

A criterion strip for Content is included as an example on the blank form for the Pictorial Rubric Generator. Use this criterion as it is modeled, rewrite it, or simply paste another criterion over it if content is not one of the criteria selected for the rubric.

Kingore, B. (2005). *Assessment,* 3rd ed. Austin: Professional Associates Publishing.

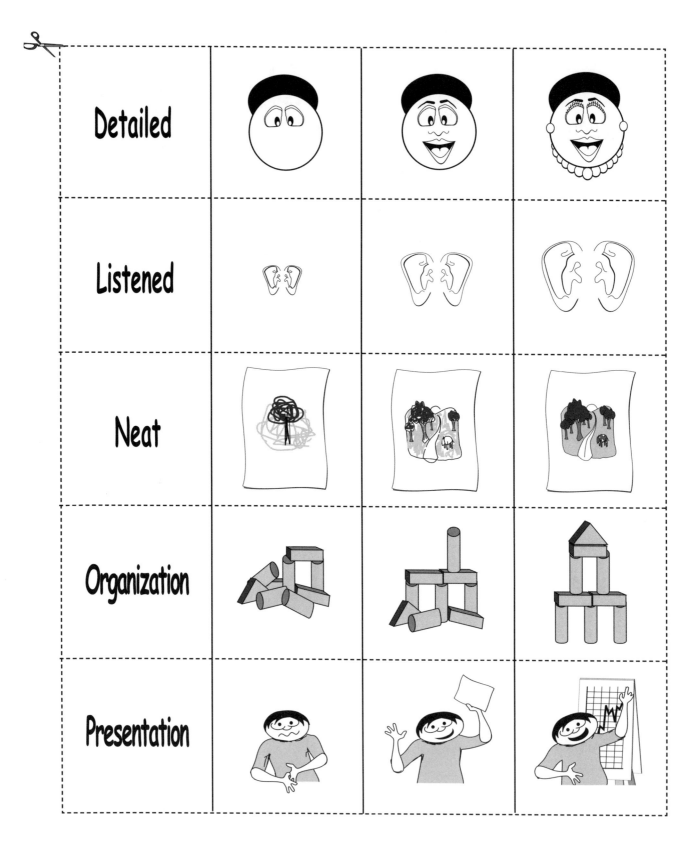

This Pictorial Rubric Generator is intended to serve as a model for developing customized rubrics. If some parts of the Pictorial Rubric Generator are appropriate, add them and rewrite any descriptors that can be better adapted to specific needs.

Kingore, B. (2005). *Assessment,* 3rd ed. Austin: Professional Associates Publishing.

Problem solving			
Punctuation and Capitalization	do you hear the dog he is very loud	Do you hear the dog he is very loud.	Do you hear the dog? He is very loud!
Shared			
Thinking			
Vocabulary	big say look draw write	huge express view sketch record	enormous articulate examine illustrate compose

Enlarge the pictures of the Pictorial Rubric Generator and create a class rubric poster for the wall instead of providing a paper copy for each child. The directions and suggestions for adapting this tool into a poster are shared in Appendix B.

Kingore, B. (2005). *Assessment,* 3rd ed. Austin: Professional Associates Publishing.

FROM TEACHER TO TEACHER: WORDS OF EXPERIENCE

Teachers across the nation shared advice, support, and ideas for simplicity. This section presents a composite of some of the most frequent suggestions from teachers in prekindergarten through first grade who implemented portfolios and authentic assessment.

I never thought kindergartners could do all this. They are so proud of themselves when they file their papers.

Be comfortable hamming it up with your class as you **model** *the importance of rubrics and portfolios. I found that my enthusiasm for the process was infectious to students and parents!*

The more I observe and use open-ended assessments with my students the better I understand them as individuals.

When conferencing with young children, put on a hat, shawl, bangally necklace or crown to signal the other children that you are not to be disturbed.

Tell everyone that picture rubrics work! My kids really took them seriously and worked to **earn** *a grade.*

Rubrics got me lots of recognition from my administrators! They were impressed with how I had woven our districts' standards into rubrics that my students used.[12] I know that the most important value is to the children, but I did love the positive feedback I got about this!

My special education students in my mixed-ability class got a boost from their portfolios. They always smiled when we reviewed their products. They also greatly benefitted when I used more open-ended assessments with them. They could see that different students did it differently and that was still okay. In my classroom, it helped kids get over that idea that everything had only one way to be right.

With our youngest students, we just **begin** *the idea of having a portfolio. Any progress we make in organization, management, and reflection helps next year's teachers further the process.*

Attaching students' photographs to their portfolios was a huge success with my class! It increased their independence and simplified management.

Let young students have a small number of stickers or sticky notes in their collection folder. The students use a sticker to tag a paper they want in their portfolio. Then, they are ready to dictate their reflective caption to a Big Buddy or adult scribe.

Product selection for portfolios worked best with my little ones when we did it in small groups. They enjoyed the more individual attention. I had some children in the small group share their products with each other while I worked with one or two children and wrote captions. After once or twice, it proceeded smoothly and worked well.

Organization worked best when we used legal sized folders with kindergarten children so their larger projects fit. Legal-sized hanging files fit sideways in most plastic-crate file boxes.

Many kindergartners are unable to write captions. If there is a shortage of adults to help write the dictations, an alternative is to make special caption strips by photocopying some of young children's most common responses and add a picture clue to each. Then kindergartners choose and just checked which prepared caption they wanted to use for each selection.

---

[12] See Chapter 9 for examples of rubrics that integrate learning standards and are appropriate for young learners.

Kingore, B. (2005). *Assessment*, 3rd ed. Austin: Professional Associates Publishing.

• CHAPTER 4 •
Metacognitive Responses:
Goal Setting and Reflection

When the mind is thinking, it is talking to itself.
—Plato

METACOGNITION

Metacognition is the gear keeping the assessment process moving meaningfully. It requires students to consciously analyze their thinking processes. Jean Kerr Stenmark[13] noted that the capability and willingness to assess their own progress and learning is one of the greatest gifts students can develop. Those who are able to review their performance, explain the reasons for choosing processes, and identify their next step have a life-long head start.

Metacognition is related to students' ability to transfer knowledge from one situation to another. It involves two basic components[14]:

1. Students' awareness of the processes they need to successfully complete a task, and
2. Students' cognitive monitoring--the ability to determine if the task is being completed correctly and make the corrections as appropriate.

[13]Stenmark, J. (2001).
[14]Baker, L., & Brown, A. (1984).
[15]Cooper, J. (2002).

Use the word *think* or *thinking* often. Words reflect what is important to us, and we surely want students to value the role of thinking. Model your own thinking processes with your students. At times, engage in *think alouds* so students understand how you figured something out or arrived at a decision. In this approach, teachers orally share with students their thinking process, and then encourage students to practice the cognitive technique in small groups. Think alouds must occur in a specific context to avoid the activity becoming nothing more than modeling an isolated skill. Consider the following partial think-aloud as a teacher models inference skills.

As I read through this paragraph I can immediately tell that the topic of it is space travel because it mentions outer space, rockets, and planets. Even though mention is made of early pioneers, I can see that this is only a point of comparison. I notice that all of the points compared show me how early pioneer travel and space travel have been similar.[15]

Kingore, B. (2005). *Assessment,* 3rd ed. Austin: Professional Associates Publishing.

Students' metacognitive responses take the form of reflections and goal setting. These are explored throughout this chapter.

REFLECTIVE TECHNIQUES

Students' reflections express their perceptions of their learning process and achievements. Reflective thinking is the foundation of each of the techniques that follow.

> 1. *Ongoing investigative conversations and questioning*
> 2. *Captions or reflective statements*
> 3. *Metacognitive questions*
> 4. *Learning reflections*
> 5. *Reflective learning summaries*
> 6. *End-of-year reflection*
> 7. *Multiple-year reflection*

1. *Ongoing investigative conversations and questioning*

These dialogues are informal, verbal, and often spontaneous interactions between teachers and students or between small groups of students. The intent of these conversations is clarification or elaboration of the students' thinking. Teachers guide students' development of metacognitive strategies by asking questions that highlight the ideas that are most important, such as the Inquiry Probes in Chapter 7. These interactions provide a window into students' reasoning.

2. *Captions or reflective statements*

These statements are written responses students add to each product selected for the portfolio. A caption is a main idea statement. The term *caption* is used to signal students that the response can be short and should be the main idea of their analysis. Another commonly used term for this reflection is *entry slip* since it is an entry into the portfolio.

A caption is usually a separate strip of paper that is written on and then stapled onto a product before it is filed in the portfolio. These reflective statements can be completed on blank paper or simple duplicated forms containing open-ended prompts. The duplicated forms simplify the captioning process because students have less to write to complete each response. Having less to write is particularly helpful with students for whom handwriting is slow and laborious or for students who view handwriting as punitive.

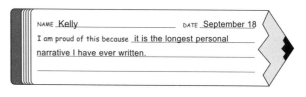

NAME Kelly   DATE September 18
I am proud of this because it is the longest personal narrative I have ever written.

NAME Kelly   DATE April 29
This work is important because this science experiment shows how I have mastered the scientific method. I clearly formulated a hypothesis and validated it by experimentation, analytical observation, and careful data recording.

Many teachers requested copies of caption forms to duplicate, so four pages of examples are included in this chapter. These caption forms progress from simple to more expansive. Figure 4.1 provides four copies of the same prompt. This form is a sound choice for beginning the captioning process as it requires only brief responses. After students gain experience writing captions, use Figure 4.2 with four different prompts so students begin making choices about which sentence stem best fits their selected product. Later, consider using the last three caption forms that invite more elaboration. Figure 4.3A and 4.3B prompt comparative reasoning, asking students to respond to two or more of the prompts as they complete their captions. Figures 4.4 and 4.5 highlight students' learning successes.

Kingore, B. (2005). *Assessment,* 3rd ed. Austin: Professional Associates Publishing.

Figure 4.1: CAPTIONS: PENCIL STRIPS

NAME _____ DATE _____

I am proud of this because _____

_____

_____

✂ -

NAME _____ DATE _____

I am proud of this because _____

_____

_____

- -

NAME _____ DATE _____

I am proud of this because _____

_____

_____

- -

NAME _____ DATE _____

I am proud of this because _____

_____

_____

Metacognitive Responses

Kingore, B. (2005). *Assessment,* 3rd ed. Austin: Professional Associates Publishing.

Figure 4.2: **CAPTIONS: FOUR CHOICES**

NAME _____ DATE _____

I think I did better work on this by _____

---✂---

NAME _____ DATE _____

This shows that I know how to _____

_____

_____

_____

NAME _____ DATE _____

I could improve this by _____

_____

_____

_____

NAME _____ DATE _____

This work is important because _____

_____

_____

_____

Kingore, B. (2005). *Assessment,* 3rd ed. Austin: Professional Associates Publishing.

Figure 4.3A: CAPTIONS: COMPARATIVE REASONING

NAME _____ DATE _____

This assignment was:

• Hard because _____
  _____

• Easy because _____
  _____

• Interesting because _____
  _____

• Fun because _____
  _____

Kingore, B. (2005). *Assessment,* 3rd ed. Austin: Professional Associates Publishing.

Figure 4.3B: CAPTIONS: COMPARATIVE REASONING

NAME _____ DATE _____

This assignment was:

• Difficult because _____
  _____

• Frustrating because _____
  _____

• Important because _____
  _____

• Enjoyable because _____
  _____

• Significant because _____
  _____

Kingore, B. (2005). *Assessment,* 3rd ed. Austin: Professional Associates Publishing.

Figure 4.4: CAPTION: CAN DO!

Can do!

NAME _____ DATE _____

This work shows that I _____

_____

_____

_____

I feel _____

_____

_____

Next time I want to _____

_____

_____

Kingore, B. (2005). *Assessment,* 3rd ed. Austin: Professional Associates Publishing.

Figure 4.5: CAPTION: WRITE ON!

NAME _____ DATE _____

This work demonstrates _____

_____

_____

_____

I have improved _____

_____

_____

_____

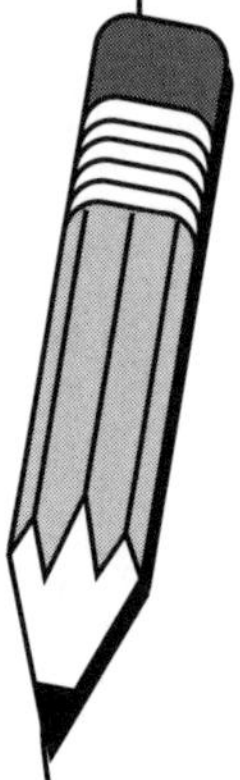

Kingore, B. (2005). *Assessment,* 3rd ed. Austin: Professional Associates Publishing.

If you intend to bind the yearly portfolio books at the end of the school year, avoid stapling the captions to the product in the usual upper left-hand corner of the paper. Staples located in that corner obstruct the cutting process when binding with plastic comb binders. Instead, staple the captions to the product in the middle at the top of the page. For younger children, place a mark on the caption strip before it is duplicated to guide students where to staple the strip to their paper.

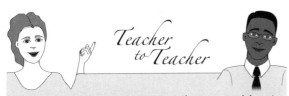

Teacher to Teacher

To save paper-management time, provide students with a page of miscellaneous caption strips to keep in their work or collection file. When they have an item for their portfolio, they simply select, cut off, and complete a caption strip.

3. Metacognitive questions

These questions focus students' thinking and reactions to learning. Figure 4.6 provides upper elementary and secondary students with a set of questions applicable to multiple learning situations. Have students store a copy of these questions in their work folder. Then, without the teacher having to develop new metacognitive devices each time, students select and respond to one or more questions as they complete different learning experiences. The intent is to guide students' reflections, prompt choice and variety, and save teachers' time in planning assessments. Encourage students to add questions to their list as quality suggestions are made during a class discussion.

> *The brain is like a muscle. When we think well, we feel good. Understanding is a kind of ecstasy.*
>
> --Carl Segan
> *Broca's Brain*

4. Learning reflections

Learning Reflection forms prompt students' reflection about a specific learning task (Figure 4.7). Asking students to relate the information to something else is a productive strategy for developing transfer and increasing in-depth understanding. *This is like... How this relates to other subjects... How this applies to my life...*

Figure 4.7: LEARNING REFLECTIONS

NAME *Trent* DATE *May 3*
TOPIC *Honeybees*

INFORMATION SOURCE:
☒ Book ☐ Magazine ☐ Newspaper
☒ Discussion ☐ Internet ☐ Graph
☐ Interview ☐ Lecture ☐ Video

How this relates to other subjects:

SUBJECT	CONNECTION
Health	*Humans also go through different stages.*
Social studies	*Bees live in a colony and have jobs like workers.*
Language arts	*Bees dance to tell each other things.*

1. Three major ideas:
   • *A honeybee dies after it stings something.*
   • *A hexagon makes the hive strong with no space wasted.*
   • *Pollen and nectar feed the hive.*

2. How this applies to me:
On the way to school, I found 11 different flowers bees like. They were yellow, blue, or purple with a sweet smell and a good landing spot to fit a bee.

3. One insight or thought:
Bees have to work so hard and don't live very long. Why? I don't want to be a bee.

4. Questions:
Why are there 25,000 kinds of bees? Why did they need to specialize so much?

Kingore, B. (2005). *Assessment,* 3rd ed. Austin: Professional Associates Publishing.

---

5. Reflective learning summaries

In summaries, students reflect about a set of learning experiences or products and interpret their learning outcomes over several

Metacognitive Responses

Figure 4.6: METACOGNITIVE QUESTIONS

❑   1.   Why is this important?

❑   2.   What are two strengths of my work?

❑   3.   What would I do differently?

❑   4.   What part caused me the most trouble?

❑   5.   How does this relate to what I already know?

❑   6.   What is something similar to this?

❑   7.   What is the most important thing I learned while doing this work?

❑   8.   How can I use this information in my life?

❑   9.   What are two questions I have about this?

❑ 10.   What have I done to help me understand or learn about this?

❑ 11.   What can I do to substantiate my conclusion?

❑ 12.   How effective have I been in working and completing this process?

❑ 13.   What do I need to do next?

❑ 14.   What is one thing I will remember?

❑ 15.   What analogy can I create to explain this?

❑ 16.   What new goal can I set because of my work on this?

❑ 17.   _____

❑ 18.   _____

❑ 19.   _____

❑ 20.   _____

Kingore, B. (2005). *Assessment,* 3rd ed. Austin: Professional Associates Publishing.

Figure 4.7: LEARNING REFLECTIONS

NAME _____ DATE _____

TOPIC _____

INFORMATION SOURCE:	❏ Book	❏ Magazine	❏ Newspaper
	❏ Discussion	❏ Internet	❏ Graph
	❏ Interview	❏ Lecture	❏ Video

How this relates to other subjects:

SUBJECT   CONNECTION

_____   _____

_____   _____

_____   _____

1. Three major ideas:

   • _____

   • _____

   • _____

2. How this applies to me:

3. One insight or thought:

4. Questions:

Kingore, B. (2005). *Assessment,* 3rd ed. Austin: Professional Associates Publishing.

Metacognitive Responses

weeks of learning. Summaries allow for a periodic review of several products and a general overview of the current status of learning. They are typically completed before conferences or at the conclusion of reporting periods such as at six-week or nine-week intervals. When completing summaries, students consider what they have accomplished thus far in their learning, what is characteristic of their learning, what needs to be done, and how they feel about their learning processes and achievements.

A summary can be expressed on blank paper or using a variety of forms. The Learning Summary, Figure 4.8, presents a framed format for product analysis. When the blank form is photocopied on the front and back of a paper, it provides four different areas to reflect the student's progress and needs over time.

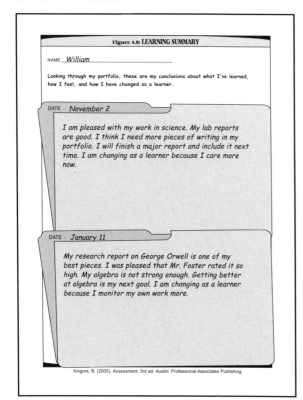

Another appealing variation of a summary is to have students write a letter to their parents from the perspective of their teacher.

Of course, the parents understand that their child is the author of the letter, but it is interesting to see the student's interpretations of the teacher's point of view. An example letter follows to illustrate the effectiveness of this writing task.

October 23

Dear Mrs. Randall,

Charlene has worked hard in school this six weeks. She is writing longer stories and checking to see that she is spelling everything correctly. She has progressed a lot.

She really likes the new newspaper software in the computer lab. She has written several articles for the school newspaper using it. She does not like the computer tests over the books she reads. I think she would rather just enjoy reading the stories than taking a test.

In math, she has mastered her division facts and is working on ratio. It is hard, but she is learning it. Debra is her math partner and they help each other.

Charlene is keeping a portfolio. She will share it with you soon.

Sincerely,
Ms. J. Dowell

6. End-of-year reflection

At the end of the school year, a summative view of learning is an effective closure task. Ask students to put their achievements in perspective by writing about what they have accomplished, what has changed with time,

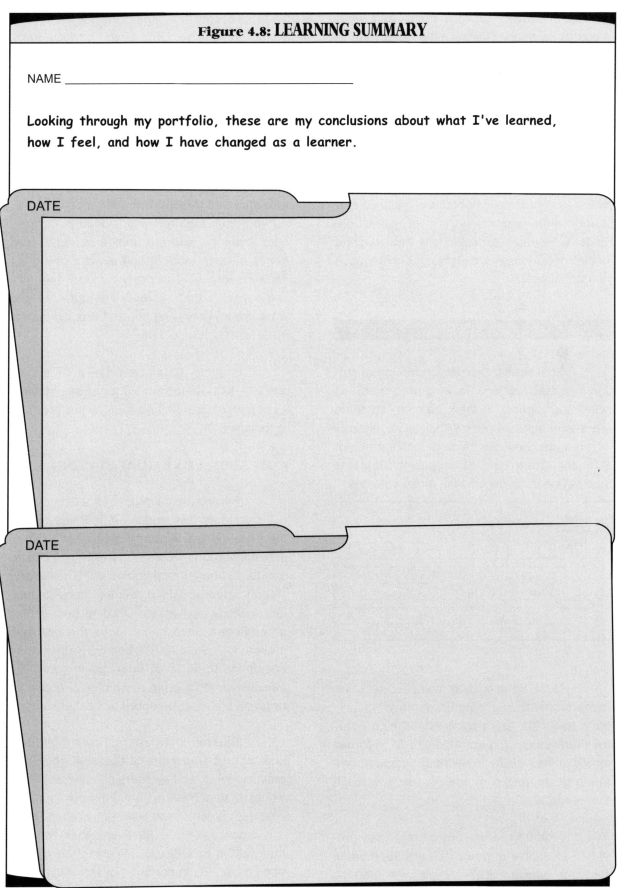

Figure 4.8: LEARNING SUMMARY

NAME _____

Looking through my portfolio, these are my conclusions about what I've learned, how I feel, and how I have changed as a learner.

DATE

DATE

Kingore, B. (2005). *Assessment,* 3rd ed. Austin: Professional Associates Publishing.

how their learning satisfies them, and what needs to be done. This reflection is a natural closure at the end of the year as students review the entire portfolio and select products for their School Career Portfolio.

7. Multiple-year reflection

One final opportunity for students' metacognitive reflections is typically completed as the School Career Portfolio is finalized and bound after several years of selection. Students review their selections and respond to their total learning experiences over those years of school.

GOAL SETTING

Goal setting is an important part of students' metacognition. To empower them as active participants in their learning, students are encouraged to review their work, assess its strengths, and determine potential areas or skills for growth and development. Students then set goals to accomplish those changes.

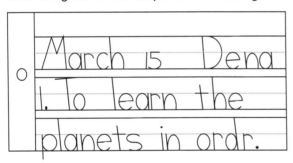

Goal setting is a complex task for many students and parents as they typically have had little experience establishing goals for themselves. Expect students to progress slowly in their ability to set realistic and appropriate goals, and plan specific steps to teach this process.

Model the goal setting process by providing examples of goals that are appropriate for your specific grade levels and learning

tasks. Teachers at the Jefferson Primary School in Findlay, Ohio suggest that educators provide students and parents with a sample bank of goals so parents understand the development of their child's individual goal plan. A sample bank of goals is included as Figure 4.9. These goal examples are not listed hierarchically or developmentally. Rather, they are intended as a sample of goals to help generate more individual ideas when working with students to establish their specific goals. As you work together with students and parents, keep in mind the unique strengths and needs of each student and avoid a one-goal-fits-all mentality. The psychology of goal setting suggests that students are more likely to work toward achieving goals in which they feel ownership.

Graphic organizers for goal setting simplify this metacogniive process. Multiple examples of goal-setting formats are provided in this chapter.

COLLABORATIVE GOAL SETTING

Parents, students, and teachers can collaborate to set goals for learners. Since there are multiple areas for goal setting, Figure 4.10 encourages students, parents, and educators to collaborate and consider the goals for a student's learning in academic, social/behavior, or study skill areas. Dividing goal setting into different units helps focus the task and makes it less overwhelming. Rather than attempting to fill in all three blank goals, the objective is to respond to whichever goal area or areas are most appropriate for that student.

Classes in Houston, Texas found that goal setting was more successful when parents, students, and teachers planned what they would do to achieve a goal. Figure 4.11 invites students, parents, and teachers to each establish a goal for the student and then list what they will do to assist in achieving the goal. In each case, it is important that the student add

Figure 4.9: GOAL EXAMPLES

ACADEMIC SKILL GOALS

❏ To master math facts
❏ To understand and apply mathematical concepts (time, fractions, ratio, etc.)
❏ To effectively use the problem solving process in math and science
❏ To create and solve story problems
❏ To implement the scientific method
❏ To transfer spelling skills in written work across the curriculum
❏ To effectively apply letter and sound relationships in reading and writing
❏ To increase reading and oral language vocabulary
❏ To develop independent reading habits
❏ To write neatly and with correct letter formation
❏ To complete a piece using the writing process
❏ To use more appropriate details, description, precise language, and elaboration in writing
❏ To develop a story with a beginning, middle, and end
❏ To incorporate unique analogies and symbols in writing

STUDY OR RESEARCH SKILL GOALS

❏ To maintain a well organized portfolio
❏ To manage time well during independent work assignments and finish on time
❏ To improve the quality of work
❏ To improve organizational skills
❏ To manage materials more effectively
❏ To accept responsibility for learning
❏ To effectively use a variety of resources to extend learning
❏ To use correct bibliographic references
❏ To develop critical thinking skills
❏ To improve application of problem-solving skills
❏ To appropriately apply more complex technology

BEHAVIOR OR SOCIAL SKILL GOALS

❏ To assume more leadership responsibilities in groups
❏ To encourage others
❏ To be an active listener
❏ To foster respect and the positive image of self and others
❏ To interact more effectively with peers and adults
❏ To improve self-esteem and confidence
❏ To be persistent in learning tasks
❏ To improve self-control
❏ To increase intrinsic motivation
❏ To understand and accept behavioral consequences
❏ To participate more comfortably in large group discussions

Kingore, B. (2005). *Assessment,* 3rd ed. Austin: Professional Associates Publishing.

Figure 4.10: COLLABORATIVE GOAL SETTING

NAME _____ DATE _____

Student's goals for self:	**Academic goal:** **Social or behavior goal:** **Study skills or research goal:**
Parent's goals for student:	**Academic goal:** **Social or behavior goal:** **Study skills or research goal:**
Teacher's goals for student:	**Academic goal:** **Social or behavior goal:** **Study skills or research goal:**

Kingore, B. (2005). *Assessment,* 3rd ed. Austin: Professional Associates Publishing.

Figure 4.11: COLLABORATIVE GOAL SETTING PLAN

NAME _____ DATE _____

Student's goal for self:	What I will do to accomplish my goal: Date by which I want to reach my goal: _____
Parent's goal for student:	What I will do to assist my child in reaching this goal: **Student's response:**
Teacher's goal for student:	How I will assist my student in achieving this goal: **Student's response:**

Kingore, B. (2005). *Assessment,* 3rd ed. Austin: Professional Associates Publishing.

Metacognitive Responses

a reaction and response after the parent and teacher have written their goal suggestions for the student. These student responses help maintain the student's ownership in the process. Goal setting is something educators do *with* students, not *to* them.

accomplished and reflect upon how they view that accomplishment.

GOAL SETTING WEEKLY PLAN

Figure 4.13 is a variation for inexperienced or less organized students who are not able to handle goal setting over a long period of time. With this form, students are guided to set a short term goal and then plan the steps to achieve that goal. The top two boxes of the form would typically be completed by the student on Monday. Then on Friday of that week, students revisit their goal plan to reflect upon what they have accomplished. Initially, with students inexperienced in goal setting or students less task oriented, only part of the goal may be achieved. Students are encouraged to write how they feel about their accomplishment and plan what they will do next to continue their development. In many cases, another weekly plan would be used by students to continue their goal setting process.

Figure 4.10: COLLABORATIVE GOAL SETTING PLAN

NAME _____ DATE _____

Student's goal for self:	What I will do to accomplish my goal:
I want to research the latest information about the Titanic. I want to write about it for my history report.	*I will search new resources and the internet.*
	Date by which I want to reach my goal: __10-24__
Parent's goal for student:	What I will do to assist my child in reaching this goal:
I would like you to spell more accurately.	*I will continue to help you study for spelling tests and buy a word book for you to use as you write.*
	Student's response:
	I'll use the word book when I write and spell check when I'm using the computer.
Teacher's goal for student:	How I will assist my student in achieving this goal:
I would like you to increase your independent learning skills.	*Your titanic project is an excellent idea for independent learning. I will facilitate your resource searching, organizing, and editing.*
	Student's response:
	Thanks. I want it to be really good.

GOAL SETTING PLAN

Figure 4.12 is a format successfully used in many classrooms of upper elementary, middle school, and high school students. The value of this graphic organizer is that it asks students to state a goal and then outline the specific steps to accomplish it. Planning is an important link to success for many students as it requires them to establish a sequence to reach a goal. This plan has five steps indicated, but in reality, there is no predetermined number of steps to reach a goal. Students should be encouraged to plan the number of steps most appropriate toward reaching their goal. At a later date, students revise their goal setting plan to reflect the status of their goal. After recording the date, they state what they have

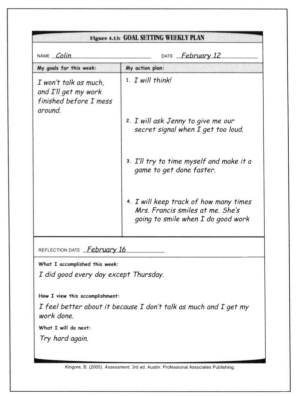

Figure 4.13: GOAL SETTING WEEKLY PLAN

NAME _Colin_   DATE _February 12_

My goals for this week:	My action plan:
I won't talk as much, and I'll get my work finished before I mess around.	1. *I will think!*
	2. *I will ask Jenny to give me our secret signal when I get too loud.*
	3. *I'll try to time myself and make it a game to get done faster.*
	4. *I will keep track of how many times Mrs. Francis smiles at me. She's going to smile when I do good work*

REFLECTION DATE _February 16_

What I accomplished this week:
I did good every day except Thursday.

How I view this accomplishment:
I feel better about it because I don't talk as much and I get my work done.

What I will do next:
Try hard again.

Figure 4.12: GOAL SETTING PLAN

NAME _____   DATE _____

My goals:	My action plan:
	1.
	2.
	3.
	4.
	5.

REFLECTION DATE _____

What I accomplished:	My reflection:

Kingore, B. (2005). *Assessment,* 3rd ed. Austin: Professional Associates Publishing.

Figure 4.13: GOAL SETTING WEEKLY PLAN

NAME _____   DATE _____

My goals for this week:	My action plan:
	1.
	2.
	3.
	4.

REFLECTION DATE _____

What I accomplished this week:

How I view this accomplishment:

What I will do next:

Kingore, B. (2005). *Assessment,* 3rd ed. Austin: Professional Associates Publishing.

MONTHLY GOAL SETTING

Some teachers find it simpler to integrate goal setting with ongoing activities in the classroom. For example, elementary and secondary students can incorporate goals in their learning logs or journals. On the first school day of each month, students review previous goals written in their journals or logs, revise those goals, and reflect upon their progress. During some monthly reviews, students add a new goal.

Primary classrooms can combine goal setting with handwriting practice. Once a month, in a primary class in Independence, Iowa, students determine the school-related goals they want to set and then write them on their lined handwriting paper. One student particularly revealed his need for organization when he set his goals as: 1) *To finish some of my writing pieces,* and 2) *To remember where I put my goals!*

GOAL SETTING BUD AND BLOOM

With more experienced or sophisticated students, the rose analogy is an effective goal setting device. Using Figure 4.14, students write a learning goal or goals for themselves and store those goals in their portfolios. At a later date, they revise their goals to reflect upon how much their learning has bloomed. If appropriate, develop the analogy further with the students.

A bud needs:	A goal needs:
Nutrients	Nurturing environment and collaboration with others
Soil	Content information, practice, positive attitude, and self-esteem
Light	Learning opportunities
Water	Task commitment

Figure 4.14: GOAL SETTING BUD AND BLOOM

NAME _____   DATE _____

Budding goal:

REFLECTION DATE _____

Idea in bloom:

Kingore, B. (2005). *Assessment,* 3rd ed. Austin: Professional Associates Publishing.

STUDENTS' METACOGNITIVE DEVELOPMENT OVER TIME

Teachers experienced in assessment report that students' metacognitive abilities mature over time. The following are three changes teachers noticed.

1. Attitude

With experience in reflection, students increase their willingness to complete captions or reflections of their learning. At first, many students are resistant because they lack experience in metacognition, they are not sure how to do it, and they are not certain why it is important. Later, students begin to enjoy the process and respect the value of their own work and progress. As one anonymous adage notes:

Attitude is the mind's paint brush. It can color any situation.

2. Self-monitoring

With time and experience, students begin to use earlier works to compare how they have improved on specific goals and skills. As one fifth grader commented after several months of product analysis: *It's cool to see how much my math has changed. I'm working harder problems now and getting them right most of the time.* As another example, a gifted first grader in Barrington, Illinois stated during a student-involved conference with his mother and teacher: *This clearly shows how much I have improved in my punctuation when I write.*

3. Breadth

With instruction and modeling, students' reflections increase in length and depth of content. Reflections stretch from a few words to sentences containing a more mature awareness of criteria for assessing the quality and value of students' learning. The second grader's and ninth grader's captions that follow are examples of this development from very simple to more thoughtful responses.

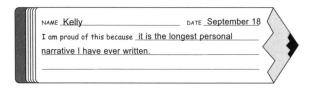

NAME Kelly   DATE September 18
I am proud of this because it is the longest personal
narrative I have ever written.

NAME Kelly   DATE April 29
This work is important because this science experiment shows
how I have mastered the scientific method. I clearly formulated
a hypothesis and validated it by experimentation, analytical
observation, and careful data recording.

• CHAPTER 5 •
Conferences

The best way to learn about a child's thinking and learning is to ask the child

—*Ministry of Education, Canada*

Ongoing student-teacher, student-student, and student-parent conversations continue spontaneously throughout the day to assist, encourage, and affirm students. However, structured conversations in the form of conferences also enhance learning. The objective of conferencing is to discuss with and listen to students in order to elicit their perceptions, gain insights into their learning, and facilitate their continued achievements. Through conferences, teachers and parents refine their understanding of the students' strengths and needs as the students discover that they have something worth saying and accomplishments worth honoring. The tone is interactive, and the information is supported and guided by specific examples of students' work.

Interactive conferences help students:
• Think about their own learning,
• Ask questions,
• Achieve new levels of understanding,
• Facilitate self-evaluation,
• Affirm their ideas and opinions are valued,
• Appreciate progress,

• Set future goals,
• Respond to comments,
• Experience positive teacher-student or parent-student relationships, and
• Become self-directed learners (Ministry of Education, 1991).

School conferences once focused on information between teachers and parents. Now, conferences invite students, teachers, and parents to openly share information with each other in order to enrich the learning experiences of the students.

STUDENT-TEACHER CONFERENCES

Authentic assessment promotes students conferencing with teachers to directly share their perceptions. The quality of a student-teacher conference is greatly enhanced by the thoughtful preparation completed by students before they conference with the teacher. Two variations of forms for students' conference preparation are included as Figures 5.1 and 5.2.

Kingore, B. (2005). *Assessment,* 3rd ed. Austin: Professional Associates Publishing.

Figure 5.1: CONFERENCE PREPARATION

NAME _____   DATE _____

Before coming to the conference, please prepare your portfolio for sharing.

❑   All products have your name, date completed, and caption strip attached.
❑   Products are in the predetermined order.
❑   Select one product added to your portfolio since your last conference that you
       especially want to discuss. Mark its place in your portfolio by attaching a sticky
       note that extends from the edge of the product to flag that piece.

Answer the following questions, please.
Why did you choose the product that you want to share first?

What was the goal you set during our last conference? What have you accomplished toward
that goal?

List two or three questions that you want to discuss.

Kingore, B. (2005). *Assessment,* 3rd ed. Austin: Professional Associates Publishing.

Figure 5.2: CONFERENCE PREPARATION

NAME _____   DATE _____

Areas of study this reporting period:

• _____

• _____

• _____

• _____

Number of products assigned: _____   Number of products I completed: _____

What I am proud of:

What I would like to improve:

The one thing I especially enjoyed learning:

One change I suggest:

My questions are:

Kingore, B. (2005). *Assessment,* 3rd ed. Austin: Professional Associates Publishing.

Conferences

Questioning is another important component of successful, interactive conferences. Plan questions, such as those in Figure 5.3, to help the conference proceed without the pauses that inevitably occur when people try to think of what to ask. Many teachers find that having prepared questions helps them gather more assessment information and use time with students more productively. When conferencing with a student, keep the page of conference questions for reference in case of being distracted or blank for a moment.

SUGGESTIONS ABOUT ASSESSMENT QUESTIONING

- Effective high-level, open-ended questions encourage students to think. Those questions are more valuable to assessment and provide richer information than low-level recall quizzing.
- Develop a list of possible leading and probing questions ahead of time, but unless assessment standards require identical questions for all students, be flexible in which ones you actually use with different students at different times.
- Conferences are more productive when students are prepared for the questions to be discussed. Provide students with a list of possible questions before conferencing with them. Allow them to ponder their responses rather than feel put on the spot.
- Invite students to prepare questions they think are significant. *What do you want someone to ask you? What would you like to ask others?*
- Provide wait time during the conference to allow students to be more thoughtful in their responses.
- Follow the student's leads. Let the student's information naturally guide your questioning responses.
- A brief written record of observations and conclusions from the conference may be more appropriate and informative than a simple checklist.

End the conference with a moment for both the student and teacher to write a brief note about the conference and future goals. These notes are valuable memory prompts before the next conference. Provide the student with a blank paper, conference note, or reflection form (Figures 5.4 through 5.6) to write notes of her or his perception of the conference. On another paper, simultaneously record important notes for guiding the student's continued growth.

Duplicate conference forms front and back so the same paper can be used for multiple conferences. If the students' copies are duplicated on colored paper, the paper is more easily found when it is needed again. The student's conference notes are usually filed in the back of the portfolio and thus the colored page signals that the work in front of it has already been discussed in a conference. The teacher's conference notes are typically stored by the teacher.

How can teachers find the time to have student conferences? Write one student's name on each day or so of your class or section planner. By rotating among the students, you can complete a five-to-ten minute conference with each student once every six to nine weeks.

Kingore, B. (2005). *Assessment,* 3rd ed. Austin: Professional Associates Publishing.

Figure 5.3: CONFERENCE QUESTIONS

1. What have you chosen to share with me first?
   - Why did you choose this product?
   - How did you think of that idea?
   - What could you say to your parent about this to explain what you've learned?

2. What questions or concerns do you want to discuss today?
   - What is the problem as you see it?
   - Who can best help you? How?

3. What should I learn about you from your work?
   - How is that important?
   - What else do you want me to know?

4. Are your learning achievements satisfying or not satisfying to you? Why?
   - What do you feel is a strength?
   - What would you like to change?

5. What product shows something important you've learned?
   - Why is this important?
   - What did you do to learn it?

6. Show me something in your portfolio that you think we should do again.
   - What do you like about it?
   - How is it important to next year's class?
   - How could we change it to make it better?

7. Tell me about something on your reading review.
   - Have you encouraged others to read this?
   - Have you read anything else like it?
   - What do you plan to read next?

8. What is something you can do now that you could not do well before?
   - What did you do to learn it?
   - Give an example of how you use this ability.

9. Which product do you feel is not your best work? Why?
   - What would you change about it?

10. What changes have you noticed in your work?
    - How do you feel about these changes?
    - What additional help or resources do you need?

11. What was the goal you set during our last conference?
    - How have you progressed toward that goal?
    - How or when did you achieve it?

Kingore, B. (2005). *Assessment,* 3rd ed. Austin: Professional Associates Publishing.

Figure 5.4: CONFERENCE NOTES

NAME _____   DATE _____

What I would like to learn:

How I feel about our conference:

Kingore, B. (2005). *Assessment,* 3rd ed. Austin: Professional Associates Publishing.

✂ -

Figure 5.5: CONFERENCE NOTES

NAME _____   DATE _____

What we talked about:

What I have learned:

My next goal:

Kingore, B. (2005). *Assessment,* 3rd ed. Austin: Professional Associates Publishing.

Figure 5.6: CONFERENCE REFLECTION

NAME _____   DATE _____

What I did:	What I will do next time:

What I enjoyed:	What I would change:

Conferences

When conferencing or observing, develop codes to monitor students' progress and goals. The codes enable you to jot ideas faster and provide a consistent format for data. The following example of a quick note code was shared by primary teachers in Hurst-Euless-Bedford schools in Texas.

✳	✓
	✗

✓ = STRENGTHS   ✗ = CONCERNS
✳ = SKILLS TO TEACH

Teachers do not want students to think the only time they can meet with the teacher is when a conference is scheduled. Provide a form, such Figure 5.7, that allows students to request a conference with you. This particular form helps students think through what they need to discuss so your conference time is more productive.

PARENT-TEACHER CONFERENCES

Teachers are familiar with traditional conferences between teachers and parents. A portfolio enhances the information typically

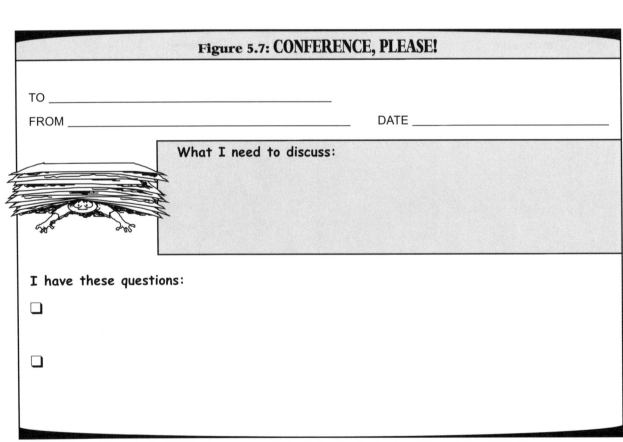

Kingore, B. (2005). *Assessment,* 3rd ed. Austin: Professional Associates Publishing.

shared during a conference because teachers use specific product examples from the portfolio to support and clarify each point regarding the student's growth and needs.

When sharing information, the parent and teacher must sit side by side to more comfortably review pieces from the portfolio. This seating arrangement signals a more collaborative environment rather than a confrontational one.

GUIDELINES FOR PARENT-TEACHER PORTFOLIO CONFERENCES

1. Establish rapport by showing the parents a successful product their child chose from the portfolio and wanted them to see first.

2. Accent student growth and the strengths of the portfolio rather than just allow the parent to comment on deficiencies.

3. Use specific product examples to share information more concretely and to document the instructional points you make. Avoid educational jargon.

4. Use a triplet to focus the discussion on the main idea you want to communicate.[16]

5. Do not overwhelm parents by attempting to discuss every item in the portfolio. Pre-plan and be selective.

6. Remind parents that they will have other opportunities to review the portfolio, such as a portfolio conference with their child and that the bound portfolio will be sent home at the end of the school year.

7. Listen to the parent's comments and their questions.

8. Offer specific suggestions regarding how parents might support their child's continued development at home.

9. Conclude by summarizing major points and inviting continued collaboration.

---

[16] See Chapter 2 for more information about triplets.

STUDENT-INVOLVED CONFERENCES

Most student-involved conferences are conducted at the school. One type of student-involved conference involves only the student and a parent or other significant adult of the student's choosing. This type of conference involves less school or teacher time because multiple student-parent conferences occur simultaneously while the teacher facilitates. These conferences can also add depth and authenticity to parents' nights at schools.

A second type of conference is a three-way conference where the student, parent, and teacher are all participants. This type of conference requires significantly more teacher time as only one conference is completed at a time. However, the three-way conference produces valuable communication as all three people vested in the student's needs and achievements sit down to learn and share together.

Model a student-involved conference during a parent meeting early in the year by using a parent and former student or two teachers role playing the conference in front of the parents. Then, parents know what to expect when they have a conference with their child later.

OBJECTIVES OF STUDENT-INVOLVED CONFERENCES

The intentions of successful student-involved conferences are to:
*   Elicit the students' perspectives of their learning;
*   Showcase what students have produced and accomplished;

Kingore, B. (2005). *Assessment,* 3rd ed. Austin: Professional Associates Publishing.

- Accent the students' active role in their assessment;
- Require students' to plan, organize, present, respond, and self-evaluate;
- Encourage students to set goals for their learning;
- Provide authentic audiences for students' work; and
- Increase students' accountability.

The process of students sharing their portfolios with adults vests the students with status and accents their responsibility for their own learning. When students are truly accountable, they become more motivated to improve.

STUDENTS' PREPARATION FOR THE CONFERENCE

Student preparation is necessary for productive and successful student-involved conferences. Students will not be confident communicators unless they are well prepared and have practiced the procedure. Their preparation encourages them to focus on a few specific items from their portfolios that they most want or need to share since it is not practical to conference on every piece in most portfolios. Parents also appreciate knowing their child has worked to prepare for their conference together.

Sequence for Students' Preparation

1. Students list how they have changed as a learner and select specific portfolio products to support those changes. They prepare for the conference by completing the student section of the Student-Involved Conference form (Figure 5.8) to help them synthesize their work and focus on what their achievements represent.

2. Students select the first product they want to share and plan what they want to say about it to communicate their perceptions about their learning.

3. Students then select two or three additional products and prepare what to say about each of them.

4. The teacher selects benchmark pieces to share. These products represent district learning standards, skills, and achievement levels that the teacher believes every parent should review with his or her child. Parents need to be informed which of the pieces they discuss during the conference are selected by the student and which are required by the teacher.

5. As a class, discuss the Procedures for Students, Figure 5.9, and incorporate any additional procedures brainstormed by the students.

6. A student volunteer and the teacher model in front of the class what a student-involved conference looks and sounds like. This demonstration gives students a better idea of the process and a better ability to prepare.

7. Next, students work in pairs to role play their portfolio conferences and practice the specific procedures listed in Figure 5.9 that will be used for student-parent conferences. One student role plays a parent while the other student shares and discusses her or his portfolio. Then, the two reverse roles and continue role playing a conference using the second student's portfolio. Role playing develops students' confidence and increases their fluency for a conference with their parent or family representative. It is fascinating to observe this role playing as students are surprisingly perceptive when playing adults' roles.

8. Student committees can be formed to complete any needed arrangements for

Kingore, B. (2005). *Assessment,* 3rd ed. Austin: Professional Associates Publishing.

Figure 5.8: STUDENT-INVOLVED CONFERENCE

NAME _____   DATE _____

STUDENT

While you look at my work, I want you to notice these things about it:

• _____

• _____

• _____

• _____

These are things I think I do well:

• _____

• _____

• _____

• _____

My next academic and study skill goals are:

• _____

• _____

• _____

• _____

PARENT/GUARDIAN

After looking at your work and listening to your explanations, I want to comment:

GUARDIAN _____   DATE _____

Kingore, B. (2005). *Assessment,* 3rd ed. Austin: Professional Associates Publishing.

the conferences. Some examples include arranging for refreshments, organizing the classroom space, preparing welcome signs, and duplicating needed papers.

9. Students write a letter to their parent or family representative asking them to attend the conference.

Students should avoid removing products from their portfolios during conferencing; it is difficult for them to get the pieces back in the correct order, even when the pages are numbered. Instead, have students place sticky notes on the edge of each selected piece so the note stands out like a flag. Then, the student simply turns to each piece as the portfolio is shared.

*DeBono, E. (1993).

STUDENT CLOSURE

Debrief the experience with students after each conference by asking them to reflect on the process orally or in writing. A PMI format* or one of the various conference forms in this chapter effectively prompt individual or small group conference reflections. For three-way conferences, Figure 5.11, provides an effective format for debriefing.

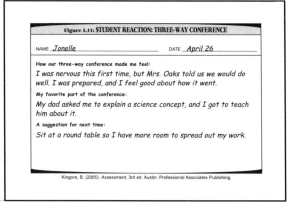

Figure 5.11: STUDENT REACTION: THREE-WAY CONFERENCE

NAME *Jonelle*   DATE *April 26*

How our three-way conference made me feel:
I was nervous this first time, but Mrs. Oaks told us we would do well. I was prepared, and I feel good about how it went.

My favorite part of the conference:
My dad asked me to explain a science concept, and I got to teach him about it.

A suggestion for next time:
Sit at a round table so I have more room to spread out my work.

Kingore, B. (2005). *Assessment*, 3rd ed. Austin: Professional Associates Publishing.

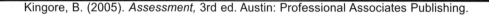

Figure 5.9: PROCEDURES FOR STUDENTS

❑   1.   Have your prepared portfolio at your desk or conference site.

❑   2.   Introduce your parent(s) or family representative to your teacher.

❑   3.   Sit between your parents if both are present, or sit in a close circle.

❑   4.   Share your work in the order and manner you planned.

❑   5.   Ask your parent(s) if they have any questions or other items that they want to discuss.

❑   6.   Invite your parent(s) to join you in goal setting what you should accomplish next.

❑   7.   Show your parent(s) around the room and use the entire classroom environment to support your learning process and achievements.

❑   8.   Invite your parent(s) to complete a Portfolio Response Letter (Figure 5.10).

❑   9.   Thank your parent(s) for attending.

Kingore, B. (2005). *Assessment*, 3rd ed. Austin: Professional Associates Publishing.

Figure 5.10: PORTFOLIO RESPONSE LETTER

DATE _____

DEAR _____,
Name of the student

The product that impressed me the most:

What I learned from your portfolio sharing:

A compliment:

Something to work on:

Comments:

Sincerely,

Kingore, B. (2005). *Assessment,* 3rd ed. Austin: Professional Associates Publishing.

Conduct a class discussion to combine responses and allow students to share anecdotes about their conferences. Elicit their perceptions about the conference process and develop a list of suggestions for refining the process next time.

Discuss how the students feel about the Portfolio Response letters they received from their parents. (Most students choose to file those responses in their portfolios because parents' written notes of positive feedback and compliments are highly valued by the students.) Encourage students to write a follow-up letter to their parents thanking them for attending the conference and sharing their learning experiences.

CONFERENCE FACTORS FOR TEACHERS TO CONSIDER

Teachers in Iowa, Ohio, Michigan, Oregon, and Texas held debriefing sessions to discuss the values and problems of implementing student-involved conferences. Their comments are presented on a PMI chart,[17] Figure 5.12. While looking toward implementing or refining the use of student-involved conferences, refer to the PMI chart and keep in mind their observations and experiences with the process.

The concept of student-involved conferences is difficult at first for many educators to adopt because it requires a significant shift from the educational procedures of the past. The following nine factors help guide the

[17]DeBono, E. (1993).

✂ -

Figure 5.11: STUDENT REACTION: THREE-WAY CONFERENCE

NAME _____   DATE _____

How our three-way conference made me feel:

My favorite part of the conference:

A suggestion for next time:

Kingore, B. (2005). *Assessment,* 3rd ed. Austin: Professional Associates Publishing.

Figure 5.12: PMI CHART ON STUDENT-INVOLVED CONFERENCES

PLUS (+)	MINUS (-)	INTERESTING (?)
Student-centered; students are responsible, accountable, and involved	Need to teach skills of conferencing to students	Positive interaction between student and parent
Encourages students to organize, communicate, and evaluate their work	Not all parents attend the conference	A majority of parents do attend
Opportunity for teachers to observe students in new light	Lack of time; time intensive with young children	Self-esteem builder for students
Demonstrates progress to parents more concretely than grades alone	Some teachers feel students lacked verbal skills to lead conferences	Most students seemed excited and surprised that their parents were responsive and interested
Demonstrates the importance of authentic assessment	Communication issue with ESL families; need translators	Working parents were willing to take off from work to attend
Positive parental response; they liked the specific academic examples to discuss	Parents need information about their role; unsure how to appropriately interact and question their child	Students were empowered; their leadership role gave them status
Students felt motivated to do their best	Teachers have had little if any experience with this process; training is needed	Teachers were amazed how positive an experience it was for parents and students
Multiple opportunities for students' analytical thinking	Students need more thoughtful captions for more in-depth parent communications	Students have lots of ideas about how they can improve next time

Kingore, B. (2005). *Assessment,* 3rd ed. Austin: Professional Associates Publishing.

Conferences

preparation for student-involved parent conferences.

1. The teacher's role changes from being the authority to becoming a facilitator and a supportive commentator.

2. Clarify to students that you play a critical role in guiding learning and helping students prepare for conferences but that they will be the leaders responsible for the conferences. Your intent during the actual conference is to remain in the background as much as possible so the spotlight is clearly focused on the students.

3. Encourage the parents to direct their attention and responses to the student rather than to you.

4. When initiating student-involced conferences, provide the parents with a list of sample questions they can use to discuss products with their child.[18] In this way, parents can prompt their child if needed during the conference. Also, include a reminder to parents that their child is learning and that they will see mistakes in products as well as growth in learning. Accent that the conference is to celebrate the student's accomplishments and understand achievement levels rather than to criticize.

5. Avoid giving *canned* information to parents. Each student-parent conference should reflect the unique learning of the student and address the concerns of the parent.

6. Avoid interrupting any student-involved conferences. If the teacher frequently intervenes, the students typically stop leading and expect the teacher to take over.

7. Understand that you may also schedule traditional parent-teacher conferences as you deem necessary. You may want to conference alone with parents at another time when your perception of the student's learning is different from the student's or when you have special student needs to address with parents.

8. Understand that some parents may still want to request a conference with you. Teachers generally find, however, that holding the student-involved conferences provides most parents with so much information that few request a parent-teacher conference.

9. At the conclusion of a conference, encourage the parents to debrief with each other and share their opinions. Provide them with a copy of the Parent Reaction: Student-Involved Conference form, Figure 5.13, to record their ideas.

While student-involved conferences may seem a difficult task to conquer, teachers and parents both express surprise at how well students rise to the occasion. Even primary students can conduct conferences with their parents and delight the participants with how much they have to say about their school work. Kindergarten teachers in Georgia suggest that kindergarten children are the most successfully involved in three-way conferences when they rotate with their parents among the learning centers or learning stations set up in the room. In this way, the child's work and the class activities prompt what the child wants parents to know about school.

Students can also conference at home. Students simply take the portfolio home overnight and have a portfolio conference with a parent or parents. The parents

---

[18]Refer to the questions in the parent letter, Figure 10.2.

Kingore, B. (2005). *Assessment,* 3rd ed. Austin: Professional Associates Publishing.

Figure 5.13: PARENT REACTION: STUDENT-INVOLVED CONFERENCE

STUDENT _____ DATE _____

RELATIONSHIP TO STUDENT _____

1. How do you feel about having your child involved in the conference?

2. What did you notice about your child's reactions to the conference?

3. What information or which part of the conference was most helpful to you?

4. Were your concerns and interests addressed?

5. Were the arrangements and setting comfortable for you? Is there anything that would work better for you in the future?

6. What are your comments or suggestions to make future conferences more effective?

Kingore, B. (2005). *Assessment,* 3rd ed. Austin: Professional Associates Publishing.

then record their reactions on a Portfolio Response Letter (Figure 5.10). This procedure alarms some educators because they assume the portfolio contents will be lost or damaged. However, when the home environment supports learning, teachers can successfully send portfolios home for conferences and have the portfolios returned safely the next day.[19] It is vital to schedule portfolio sharing at home after students have grown to value their work and take pride in the portfolio. That pride motivates them to handle their portfolio with care.

PEER REQUEST FOR HELP

Students know that their teacher is there to help them, but they also need to view their classmates as sources of assistance. Often, both students benefit when one helps another clarify an idea or process. Consider providing a small area where students post messages and requests. This procedure is especially useful in departmentalized situations where multiple sections of a course meet in the same room but the students do not have opportunities to see or talk with one another about class topics. The Peer Request for Help form, Figure 5.14, and the Response to Peer Request form, Figure 5.15, are one way to organize this interaction.

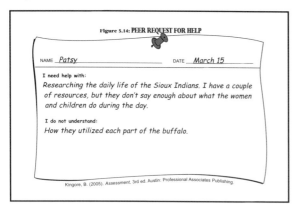

PEER REVIEW

Encourage students to help each other refine their work through peer conferences. Allow each student to select a product that is in process and then collaborate with another student to review the work. Math story problems, written compositions, and science lab reports are examples of products for student review. Encourage each student to read the piece aloud. This process enables both the ear and the eye to guide the review for editing and revision. The Peer Review Response forms, Figures 5.16 and 5.17, help students organize their responses.

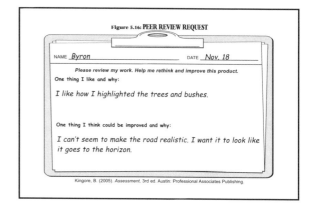

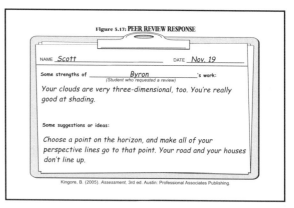

[19] A sample letter informing parents about portfolio sharing at home is included in Chapter 10.

Kingore, B. (2005). *Assessment,* 3rd ed. Austin: Professional Associates Publishing.

Figure 5.14: PEER REQUEST FOR HELP

NAME _____   DATE _____

I need help with:

I do not understand:

Kingore, B. (2005). *Assessment,* 3rd ed. Austin: Professional Associates Publishing.

- -

Figure 5.15: RESPONSE TO PEER REQUEST

NAME _____   DATE _____

My suggestion for _____:
                        (Student who requested help)

A resource that might help:

Let's meet: _____ on _____

Kingore, B. (2005). *Assessment,* 3rd ed. Austin: Professional Associates Publishing.

Figure 5.16: PEER REVIEW REQUEST

NAME _____   DATE _____

Please review my work. Help me rethink and improve this product.

One thing I like and why:

One thing I think could be improved and why:

Kingore, B. (2005). *Assessment,* 3rd ed. Austin: Professional Associates Publishing.

Figure 5.17: PEER REVIEW RESPONSE

NAME _____   DATE _____

Some strengths of _____'s work:
                              (Student who requested a review)

Some suggestions or ideas:

Kingore, B. (2005). *Assessment,* 3rd ed. Austin: Professional Associates Publishing.

· CHAPTER 6 ·
Rubrics

*Rubrics represent not only scoring tools but also,
more importantly, instructional illuminators.*
—W. James Popham

Rubrics are a significant assessment and evaluation tool. The ongoing process of constructing effective rubrics invites professional conversations among grade-level teams and across grade levels of educators. These conversations clarify the instructional priorities that precede assessment. Together, educators determine the key attributes of learning tasks and discuss which criteria can be measured and taught. Thus, thoughtfully developed rubrics contribute to the quality of instruction.

Well-constructed rubrics can be used three ways: goal setting, students' self assessment, and teacher evaluation. Initially, provide a copy of a rubric and ask students to set goals before they begin by checking the levels they intend to achieve. When the task is complete, students use the same rubric copy, marking with a second color of pen, to self-assess their achievement level. Finally, teachers use the same rubric copy and a third color of pen to mark their evaluation of the achievement. Many teachers report that achievement increases when students use a rubric to goal set their intended levels of success before they begin the task. Setting their own target increases the students' determination to reach it.

WHAT ARE RUBRICS?

Rubrics are *guidelines to quality* that describe the requirements for various levels of proficiency on a learning task. They challenge students to think about the characteristics of quality work and how to plan for success. They enable teachers to clarify to students what is expected in a learning experience and what to do to reach higher levels of achievement.

Rubrics are *standards for evaluation*, providing clear, quantified criteria that state the parameters of quality work. They specify evaluation criteria and describe each level on a scoring scale. Thus, a rubric is a scoring guide that distinguishes acceptable from unacceptable responses and establishes a clearer standard to more accurately and fairly determine grades.

Rubrics are *task specific* or *generalizable.* Specific rubrics relate to one topic or task

Kingore, B. (2005). *Assessment,* 3rd ed. Austin: Professional Associates Publishing.

and assess a particular learning experience. Generalizable rubrics allow repeated applications and conserve preparation time; they can be modified as needed. While both are useful, generalizable rubrics are more practical for busy teachers.

Rubrics are *holistic* or *analytical*. Holistic rubrics aggregate all of the evaluative criteria into a single qualitative score. The format of a holistic rubric is hierarchically arranged statements or paragraphs. The evaluation is based on a consensus of the entire work and is useful when the objective is to focus on the process or product as a whole.

To initially develop holistic scoring, sort students' work into stacks that represent different levels of quality, such as *strong, adequate, below level,* and *inadequate.* Then, describe each stack in terms of the attributes common to those works and hierarchically arrange those descriptions on a holistic rubric. Holistic rubrics are useful in many instructional situations. Children use the Behavior (Figure 6.1) or Achieving at Centers (Figure

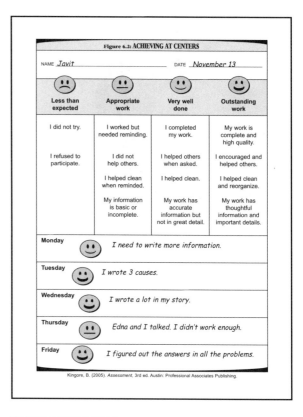

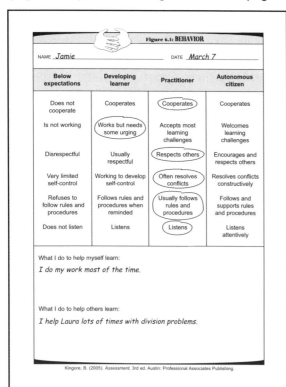

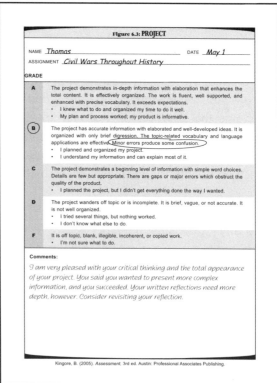

6.2) rubric to self-evaluate their classroom behaviors as they complete a learning experience. Students use the Project rubric (Figure 6.3) to focus their goals before they begin;

Kingore, B. (2005). *Assessment,* 3rd ed. Austin: Professional Associates Publishing.

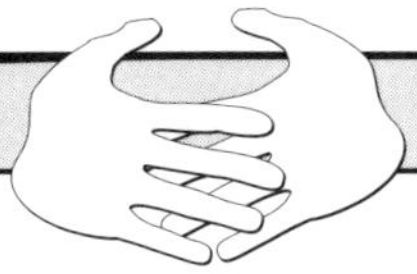

Figure 6.1: BEHAVIOR

NAME _____ DATE _____

Below expectations	Developing learner	Practitioner	Autonomous citizen
Does not cooperate	Cooperates	Cooperates	Cooperates
Is not working	Works but needs some urging	Accepts most learning challenges	Welcomes learning challenges
Disrespectful	Usually respectful	Respects others	Encourages and respects others
Very limited self-control	Working to develop self-control	Often resolves conflicts	Resolves conflicts constructively
Refuses to follow rules and procedures	Follows rules and procedures when reminded	Usually follows rules and procedures	Follows and supports rules and procedures
Does not listen	Listens	Listens	Listens attentively

What I do to help myself learn:

What I do to help others learn:

Kingore, B. (2005). *Assessment,* 3rd ed. Austin: Professional Associates Publishing.

Figure 6.2: ACHIEVING AT CENTERS

NAME _____   DATE _____

Less than expected	Appropriate work	Very well done	Outstanding work
I did not try. I refused to participate.	I worked but needed reminding. I did not help others. I helped clean when reminded. My information is basic or incomplete.	I completed my work. I helped others when asked. I helped clean. My work has accurate information but not in great detail.	My work is complete and high quality. I encouraged and helped others. I helped clean and reorganize. My work has thoughtful information and important details.

Monday

Tuesday

Wednesday

Thursday

Friday

Kingore, B. (2005). *Assessment,* 3rd ed. Austin: Professional Associates Publishing.

Figure 6.3: PROJECT

NAME _____ DATE _____

ASSIGNMENT _____

GRADE

A	The project demonstrates in-depth information with elaboration that enhances the total content. It is effectively organized. The work is fluent, well supported, and enhanced with precise vocabulary. It exceeds expectations. • I knew what to do and organized my time to do it well. • My plan and process worked; my product is informative.
B	The project has accurate information with elaborated and well-developed ideas. It is organized with only brief digressions. The topic-related vocabulary and language applications are effective. Minor errors produce some confusion. • I planned and organized my project. • I understand my information and can explain most of it.
C	The project demonstrates a beginning level of information with simple word choices. Details are few but appropriate. There are gaps or major errors which obstruct the quality of the product. • I planned the project, but I didn't get everything done the way I wanted.
D	The project wanders off topic or is incomplete. It is brief, vague, or not accurate. It is not well organized. • I tried several things, but nothing worked. • I don't know what else to do.
F	It is off topic, blank, illegible, incoherent, or copied work. • I'm not sure what to do.

Comments:

Kingore, B. (2005). *Assessment,* 3rd ed. Austin: Professional Associates Publishing.

teachers and/or students use the same rubric to analyze students' levels of achievement at the completion of the task.

Analytical rubrics allow an evaluation of each criterion instead of scoring the product as a whole. The format of an analytical rubric is a list of specific criteria with the characteristics for multiple levels of success for each criterion listed as separate proficiencies beside or under each criterion. Thus, analytical rubrics enable teachers and students to recognize that a student's degree of proficiency may vary among the different criteria of the work. For example, a student might score at grade level on several criteria and slightly higher or lower on another criterion. The Open-Ended Product rubric (Figure 6.4) and the Writing rubric (Figure 6.5) are examples of analytical rubrics. The Rubric Generator at the end of this chapter (Figure 6.8) enables teachers to develop analytical rubrics for any learning task.

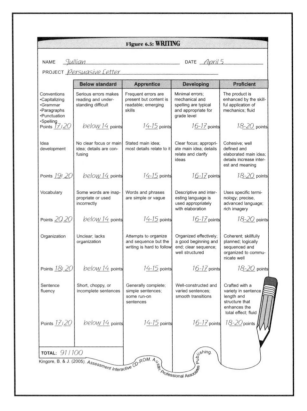

There are no absolutes in terms of how many levels best communicate the different degrees of success for each criterion. The goal is a valid differentiation of levels that is more broad than just right or wrong yet is not so broad that differences seem minute.[20] An even number of degrees helps avoid the problem of someone just settling on the center too often instead of more carefully analyzing levels.

To challenge advanced and gifted students, use a rubric with six levels. Level four represents grade-level standards and scores an *A* in terms of a grade. Five and six also score an *A*, but delineate what a student can do to achieve the next levels of expertise. This hierarchy encourages many advanced students to set higher expectations and challenge themselves to excel beyond grade-level standards.

[20] Parents and students often associate a five-degree rubric with the traditional A-B-C-D-F of letter grades. Hence, it is best to avoid a five-degree rubric if letter grades are not your intent.

Kingore, B. (2005). *Assessment,* 3rd ed. Austin: Professional Associates Publishing.

Figure 6.4: OPEN-ENDED PRODUCT

NAME _____ DATE _____

OPEN-ENDED PRODUCT _____

	Information	Writing conventions	Vocabulary	Organization
Getting started	Little information not accurate	Serious errors make it hard to understand	Incorrect	Unorganized
On the right track	Basic facts; needs elaboration	Frequent errors but readable; emerging skills	Simple words and phrases	Hard to follow at some places
Got it	Develops topic well; includes most of the key ideas and concepts; some substantiation	Few errors; appropriate for grade level in __capitalization __punctuation __spelling __complete sentences __grammar	Descriptive; uses interesting and varied word choices	Organized; a clear sequence
Wow!	In-depth information; well supported ideas; elaborates	Skillful application of mechanics in __capitalization __punctuation __spelling __complete sentences __grammar	Advanced; uses specific terms and multiple-syllable words; rich adjectives	Skillfully planned, organized, and sequenced; fluent

Total Grade Points

/

COMMENTS

Kingore, B. (2005). *Assessment,* 3rd ed. Austin: Professional Associates Publishing.

Figure 6.5: WRITING

NAME _____   DATE _____

PROJECT _____

Conventions •Capitalizing •Grammar •Paragraphs •Punctuating •Spelling Points __/__	Serious errors makes reading and under-standing difficult _____ points	Frequent errors are present but content is readable; emerging skills _____ points	Minimal errors; mechanical and spelling are typical and appropriate for grade level _____ points	The product is enhanced by the skillful application of mechanics; fluid _____ points
Idea development Points __/__	No clear focus or main idea; details are confusing _____ points	Stated main idea; most details relate to it _____ points	Clear focus; appropri-ate main idea; details relate and clarify ideas _____ points	Cohesive; well defined and elaborated main idea; details increase interest and meaning _____ points
Vocabulary Points __/__	Some words are inap-propriate or used incorrectly _____ points	Words and phrases are simple or vague _____ points	Descriptive and inter-esting language is used appropriately with elaboration _____ points	Uses specific termi-nology; precise, advanced language; rich imagery _____ points
Organization Points __/__	Unclear; lacks organization _____ points	Attempts to organize and sequence but the writing is hard to follow _____ points	Organized effectively; a good beginning and end; clear sequence; well structured _____ points	Coherent; skillfully planned; logically sequenced and organized to commu-nicate well _____ points
Sentence fluency Points __/__	Short, choppy, or incomplete sentences _____ points	Generally complete; simple sentences; some run-on sentences _____ points	Well-constructed and varied sentences; smooth transitions _____ points	Crafted with a variety in sentence length and structure that enhances the total effect; fluid _____ points

TOTAL:

Kingore, B. & J. (2005). *Assessment Interactive CD-ROM.* Austin: Professional Associates Publishing.

CHARACTERISTICS OF A QUALITY RUBRIC

Quality rubrics:

- Reflect the most significant elements related to success in a learning task. The criteria focus on the *main ideas* of the work rather than a narrow list of skills or procedures. Each level of a criterion elaborates the *details* of successful achievement by describing important aspects that represent the best thinking in the field.[21]
- Organize elements in a progression from least developed to most stellar (or most to least, if preferred).[22]
- Are practical. They are easily used by students and teachers to accurately and consistently identify the level of competency or stage of development.
- Promote a standard for more accurate and fair grading.
- Encourage students' self-evaluation, higher expectations, and achievement.
- Are shared with students prior to beginning the task so they know the characteristics of quality work.

EVERYONE BENEFITS FROM RUBRICS

Rubrics provide teachers, students, and parents with standards of achievement instead of relying on more subjective decisions.

Teachers benefit

- Teachers use rubrics to set clear expectations for assignments and to assess learners' current levels of proficiency.
- Carefully constructed rubrics are relevant to instruction and guide teachers in designing lessons that enable students to reach higher levels of proficiency.

- Rubrics provide a standard by which to explain grades to parents and students.
- Once fully established, rubrics can make the grading process more interesting and efficient.

Students benefit

- Rubrics can help students set individual goals and provide students with a clearer view of the merits and demerits of their work than grades alone communicate.
- Rubrics communicate to students that they are responsible for the grades they *earn* rather than to continue to view grades as something someone *gives* them.
- Quality rubrics affect achievement. Marzano discusses research supporting rubrics' direct effect on student learning, increasing achievement by 14 to 32 percentile points.[23] Apparently, rubrics encourage teachers to analyze the strengths and weaknesses of desired knowledge and skills and then pass this perspective on to students in the form of rubrics that, in turn, improve student achievement by helping them think more clearly about the characteristics of quality and success.

Parents benefit

- Rubrics help inform parents about which learning concepts and skills are required at a specific grade level.
- Rubrics more concretely explain to parents the student's learning needs and levels of achievement.
- Rubrics communicate more clearly the standard behind grades so parents understand why a child earns certain grades.

---

[21] Stiggins, R., 2001. Stiggins stipulates that rubrics must be *on target* which he defines as clear, complete, and compelling to represent the best thinking in the field.

[22] A history of rubric applications suggests that either progression is effective and simply a matter of teacher/student preference.

[23] Marzano, 2000.

Kingore, B. (2005). *Assessment,* 3rd ed. Austin: Professional Associates Publishing.

Figure 6.6:
PRODUCT DESCRIPTORS AND RUBRICS

Evaluation Tool	Example	Advantages	Disadvantages
Product descriptor	**SCIENCE LAB REPORT** ☐ Components ☐ Procedure ☐ Data ☐ Conclusions ☐ Appearance	• Lists the different elements or attributes of the product • A useful checklist for students to determine which elements to include	• Fails to clarify that there are degrees of achievement • Vague; teachers and students are less likely to agree on the ratings
Product descriptor with a grading scale	**SCIENCE LAB REPORT** Components 10 ·· 7 ·· 4 ·· 0 Procedure 20 ·· 15 ·· 10 ·· 0 Data 30 ·· 20 ·· 10 ·· 0 Conclusions 30 ·· 20 ·· 10 ·· 0 Appearance 10 ·· 7 ·· 4 ·· 0	• Has all of the advantages of a product descriptor • Provides points or a scale to clarify that there are different degrees of quality	• Points do not explain to students what to do to improve their grade or achievement • Vague; fails to specify what constitutes differences among the points on the scale so teachers and students are less likely to agree on ratings
Rubric	Figure 6.7: Science Lab Repoprt	• Lists the evaluative criteria and elaborates the ascending or descending levels of achievement for each criterion so students see what to do to increase achievement • Well-constructed rubrics require teachers to carefully analyze and communicate the learning task and the teacher's objectives • Well-constructed rubrics clarify the characteristics of quality work so teachers and students are more likely to agree on the ratings	• Is more time-consuming to produce

Kingore, B. (2005). *Assessment*, 3rd ed. Austin: Professional Associates Publishing.

Figure 6.7:
SCIENCE LAB REPORT

NAME _____ DATE _____

EXPERIMENT _____

A Lab Report should include: Heading, Title, Problem, Hypothesis, Materials, Procedures, Data, Drawings/diagrams, and Conclusions.

	Components	Procedures	Data	Conclusions	Appearance/Mechanics
Below standard	Elements are missing or flawed Below 7 points	Steps are missing or not accurate Below 14 points	Inaccurate and/or incomplete Below 21 points	Illogical or inaccurate understanding Below 21 points	Inadequate; not neat; little care evident Below 7 points
Apprentice	One or more elements are missing or flawed 7 points	Not sequential; confusing 14-15 points	Measurements/observations are accurate; lacks graphs or tables 21-23 points	Limited understanding of scientific concepts underlying the lab; simple or vague 21-23 points	Adequate; needs more careful attention to detail; frequent errors present but readable 7 points
Proficient	Required elements are complete and appropriate 8 points	Adequate; in logical order but lack detail 16-17 points	Accurate representation of data in tables, graphs, and written form 24-27 points	Accurate understanding; addresses problem and states knowledge gained 24-27 points	Attractive; neatly completed; typed; mechanics and spelling are appropriate 8 points
Exceeding	All required elements are complete and add to the report 9-10 points	Logical; numbered; detailed; complete sentences 18-20 points	Professional and accurate graphs, charts, drawings and written form; specific terminology 28-30 points	Accurate and thorough interpretation; logical explanation addresses most of the questions 28-30 points	Professionally completed; aesthetically pleasing; typed; skillful application of mechanics 9-10 points

Kingore, B. (2005). *Assessment*, 3rd ed. Austin: Professional Associates Publishing.

Rubrics are effective preassessment tools. Teachers or students use a rubric before instruction begins and then revisit the rubric after instruction to assess growth and continuing learning needs.

> *Rubrics have been successfully used for years in the Olympics, Wall Street stock analysis, beauty contests, state and national level tests, and many professional competitions.*

THE ACCURACY OF RUBRICS

Some adults are suspicious of the assessment validity of rubric applications and assume that rubrics introduce grading subjectivity. Marzano argues that the current system based upon points and percentages is inherently *more* subjective. His research found that the correlation between the rubric score and a standardized test was much higher than the correlation between a point or letter-grade and a standardized test.*

Conduct the following experiment to illustrate the efficacy of rubrics. At a faculty meeting or workshop, ask teachers to independently grade a paper you provide. Invariably, the responses lack consensus and cover a wide range of grades. The obvious problem is that if teachers are unclear of a common standard of quality, students are also likely to be confused. A rubric defuses this dilemma by providing a shared standard of quality. Rubrics are essential to help ensure consistency and fairness in evaluation, e.g., that different educators would assign similar grades to a work sample. Without a rubric, a grade of *A* may not mean the same thing in different classes.

Rubrics are standard in real-life situations. Increase parents', students' and other professionals' confidence in rubrics by reminding them of the large number of situations in addition to education in which rubrics are consistently used.

When Students Aren't Accurate

Some teachers report that all students are not accurate or honest when using rubrics. The following suggestions guide responses to this problem.

- Review the assessment tools in use. Some teachers refer to product descriptors as rubrics. Product descriptors are a fine tool to provide students with a list of the elements to include in the product but they are less likely to produce accurate student self-evaluations for the reasons compared in Figure 6.6. Clearly articulated levels of proficiency produce more accurate student responses

- Refine the language used to delineate levels. Strive to replace generalized words, such as *good* or *excellent* and *frequently* or *sometimes,* with more precise words to clarify intended traits.

- Invest class time in thoroughly training students to use rubrics. Conduct mini-lessons that demonstrate the process of accurately evaluating with rubrics. Provide examples of a lower and higher learning response. Direct the class through the process of evaluating each work using a rubric. Emphasize procedural steps. Later, small groups of students work together using a rubric to evaluate another set of products.

- Model a *think aloud.* Teachers or students share with others the cognitive processes

---

[24] See Marzano, R., 2000.

or thinking that they go through as they evaluate a product with a rubric.

- Actively follow through on the accuracy of students' self evaluations. If only one or two students have accuracy issues, meet with each individually to briefly review specific use of a self-assessment rubric. Ask the student to justify each level response with examples in the product. Listen and clarify when misunderstandings exist.

- Continue discussing the process with the class. Model and share different examples.

Teachers have found a place for both product descriptors and rubrics in their instruction. Some teachers prefer a product descriptor to introduce the learning experience and concretely outline the components of the learning task. Then, they combine the descriptors into major category criteria and clarify each degree of success to construct a rubric for the task. Thus, the product descriptor becomes a checklist for students to mark their progress and inclusion of the requirements as they work; the rubric is their evaluation tool.

Guidelines for Constructing Quality Rubrics

1. Articulate your definition of a quality response. Discuss with other professionals the measurable characteristics that distinguish stellar from mediocre work.

2. Collect samples of rubrics as models to adapt for your needs.

3. Determine potential criteria by collecting a wide quality range of students' work and then analyzing attributes common to performances at different levels of achievement.

4. As often as appropriate, limit the number of criteria so the rubric fits on one page.

Lengthy rubrics appear more overwhelming and, therefore, less practical to use. Limit the number of criteria by focusing on the main ideas of the learning task.

5. For each criterion, write descriptors for the degrees of proficiency exhibited in students' work. Circle the words that can vary and adjust those words as you write the different levels.

6. As often as possible, accent *what to do* in the proficiency levels of each criterion rather than just relating what is wrong or calculating the number of errors. In other words, try to tell the student how to achieve a higher level instead of just label the problem.

7. Your first priority is to clearly determine and communicate the most appropriate degrees of success for each criterion. It is tempting to lapse into humorous or clever phrases (*1st base, 2nd base, 3rd base, and home run*), but save those ideas for later.

8. As much as possible, avoid generalities such as *good-better-best* or *little-some-frequently*. When you do use generalities because you just can't think of a stronger explanation, challenge yourself to review the rubric later to refine terminology.

9. Use points, percentages, or grades to weight each criterion. Weighting designates the relative importance of each criterion so students understand where to focus their learning time and effort.

10. Ask others to read or use your rubric and offer suggestions.

11. When feasible, use the rubric in more than one class. Rewrite specific word choices based on those results. When appropriate, elicit ideas for clarification and change from students.

12. The process of creating rubrics can seem difficult and time-consuming. It is often developmental--as soon as you use a rubric, you know ways you want to change it. Give yourself permission to reevaluate, revise, and rewrite.

Kingore, B. (2005). *Assessment,* 3rd ed. Austin: Professional Associates Publishing.

THE RUBRIC GENERATOR

The Rubric Generator is a device I began developing in 1990 to enable teachers to create rubrics in less time and with less frustration by duplicating, cutting, and pasting components. It has evolved and greatly expanded into the rubric generator shared following Figure 6.8 at the end of this chapter. Skim the Rubric Generator and other rubrics you have developed to determine the criteria crucial to contents, processes, and products typical in your curriculum. Photocopy the applicable criterion strips--a criterion and levels of achievement. Then, as you plan a specific learning experience and evaluation, select which of your photocopied criterion strips apply to that task. Rewrite and adapt each as needed, organize and paste them on a paper, and complete your new rubric. In this manner, you can readily customize and construct needed rubrics for learning tasks without starting from scratch each time. Figure 6.8 is designed so that the criterion strips on the Rubric Generator fit in place.

Inasmuch as many criteria are applicable to multiple contents, the generator is presented as an alphabetical listing of criterion strips rather than organized by content areas. *Complexity* and *organization*, for example, are criteria applicable to products in science, social studies, language arts, and math.

This Rubric Generator may prove useful for your evaluation needs or serve as a model for developing your own rubric generator. It is first presented with expanded descriptors to more specifically communicate what constitutes quality work. This version is most useful when communicating with adults, mature students, or when detailed rubrics are needed. The Rubric Generator is then presented in a simplified version. This version is useful when brief rubrics are preferred or when more simple rubrics would communicate clearly to a specific student population.

USING THE RUBRIC GENERATOR

1. **Select applicable criteria.**
   Skim the Rubric Generator and any rubrics you have developed to determine the specific criteria crucial to your intended content, process, or product evaluation.

2. **Copy criteria strips.**
   Photocopy the applicable criteria and levels of proficiencies. Cut each criterion as a separate strip to more easily maneuver into a new rubric.

3. **Organize the criteria.**
   Place the criteria strips on one or more copies of the blank rubric page (Figure 6.8).

4. **Review and rewrite the criteria strips.**
   When planning a specific learning experience evaluation, rewrite and adapt any of the descriptors for which you have a better idea.

5. **Weight each criterion.**
   Use points, percentages, or grades to weight each criterion and designate its relative importance within the total learning task.

Process

The following analytical rubric for mathematics was constructed using four criterion strips from the Rubric Generator. Each criterion is weighted using point values and multiplying by the grading scale to determine the range for

Kingore, B. (2005). *Assessment,* 3rd ed. Austin: Professional Associates Publishing.

each achievement level. Specifically, if 90 percent is an *A*, then .9 times 20 points equals 18 to 20 points for the highest level on the rubric. Because values are rounded up or down when not whole numbers, some numerical adjustments may be needed to ensure that each level has the appropriate total of points. For example, if the highest level is equivalent to an *A*, then that level's points must total 90 to 100.

Figure 6.8: RUBRIC GENERATOR

	Math applications	Communication	Concepts	Strategies
Below standard	Attempts a solution; limited mathematical applications Below 20 points	Incorrect or no explanation provided Below 20 points	Misunderstood; process and/or solution are incorrect Below 15 points	Inappropriate; no apparent logic to the solution Below 15 points
Apprentice	Hesitant to proceed independently; computational errors are present 20-23 points	Explanation is minimal; basic terminology and/or no graphic support 20-23 points	Problem is understood but solution and/or procedures are flawed 15-16 points	Approach is oversimplified; strategies are flawed in application 15-16 points
Proficient	Correct solution is achieved; minimal prompting or errors 24-26 points	Appropriate terminology and graphics; clear explanation 24-26 points	Problem and intended solution are generally correct; used relevant information correctly 17-18 points	Appropriate, efficient strategies; applied correctly and logically 17-18 points
Exceeding	Formulas are executed correctly; precisely applied; higher-level response than expected 27-30 points	Exceptional explanation; uses advanced, precise terminology and graphics 27-30 points	All important elements of the problem are correctly interpreted 19-20 points	Innovative and advanced strategies; independently implemented; sophisticated approach and thinking 19-20 points

NAME _____ DATE _____

ASSIGNMENT __Mathematics Problem Solving:_____

Total Grade Points / COMMENTS

Kingore, B. (2005). *Assessment*, 3rd ed. Austin: Professional Associates Publishing.

STUDENT-DEVELOPED RUBRICS

After students are experienced using rubrics, increase their involvement in rewriting or developing rubrics. The objectives are:

- To promote students' ownership in their assessment;
- To increase students' involvement in interpreting levels of achievement for each criterion on a rubric; and
- To customize a rubric more directly to a specific learning assignment.

The following procedure is easily implemented and typically takes twenty to twenty-five minutes of class time to complete.

1. To control the time required for the decision-making process, the teacher preselects five to eight criteria strips from the Rubric Generator that are applicable to the intended learning experience.

2. The teacher provides copies of the selected criteria strips to the class and involves them in determining which four to six criteria they think are most important for the assignment. Frequently, the teacher designates that one or two of the criteria are required. For example, a teacher may announce that *content depth* is vital to the assignment and must be one of the final five criteria.

3. The class is then divided into groups and each group is given one criterion strip to evaluate and rewrite for five minutes. Some teachers allow informal and clever but classroom-appropriate phrases instead of more formal terminology. To facilitate class sharing, give each group a strip of an overhead transparency sheet on which to copy their final criterion levels.

4. The rewritten criteria strips are placed on the overhead to facilitate review and organization by the entire class. Additional suggestions and responses are considered before the final copy is adopted.

5. The edited criteria strips are then photocopied or typed by one student on the computer and then distributed to the class as the task rubric when the assignment begins.

With time and experience, students become surprisingly sophisticated in their understanding of the value of rubrics. Kim Cheek, a teacher of gifted students at Wylie Middle School, discovered her students truly understood the process when they were asked to judge a writing contest for young children. Her students decided that they should write a rubric so their judging would be more fair. They then created a rubric to guide their decisions before they proceeded to judge the contest.

Figure 6.8: RUBRIC GENERATOR

NAME _____ DATE _____

ASSIGNMENT _____

Total Grade Points **COMMENTS**

/

Kingore, B. (2005). *Assessment,* 3rd ed. Austin: Professional Associates Publishing.

RUBRIC GENERATOR

Simple Criteria Descriptors

Consider using the following descriptive terms for the achievement levels. The descriptors communicate the desired behaviors of the students as well as the ascending levels of achievement.

Novice	Apprentice	Practitioner	Expert

Emerging	Developing	Proficient	Exemplary

Below standard	Intermediate	Advanced	Exceeds standard

Beginning	Developing	Competent	Distinguished

Below expectations	Basic	Proficient	Advanced

Started	On the right track	Got It!	WOW!

Carried out plan	No plan; not complete	Completed with frequent help	Good plan; completed with little help	Well planned; followed through well; self-motivated
Calculations	Not correct	Some errors	Some calculations shown; correct results; labeled	All calculations shown; correct results; appropriately labeled
Application	Little effort	Not able to complete independently; errors	Correct; little prompting; few if any errors	High-level; skillful
Appearance	Not neat	Needs more careful detail	Attractive; neat	Eye catching; beyond expectation

Kingore, B. (2005). *Assessment,* 3rd ed. Austin: Professional Associates Publishing.

Communication	No discussion	Needs prompting and focus	Explains or discusses	Clear; confident; strong vocabulary
Complexity	Too simple	Simple information; little critical thinking	Uses critical thinking; compares and contrasts	Beyond expected level; analyzes from multiple points of view
Comprehension	Does not under-stand	Beginning level of understanding	Adequate under-standing; good details	Thorough understanding; uses precise vocabulary, details, and concepts
Constructs meaning	Nonsense	Unclear; rambles	Clear and understandable	Meaningful; clear focus; well developed
Content depth	Lacks correct information	Needs depth or elaboration	Develops topic well; goes beyond basic facts	In-depth information; well-supported content; elaborates
Creativity	Copied	Little creativity	Creative; expanded typical ideas	Unique; novel; fresh perspective

Kingore, B. (2005). *Assessment,* 3rd ed. Austin: Professional Associates Publishing.

Critical Thinking	Discussion	Effort/task commitment	Fluency	Graph	Graphics
Basic	No discussion	Did not try	Choppy; incomplete	Incorrect	Inaccurate
General understanding	Needs prompting	Little effort	Simple sentences; some run-on sentences	Hard to understand	Neat but little information
Understands problem and considers issues; examines evidence	Appropriate nonverbal and verbal interaction	Works and completes task	Well-constructed sentences	Adequate use of data	Carefully prepared; accurate
Clear understanding; thorough examination of evidence and alternatives	Verbally and nonverbally shows analysis and active listening	Works productively; uses time well; self-motivated	Sentences vary in length and structure; fluid	Plots the data well; easy to interpret	Artfully prepared; neat and accurate; clarifies content

Kingore, B. (2005). *Assessment,* 3rd ed. Austin: Professional Associates Publishing.

Rubrics

Criterion	Level 1	Level 2	Level 3	Level 4
Group cooperation	Did not cooperate	Cooperates but interrupts others	Listens well; helps others; shares	Engaged; encourages and redirects others back to the task
Idea development	Confusing	States a main idea; most details fit	Appropriate main idea and details; clear	Well developed main idea with meaningful details
Integration of skills	Unable to apply skills	Applies some skills; inconsistent	Accurately applies skills in multiple subject areas; minor errors	Consistently integrates skills and information; skillful
Knowledge	Little knowledge; not accurate	Basic facts	Offers most key ideas and concepts; some substantiation	In-depth knowledge; well supported ideas
Math applications	Attempts a solution	Errors are present	Correct solution; minimal prompting or errors	Correct and precisely applied; higher-level response
Math communication	Incorrect	Minimal explanation	Clearly explained; appropriate terminology and graphics	Exceptional explanation; precise terminology and graphics

Kingore, B. (2005). *Assessment,* 3rd ed. Austin: Professional Associates Publishing.

Math concepts	Math strategies	Oral presentation	Organization	Participation	Personal connection
Incorrect	Inappropriate	Needs help to proceed	Unorganized	Does not participate	Lacking
Flawed solution and/or procedures	Flawed application	Needs some help; lacks fluency, eye contact, or gestures	Hard to follow	Responds when asked	Limited
Generally correct solution	Correct and logical; efficient strategies	Well prepared; good gestures and eye contact; well paced	Organized; a clear sequence	Volunteers and responds when necessary	Relates topic to self
Correctly interpreted all important elements	Above expectations; advanced	Exceptional; fluent; mannerisms add to the total effect	Skillfully planned, organized, and sequenced; logical	Volunteers, responds, and elaborates information willfully	Clearly explains and supports connection between self and topic

Kingore, B. (2005). *Assessment,* 3rd ed. Austin: Professional Associates Publishing.

Rubrics

Problem interpretation	Problem solving	Resources	Strategies	Summarization	Technology
Misunderstands	Inappropriate	Inappropriate	Inappropriate	Not well done	Needs assistance
Only a basic understanding	Incomplete or flawed	A few resources used appropriately	Incomplete or flawed	Describes part of the information	Limited success
Generally correct interpretation and explanation	Appropriate process and application	Appropriate in number, kind, and use	Uses limited strategies but applies them appropriately	Summarizes information accurately	Independently uses suggested internet sites
Well analyzed interpretation; clearly understands and explains problem	High-level solution; analyzes well	Extensive and varied; independently uses technology	Effective use of advanced strategies; flexible	Summary is appropriately brief and clearly developed	Advanced; independently navigates with ease

Kingore, B. (2005). *Assessment,* 3rd ed. Austin: Professional Associates Publishing.

Rubrics

Time management	Visual aids	Vocabulary	Voice/style	Writing conventions	Written reflection
Did not complete task	Inappropriate; misused	Incorrect	Not original	Serious errors make it hard to understand	Lacks content
Needed frequent help	Little value; limited use	Simple words and phrases	A little style	Frequent errors but readable; emerging skills	Beginning content level
Used time appropriately	Appropriate in number, kind, and appearance; appropriately used	Descriptive; interesting; uses elaboration	Interesting	Few errors; appropriate for grade level	Appropriate content and effort
Mature management; self-motivated	Very attractive; varied; enriches information; well used	Advanced; uses specific terms; rich imagery	Original, personal, and interesting	Skillful application of mechanics	High-level response and effort; clear interpretation

Kingore, B. (2005). *Assessment,* 3rd ed. Austin: Professional Associates Publishing.

RUBRIC GENERATOR

Expanded Criteria Descriptors

Consider using the following descriptive terms for the achievement levels. The descriptors communicate the desired behaviors of the students as well as the ascending levels of achievement.

Below standard	Intermediate	Advanced	Exceeds standard

Beginning	Developing	Competent	Distinguished

Below expectations	Basic	Proficient	Advanced

Started	On the right track	Got It!	WOW!

Novice	Apprentice	Practitioner	Expert

Emerging	Developing	Proficient	Exemplary

Appearance	Application	Calculations	Carried out plan
Inadequate; not neat; little care evident	Attempts task with limited skill	Inaccurate or mislabeled	Did not complete plan or lacked plan
Adequate; needs more careful work and attention to detail	Hesitant to proceed independently; errors are present	Some calculations shown; some errors	Completed with frequent assistance and prompting
Attractive and visually appealing; neatly completed	Correct response or solution with minimal prompting or errors	Some calculations shown; results are correct and labeled	Completed plan; limited prompting needed
Eye catching; aesthetically pleasing; beyond expectations	Skillful application; higher-level response than expected	All calculations shown; results are correct and appropriately labeled	Followed through well; autonomous; exceeded expectations

Kingore, B. (2005). *Assessment,* 3rd ed. Austin: Professional Associates Publishing.

Communication	Complexity	Comprehension	Constructs meaning	Content depth	Creativity
Not able to discuss; confused or disjointed	Insufficient or irrelevant information	No comprehension is demonstrated of some information	Needs clarity and focus; undeveloped	Needs more information or more accurate information	Used others' ideas or responses
Needs prompting to explain or discuss; lacks a clear focus	Simple and basic information; limited critical thinking is evident	Response reflects a beginning level of understanding of some information	Attempts to construct meaning, but rambles; unclear	Valid but little depth or elaboration; sparse	Typical or cliched responses; little original thinking
Adequate explanation or discussion; appropriate vocabulary	Critical thinking evident; compares and contrasts; integrates topics, time, or disciplines	Appropriate use of details and vocabulary; adequate understanding	Information is generally clear and understandable	Covers topic effectively; well developed and supported; explores the topic beyond facts	Creative integration; enhances more typical ideas or responses
Explains independently, clearly, and confidently; precise vocabulary	Beyond expected level; analyzes multiple perspectives and issues; abstract thinking	Precise vocabulary; supportive ideas; related concepts; demonstrates thorough understanding	Cohesive; meaningful; clearly focused; in-depth analysis	Precise data; in-depth; well supported with details and examples; develops complex concepts and relationships	Unique ideas or responses; insightful; fresh perspective; novel; imaginative

Rubrics

Kingore, B. (2005). *Assessment,* 3rd ed. Austin: Professional Associates Publishing.

Critical thinking	Discussion	Effort/task commitment	Fluency	Graph	Graphics
Vague; basic	No verbal or nonverbal participation demonstrated	Apathetic; resistant	Short, choppy, or incomplete sentences	Messy; incorrectly plotted	Inaccurate
General understanding; focuses on single issue; limited examination of evidence	Some participation with prompting	Incomplete or inadequate for task	Generally complete; simple sentences; some run-on sentences	Distorts the data	Neat and accurate but minimally informative
Understands scope of problem and more than one of the issues; conclusion reflects examination of information	Nonverbally interacts; appropriate verbal participation	Appropriate effort; successful	Well-constructed and varied sentences; smooth transitions	Adequate, but the data is somewhat difficult to interpret	Carefully prepared; accurate; adds to understanding of the topic
Clearly understands scope and issues; conclusions based upon thorough examination of evidence; explores reasonable alternatives; evaluates consequences	Nonverbally encourages others; verbal responses reflect analysis and active learning	Extensive commitment; rigorous effort; autonomous	Crafted with a variety in sentence length and structure that enhances the total effect; fluid	Plots the data well and is easy to interpret	Artfully prepared; neat and accurate; clarifies and embellishes the content

Kingore, B. (2005). *Assessment,* 3rd ed. Austin: Professional Associates Publishing.

Group cooperation	Idea development	Integration of skills	Knowledge	Math applications	Math communication
Inappropriate; resistant	No clear focus or main idea; details are confusing	Unable to apply skills; weak	Little knowledge evident; reiterates one or two facts without complete accuracy	Attempts a solution; limited mathematical applications	Incorrect or no explanation provided
Cooperates but interrupts and needs some prompting to stay on task	Stated main idea; most details relate to it	Attempts to integrate information and skills; inconsistent	Provides basic facts; lacks key ideas; fair degree of accuracy	Hesitant to proceed independently; computational errors are present	Explanation is minimal; basic terminology and/or no graphic support
Engaged; listens attentively; helps others; shares appropriately	Clear focus; appropriate main idea; details relate and clarify ideas	Demonstrates skill mastery by applying skills in multiple subject areas	Accurately relates major ideas and concepts; some appropriate substantiation and analysis	Correct solution is achieved; minimal prompting or errors	Appropriate terminology and graphics; clear explanation
Engaged; encourages and redirects others back to task; negotiates; resolves conflict	Cohesive; well defined and elaborated main idea; details increase interest and meaning	Consistently integrates information and skills in process and product; skillful	Relates in-depth knowledge of concepts and relationships; well supported; examines issues	Formulas are executed correctly; precisely applied; higher-level response than expected	Exceptional explanation; uses advanced, precise terminology and graphics

Kingore, B. (2005). *Assessment,* 3rd ed. Austin: Professional Associates Publishing.

Rubrics

Math concepts	Math strategies	Oral presentation	Organization	Participation	Personal connection
Misunderstood; process and/or solution are incorrect	Inappropriate; no apparent logic to the solution	Needs prompting and assistance	Unclear; lacks organization	Does not willingly participate; resistant	Lacking, insufficient, or irrelevant
Problem is understood but solution and/or procedures are flawed	Approach is oversimplified; strategies are flawed in application	Addresses topic; needed prompting; lacked fluency, eye contact, or gestures	Attempts to organize and sequence but is hard to follow	Does not volunteer but responds when asked	Limited attempt to relate the topic to self
Problem and intended solution are generally correct; used relevant information correctly	Appropriate, efficient strategies; applied correctly and logically	Well prepared; clear; well paced; generally effective speaking techniques	Organized effectively; a good beginning and ending; a clear sequence; well structured	Volunteers once or twice and willingly responds when asked	Credible connection made between self and topic; analysis is evident
All important elements of the problem are correctly interpreted	Innovative and advanced strategies; independently implemented; sophisticated approach and thinking	Exceptional; dynamic; fluent; speech and mannerisms enhance communication	Coherent; skillfully planned; logically sequenced and organized to communicate well	Routinely volunteers; responds and elaborates information	Fully supported and cohesive connection; complex analysis demonstrated

Kingore, B. (2005). *Assessment,* 3rd ed. Austin: Professional Associates Publishing.

Problem interpretation	Problem solving	Resources	Strategies	Summarization	Technology
Misunderstands the problem	Inappropriate process or solution	Inappropriate, unrelated, or no resources used for documentation	Inappropriate	Inadequate and/or inaccurate	Needs assistance to use internet
Basically understands the problem; flaws in interpretation	Incomplete or limited in application; logic is flawed	Minimal resources used appropriately; some resources are not reputable	Limited application; not sure of process; incomplete or flawed	Uses several sentences to describe part of the information	Limited success using internet links to find information
Generally correct interpretation and explanation; appropriate response	Appropriate process and application; analytical thinking is evident	Appropriate in quantity, quality, and application; accurately documented	Successfully applies a limited number of strategies; appropriate process	Correctly and accurately summarizes information	Independently uses suggested internet links to access information; navigates well within sites
Well analyzed and explained interpretation; clearly understands the problem	High-level solution; innovative; synthesizes; evaluates	Extensive, varied, and appropriate; high caliber; accurately documented; incorporates advanced technology	Advanced strategies are independently implemented; flexible and innovative	Clearly and succinctly describes the information; thoughtfully developed	Advanced application; successfully goes beyond suggested links to access information; independently navigates with ease

Kingore, B. (2005). *Assessment,* 3rd ed. Austin: Professional Associates Publishing.

Criterion	Level 1	Level 2	Level 3	Level 4
Time management	Did not complete task	Needed frequent assistance	Used time appropriately	Autonomous; mature time management
Visual aids	Incomplete or inappropriate; misused	Ineffective; minimal visual aids; limited application	Appropriate in quantity, quality, and appearance; appropriately used to support information	High visual appeal; extensive and varied; enhances and integrates information; skillfully used
Vocabulary	Some words are inappropriate or used incorrectly	Words and phrases are simple or vague	Descriptive and interesting language is appropriate with elaboration	Uses specific terminology; precise, advanced language; rich imagery
Voice/style	Formalized	Some personal style	Personal; evokes feelings and interest in the topic	Personal voice enhances appeal and interest; the originality of the ideas linger in your mind
Writing conventions	Serious errors makes reading and understanding difficult	Frequent errors present but content is readable; emerging skills	Minimal errors; mechanics and spelling are typical and appropriate for grade level	Product is enhanced by the skillful application of mechanics; fluid
Written reflection	Content lacks understanding; no effort evident	Content reflects a beginning level of understanding; tried to address the topic	Addresses major content points; some interpretation; appropriate effect	Clearly interprets and synthesizes content; high-level response and effort

• CHAPTER 7 •
Open-Ended Techniques

The same classroom experience often affects different learners in different ways.

—Carol Ann Tomlinson.

<u>*Fulfilling the Promise of the Differentiated Classroom*</u>

Open-ended techniques for assessment and evaluation promote multiple processes and diverse responses. They are less restricted and elicit the student's perceptions of learning through an invitation for high-level thinking. Open-ended techniques increase both students' and teachers' comfort levels with considering different responses and different ways of learning. Inasmuch as they can be used multiple times, they save instruction time and simplify the assessment process.

In order to incorporate a variety of effective open-ended assessment and evaluation techniques, teachers need format samples to prompt their own development of procedures and assessment tools. Effective open-ended formats with less writing are requested by teachers in primary through secondary classrooms to prompt students' reflections and scaffold their thinking. Open-ended techniques include observation, inquiry, checklists, inventories, interviews, and self-assessment devices.

When implementing more open-ended assessment techniques:
- Be flexible.
- Maximize students involvement and responsibilities for record-keeping.
- Take a risk and try something different.
- If a tool does not meet your needs or provide valid diagnostic information, try a different one.

After using an open-ended form, save the results and consider repeating the task at a later date to note students' growth and changes.

Open-Ended Techniques

Kingore, B. (2005). *Assessment,* 3rd ed. Austin: Professional Associates Publishing.

ASSESSMENT THROUGH ANALYTICAL OBSERVATION

Dynamic teachers want to better understand the multiple facets of students and their learning needs. These teachers continually analyze students' behaviors to understand what is occurring in learning situations. Observations during authentic learning experiences enable educators to formulate and substantiate the students' strengths and needs. Analytical observation infers that teachers do more than merely watch; they analyze as they observe to guide instructional decision making.

VALUES OF ANALYTICAL OBSERVATION

- Analytical observation helps define and refine students' levels of development, acquired proficiencies, learning needs, and the multiple facets of their talents and potential.
- It enables teachers to assess the *process* of students' learning as well as the *products* they produce.
- It signals the students' integration and transfer of skills taught in previous classroom learning experiences.
- It increases awareness of different special populations and learning needs that may be clouded by standardized tests results.
- It supports and integrates with other assessments and evaluations.
- It enhances teachers' interpretations and insights about their students.
- It encourages teachers to focus on each student at reoccurring intervals so quiet children do not slip through the cracks.

WHAT DO TEACHERS OBSERVE?

- ### *Skill mastery*
  Which skills have specific students mastered? Which students require additional teaching, continued guided practice, or acceleration of instruction?

- ### *Skill integration*
  Are students appropriately applying the specific skills they have been taught? Are students successfully applying the skills in new learning situations and across content areas? How have advanced children extended the skill applications?

- ### *Modality preferences*
  Which learning experiences do specific students most enjoy? Which learning experiences enable specific students to best succeed?

- ### *Learning needs*
  Is a student frequently demonstrating behaviors typical of students with learning differences or disabilities? What types of additional asssessment information should be requested? What pacing adjustments might benefit this learner?

- ### *Advanced potential*
  Which students consistently demonstrate responses that exceed grade-level expectations? What are their advanced areas? Which students would benefit from an accelerated pace and/or advanced level of instruction?

DOCUMENTATION OF OBSERVATIONS

Analytical observations must be appropriately documented so other educators understand what a teacher has come to know. A combination of assessment procedures effectively documents learning and ensures a valid assessment of students' readiness levels and learning needs.

- Conversations among children reveal the process of their learning. Listening to children as they work and brainstorm together provides insight into each student's prior knowledge, vocabulary, and level of achievement.

Kingore, B. (2005). *Assessment,* 3rd ed. Austin: Professional Associates Publishing.

- DOCUMENTATION: Written anecdotes[25] and checklists

• The products students work on support teachers' observations of the special needs of students. This documentation provides information for more appropriate services for those learners who have different learning and pacing needs.

- DOCUMENTATION: Checklists, lists of learning standards, written anecdotes, and portfolios

INQUIRY

Teachers frequently interpret and respond to what students are trying to do when engaged in learning tasks by questioning and probing for clarity of their thinking. As teachers analyze behaviors, they talk with the students because kids often have significant information to share if only we know to ask. Talking with children about what they are doing or how they feel about their work provides a window that increases adults' understanding of students' behaviors and invites students to bring their thinking to a conscious level. Hence, teachers use inquiry to interpret and respond to what students are trying to do when engaged in learning tasks. The objective is for teachers to model and guide the reflective process so metacognitive or self-monitoring strategies are an internalized part of students' learning.

Inquiry allows teachers to assess the process involved in students' learning rather than only evaluating the product. Inquiry probes are suggested in Figure 7.1 to stimulate your thinking of the questions that would most enhance your understanding of students' learning. Consider which probes might help guide your instructional decisions, and write other questions as they occur to you.

I noticed in many classrooms that when teachers question students about an answer, students frequently change that answer. We infer from this response that students are used to being questioned when they are wrong. Hence, they respond by thinking of another answer. It would be more productive to students' thinking skills and self-confidence if we question them more when they are correct! Then, they will be modeling to other students the thinking behaviors that work.

Teacher to Teacher

Exciting moments and increased mental engagement occur in a lesson when teachers encourage students to produce their own questions. As producers, students are more motivated to offer original ideas, suggest solutions, and reflect upon what they have heard, seen, and done. Model inquiry and then prompt students to develop questions to ask one another.

CHECKLISTS

Checklists are an assessment tool of choice for many teachers. At their best, checklists provide a succinct means of documenting learning and focusing on important learning standards. The caution however, is to avoid checklists that have such an infinite list of isolated skills that the marking is laborious and consumes extensive instructional time. Brief lists can guide assessment and provide a quick

[25] A set of dated, specific anecdotes for each student guides instruction and enhances the information shared at conferences and in report card narratives. See Kingore (2001), for a discussion of an observation folder to systematically and efficiently organize anecdotes for all children.

Kingore, B. (2005). *Assessment,* 3rd ed. Austin: Professional Associates Publishing.

Figure 7.1: INQUIRY PROBES

Communicating with Young Students

Tell me about your picture.
Tell me about your work.
Tell some more so I understand.
How did you figure that out?
What are you thinking about now?
What did you do to begin this work?
What do you plan to do next?
What did you think was easy or difficult?

What would you like to ask about this work?
What changes do you want to make?
What does this remind you of?
If you did not know something, what would you do to learn?
How would you share this information with others?
How is this like (previous content) ?
What is the most important thing you learned from this?

Communicating with Older Students

Talk with me about the work you are doing right now.
What is your next step or idea?
What is another way to approach that?
How did you figure that out?
Why do you think that is so?
What evidence do you have to support that?
What in the text led you to infer or conclude that?
What question is essential to this topic?
What if this happened in a different order or sequence?
If this had not worked, what would you have done?

How would you explain this to another?
What did you want to happen?
What changes do you suggest?
If you did not know, what would you ask to get the most information?
How is this like (previous content) ?
What is a possible relationship between _____ and _____?
What is the most important thing you learned from this?
How would you share this information with others?
What did you think was easy to do and what was difficult?

notation system. Figure 7.2 is an example of such a checklist. After listing the names of the students in the group, a teacher uses this checklist to quickly note skill applications while working with the group.

Students can use checklists to guide their self-assessment. For example, after teaching revision techniques, a simple checklist, such as Figure 7.3, reminds students which techniques to apply during a particular revising session. It is most productive to check one to three of the items at a time for students'

focus. This use of checklists keeps students on track and allows them to take responsibility for their continued achievements.

Checklists are also effective as assessments of students' work ethic and learning behaviors. One example is Learning Characteristics: A Collaborative Assessment (Figure 7.4). This assessment tool encourages the student, a peer, and the teacher to collaboratively analyze that student's work habits and learning behaviors. Using different colors, each person can mark the same copy of the

Figure 7.2: SMALL GROUP CHECKLIST

Jot down notes and ideas. Check *proficient* when applicable.

Students:	Skill:	Skill:	Skill:
	❑ PROFICIENT	❑ PROFICIENT	❑ PROFICIENT
	❑ PROFICIENT	❑ PROFICIENT	❑ PROFICIENT
	❑ PROFICIENT	❑ PROFICIENT	❑ PROFICIENT
	❑ PROFICIENT	❑ PROFICIENT	❑ PROFICIENT
	❑ PROFICIENT	❑ PROFICIENT	❑ PROFICIENT
	❑ PROFICIENT	❑ PROFICIENT	❑ PROFICIENT
	❑ PROFICIENT	❑ PROFICIENT	❑ PROFICIENT
	❑ PROFICIENT	❑ PROFICIENT	❑ PROFICIENT

Kingore, B. (2005). *Assessment,* 3rd ed. Austin: Professional Associates Publishing.

Open-Ended
Techniques

Figure 7.3: REVISING CHECKLIST

❑ Make the beginning catchy to grab a reader's attention.

❑ Add a powerful adjective.

❑ Combine two ideas or two sentences.

❑ Delete a word that is overused or not needed.

❑ Circle two words. Use a thesarus and substitute stronger, sophisticated, more interesting words.

❑ Substitute an action verb with more punch.

❑ Elaborate by adding an appropriate and interesting detail.

❑ Elaborate by using one or more wonder words.
   ❑ Who   ❑ When   ❑ What
   ❑ Where   ❑ Why   ❑ How

❑ Vary sentence beginnings and types of sentences.

❑ Make the ending interesting.

Kingore, B. (2005). *Assessment,* 3rd ed. Austin: Professional Associates Publishing.

---

form for comparison. Teachers in positive, respectful classroom environments, suggest that peer feedback is welcomed and often viewed as very important to their students. In addition, it is helpful in preparation for a parent conference to ask parents to complete this form and then compare their perceptions with the teacher's or student's responses.

INVENTORIES AND INTERVIEWS

Understanding the interests and preferences of everyone in a classroom is important. The more teachers and students know about each other, the more comfortable they tend to be with each other. Students are certainly more likely to risk sharing a divergent question or response in a group with which they are comfortable.

Teachers want to understand students' interests and preferences so they can more effectively match instructional tasks to students' needs. Thus, teachers incorporate interest inventories and interviews that provide insights into students' interests and learning passions. The problem, however, is that many instruments that elicit students' interests are labor intensive and require extensive hand writing. To ease that difficulty for students, this section features simplified formats that often integrate art with written responses and even invite students to collaborate. Many of these forms are appropriate for young children and special-needs learners.

Kingore, B. (2005). *Assessment,* 3rd ed. Austin: Professional Associates Publishing.

Figure 7.4: LEARNING CHARACTERISTICS: A COLLABORATIVE ASSESSMENT

STUDENT _____   DATE _____

PEER _____   DATE _____

PARENT _____   DATE _____

TEACHER _____   DATE _____

Work and Study Habits	Consistently	Sometimes	Not Yet
Stays on task			
Manages time well			
Organizes work			
Uses multiple, appropriate resources			
Reorganizes and returns materials			
Sets goals for self			
Seeks help when needed			
Does not call undo attention to self			
Completes quality work			

Persistence			
Shows patience			
Self-monitors and checks own work			
Edits and revises work			
Is willing to try something new			
Accepts responsibility for own learning			

Social Skills			
Communicates diplomatically			
Works cooperatively			
Listens attentively			
Helps others as needed			
Encourages others			
Respects others' ideas and property			
Works and interacts with others quietly			

Comments:

Adapted from: Kingore, B. (2004). *Differentiation: Simplified, Realistic, and Effective.*
Austin: Professional Associates Publishing.

. ——————— **VALUES** ——————— .

Effective inventories and interviews
- Encourage respect and appreciation for students' differences.
- Help teachers learn more about each student.
- Build students' self-esteem.
- Promote high achievement by incorporating students' interests.[26]
- Enable teachers to form flexible groups based upon interests.
- Encourage independent study responding to students' interests.
- Enable teachers to establish mentorships for students.

GUIDELINES

- Inform students before they begin if you plan to display the inventories in the room for all to view. The inventories make an interesting and often visually intriguing display for students to compare and contrast information, but they should know in advance that their work will be shared.

- Consider asking students to complete an interest inventory or interview at the beginning of the year and then again later in the year, and store both forms in their portfolios. It is interesting for students to realize how their interests can change with time.

- To a point, encourage students to consider which of their interests are school applicable and appropriate. Interests applicable to school enable teachers to plan school experiences that incorporate and extend what students know about their favorite topics. For example, a student's interest in rain forests would often have more future learning connections at school than a student's interest in an arcade game.

- Inventories and interviews provide teachers with the information to incorporate better learning options. Some students perform at a higher level when they have some power of choice. *Choice* does not provide students with a license that anything goes. Rather, inventories and interviews should help teachers and students negotiate learning experiences which are appealing to the student and applicable to the desired learning outcomes.

- Have both the interviewer and the student sign the interview when the information is completed. The signatures assure that both people understand the responses and avoid the responses seeming to be secret or something to be used against a student.

PICTURE INTEREST INVENTORY

Picture interest inventories such as Figure 7.5 invite students to illustrate and write about things they most like and want to learn. The idea of integrating art with an investigation of a student's interests is shared by Miriam Winegar in Oregon. This application results in a great visual display for your room and is particularly an asset for spatial and visual learners who benefit from using art to communicate their ideas.

Procedure

To begin, ask students to brainstorm and list what they are most interested in and want to learn more about at school. Encourage them to think about their preferences and add to their list over several days. Teachers have found that these inventories are more valid when students have time to reflect and respond rather than complete the inventory at one time.

[26]Amabile (1983) and Csikszentmihalyi (1997) support that motivation to achieve increases when a student's interests are incorporated.

Kingore, B. (2005). *Assessment,* 3rd ed. Austin: Professional Associates Publishing.

Figure 7.5: PICTURE INTEREST INVENTORY

NAME _____ DATE _____

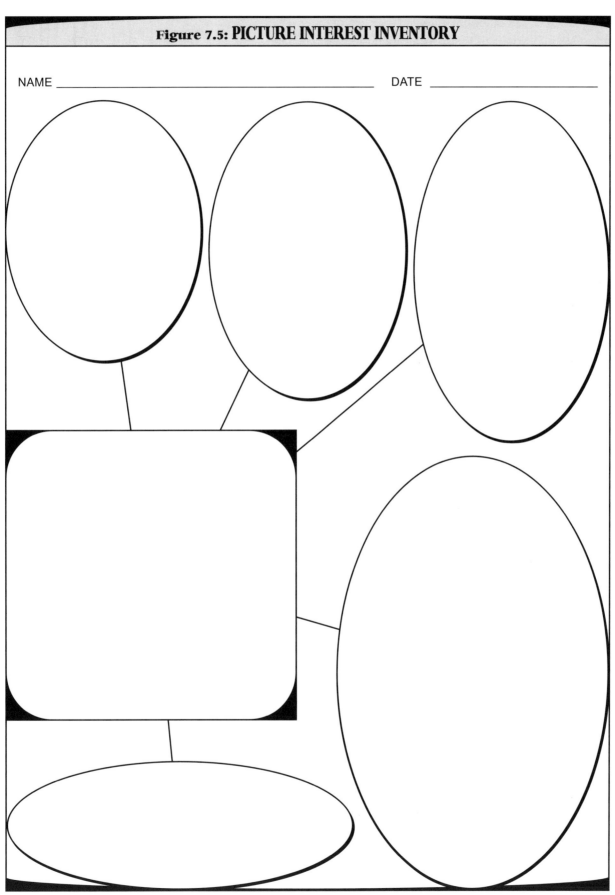

Kingore, B. (2005). *Assessment,* 3rd ed. Austin: Professional Associates Publishing.

Next, ask students to revisit their list of interests and prioritize them. With primary students, ask them to put a check or a star by the ones that they most like. With older students, ask them to rate each as a one, two, or three to denote the level of interest. Secondary students can rank their lists with one being their greatest interest and continue numbering to their lowest interest. Prioritizing is a life skill. Students cannot time manage or make decisions unless they learn to prioritize. This step effectively applies that high-level thinking skill.

Finally, students choose their highest rated interests to illustrate and write about on their Picture Interest Inventory. They paste their photograph in the box and then illustrate one interest in each of the ovals. The largest oval is for their greatest interest; descending oval sizes represent descending priorities in interests. For the best success, have students draw one picture and then write about it before beginning another illustration. Teachers found that when students completed all of the art first, their written explanations were less expansive and showed less thinking than when they went back and forth between drawing and completing their written explanations.

Applications Involving Teachers
- Develop picture inventories as a class project to celebrate individual interests, similarities, and differences.
- Develop an interest inventory for yourself. Students enjoy knowing more about their teacher.

Applications Involving Families
- For young children, encourage an adult family member to assist the student in developing a picture interest inventory at home.
- All family members can develop individual inventories to share together as a family or to use in planning family activities or vacations in which everyone's interests are actively incorporated.

With primary-aged students, use Big Buddies to more efficiently complete picture interest inventories. Arrange for upper-elementary students to work with the younger children in one or more sessions to individualize and complete the inventories. Teachers are then free to facilitate the process rather than be responsible for completing most of the writing for the children.

I'M GOOD AT... I'M NOT GOOD AT... I WANT TO LEARN...

This inventory is particularly useful in mixed-ability classrooms with a wide range of student abilities. It is an effective way to accent that all students have something they do well, something they perceive they do not do well, and something they want to learn this year at school.

Students fold a large piece of paper into thirds and label each third: *I'm Good At... I'm Not Good At...* and *I Want to Learn...* Encourage students to draw and write one or more responses in each column.

One insightful teacher in Wichita, Kansas had her class silently walk around the room to view what other students had included on their forms. Her challenge to her students: *Find a classmate who wants to learn what you know well and another classmate who is good at an area in which you need help. We are the best we can be, and we are here to learn together and help each other.*

Kingore, B. (2005). *Assessment,* 3rd ed. Austin: Professional Associates Publishing.

Teachers, consider completing this three column inventory for yourself and share your responses with your class. As you share who you are with your students, you are also modeling that you are a life-long learner. There are always wonderful things to learn at any age.

I WANT TO LEARN ABOUT _____.

Figures 7.6 provides an alternative inventory that appeals to visual and spatial learners. Encourage the students to draw multiple responses and add words or phrases, almost graffiti style, to clarify their choices. Suggest that advanced students create symbols for their interests instead of just drawing literal pictures. Explaining the symbols often invites students to discuss their inventories at greater length with each other.

PROJECT INTERVIEW

One way to respond to the individual differences of your students is to use a project interview, such as Figure 7.7. Rather than all students completing the same project, the results of these interviews will suggest a wide variety of projects to maximize student interest and motivation.

The project interview in this chapter requires students to think about their priorities and plan an appropriate project that is interesting to them but also applies related skills and learning standards. Thus, the project is a defensible learning experience rather than just *fun* and *creative*. Students are asked to plan a sequence for completing the project so they are more likely to succeed in a timely fashion.

In most cases, the student should write out responses to each item on the interview

WAYS TO COMPLETE INTERVIEWS

Student's self-reflection

A student writes responses on an interview form and then briefly meets with the teacher to discuss the results or shares the responses in a class discussion.

Student's self-taped interview

A student tape records responses to the interview questions. This option is especially helpful for special-need students for whom handwriting is difficult. It is also effective with young students when an older student or adult is available at a later time to transcribe the recording. With this option, older students can also transcribe the recording in their own classroom as an exercise to practice skills in the mechanics of writing.

Student to student interview

Students interview each other and write each others responses as the interview proceeds. This process invites interaction, discussion, and comparison between the students.

Teacher to student interview

The teacher interviews a student and writes the student's responses.

Adult to student interview

A parent at home, a parent volunteer at school, or another significant adult interviews a student and writes the student's responses.

Open-Ended Techniques

Kingore, B. (2005). *Assessment,* 3rd ed. Austin: Professional Associates Publishing.

Figure 7.6: I WANT TO LEARN ABOUT _____.

Figure 7.7: PROJECT INTERVIEW

NAME _____   DATE _____

SUBJECT AREA OR TOPIC _____

1. What are you interested in doing?

2. How is this project relevant to your topic?

3. Which learning standards and skills can be incorporated in this project?

4. What important skills or information can you gain from this project?

5. What will be your final product?

6. What resources will you need, and how will you access them?

7. How may I or others help?

8. On the back of this page, sketch a time line or flow chart of your project showing dates and steps from the beginning to the completion of your work.

STUDENT'S SIGNATURE _____

INTERVIEWER'S SIGNATURE _____

Open-Ended Techniques

Kingore, B. (2005). *Assessment,* 3rd ed. Austin: Professional Associates Publishing.

and then briefly meet with the teacher to discuss and brainstorm further. Having students complete the interview first requires them to organize their thoughts and enables a more productive use of time when the teacher and student meet to discuss the project plan.

READING OR MATH INTERVIEW

Interviewing is a valuable way to gain information about students' learning processes and strategies. Interviews also help students become more aware of their thinking as they discuss their learning process. After an interview is complete, the teacher and student can use the recorded information to analyze the student's strengths and to determine the most productive instructional decisions.

A Reading Interview and a Math Problem Solving Interview are included as Figures 7.8 and 7.9. The questions are intended to be flexible. They can be varied as appropriate to increase students' understanding and reworded to use with young students.

The Reading Interview and the Math Problem Solving Interview are particularly effective as repeated tasks. Have students complete the interview at the beginning of the year and then again later in the year to compare the changes and growth in their perceptions about their learning.

CLASSMATE INTERVIEW AND BANK OF INTERVIEW QUESTIONS

Students enjoy talking together and learning more about one another. The Classmate Interview in Figure 7.10 is a sample form to use. For more authentic interviews, students select and create their own interview

questions. The Bank of Interview Questions in Figure 7.11 encourages students to select the questions that are most appropriate to their interviewing situation and then brainstorm and plan additional questions. Discuss the value of open-ended questions that encourage multiple-word responses instead of single-word answers.

As a foreign language application, conduct the interview in a foreign language for a learning task incorporating vocabulary, fluency and grammar.

Combine all of the completed Classmate Interviews into a class Who's Who Book. Add a photograph or the interviewed student's original artwork on another page to illustrate each interview. Arrange the pages so that the illustration and the interview are on the same two-page spread as the book is read.

Primary and intermediate teachers using open-ended forms suggest that students' reflective thinking is more important than spelling and handwriting during the self-assessmenty process. Focus on students' analysis of the merits of their work and encourage them to be thoughtful in their responses. This emphasis proves more successful in motivating students to be reflective.

Figure 7.8: READING INTERVIEW

NAME _____   DATE _____

SUBJECT AREA OR TOPIC _____

1. Are you a good reader? Why?

2. What do you most like to read?

3. How do you choose something to read?

4. When are you most likely to read something?

5. What do you do when you come to a word you do not know?

6. What do you do when you do not understand what you read?

7. How do you help yourself remember what you read?

8. How would you explain "reading" to a young child who asks you how to read?

STUDENT'S SIGNATURE _____

INTERVIEWER'S SIGNATURE _____

Open-Ended Techniques

Kingore, B. (2005). *Assessment,* 3rd ed. Austin: Professional Associates Publishing.

Figure 7.9: MATH PROBLEM SOLVING INTERVIEW

NAME _____ DATE _____

SUBJECT AREA OR TOPIC _____

On the back of this paper, copy a complex story problem and solve it.

1. What can you tell me about this problem?

2. Which words are most important? Why?

3. Is there something that can be eliminated or something missing?

4. How might a diagram or a sketch be helpful?

5. Tell me the sequence of steps you went through to solve this problem.

6. What would you caution someone else about this problem? Is there a part where one should be especially careful?

7. What is a way to check your answer?

STUDENT'S SIGNATURE _____

INTERVIEWER'S SIGNATURE _____

Kingore, B. (2005). *Assessment,* 3rd ed. Austin: Professional Associates Publishing.

Figure 7.10: CLASSMATE INTERVIEW

NAME _____   DATE _____

Peer's name _____   Nickname _____

Birth date _____   Birth place _____

Brothers and sisters _____

Pets _____

Two favorite authors _____

Two favorite books _____

Favorite TV show _____   Favorite movie _____

Favorite song or group _____

Favorite place on Earth _____

What are your hobbies, collections, and interests?

Who is your role model? Why?

What is your favorite memory?

If you could meet and talk with anyone, who would it be? Why?

What four words best describe you?

• _____   • _____

• _____   • _____

What would you like everyone to know about you?

What is something you have done that made you especially proud?

What is the best gift you have ever received?

Kingore, B. (2005). *Assessment,* 3rd ed. Austin: Professional Associates Publishing.

Open-Ended Techniques

Figure 7.11: BANK OF INTERVIEW QUESTIONS, Page 1

Check the questions you want to incorporate in your interview.
Then, write additional questions that are appropriate to your interview situation.

TELL ME ABOUT YOURSELF
- ❏ Nickname
- ❏ Family members
- ❏ Where born
- ❏ Birth date
- ❏ Pets
- ❏ Hobbies
- ❏ Special interests

FAVORITE THINGS
- ❏ What is your favorite sport?
- ❏ What kind of TV programs do you like to watch?
- ❏ What is your favorite style of music?
- ❏ What are your three favorite books?
- ❏ What do you collect? What got you started with your collection?
- ❏ What is your favorite season? Why?
- ❏ What kind of weather do you like best? Why?
- ❏ What is your favorite memory?

SCHOOL
- ❏ What is your favorite subject at school?
- ❏ What would you most like to learn?
- ❏ What do you like best about school? Least about school?
- ❏ If you were a teacher, how would you teach your class?
- ❏ What changes would you make to improve the school?
- ❏ What would the perfect classroom look like?
- ❏ Do you most enjoy working alone or with others? Why?
- ❏ What is the best book you have read?
- ❏ If you wrote a book, what would it be about?
- ❏ What is the most interesting non-fiction book you have read?
- ❏ What is the most interesting problem you have solved at school?
- ❏ What is the hardest thing for you at school?

PERSONAL CHOICES
- ❏ What is the best thing about being you? What is the worst?
- ❏ What is your idea of a schedule for a perfect Saturday ?
- ❏ Have you ever invented anything or had an idea for an invention? What?
- ❏ What do you think is the most important invention ever created? Why?
- ❏ Which five words best describe you?
- ❏ Which two words are least like you?

Kingore, B. (2005). *Assessment,* 3rd ed. Austin: Professional Associates Publishing.

Figure 7.11: BANK OF INTERVIEW QUESTIONS, Page 2

- ❑ What is the best news you could get now?
- ❑ What is something you heard on the news that interests you? Why?
- ❑ What is the best thing that has ever happened to you?
- ❑ What is something important others should know about you?
- ❑ Who is the person you would most like to meet?
- ❑ Who is a person you hope you never meet?
- ❑ What do you think is the perfect age to be? Why?
- ❑ How do you best express yourself?
- ❑ When alone, what do you most like to do?

FEELINGS
- ❑ What is the most beautiful thing you've ever seen?
- ❑ What makes you feel grouchy or annoyed?
- ❑ What fascinates you?
- ❑ What do you most like about TV or the movies? What do you least like?
- ❑ What do you feel is the most important thing about living in the U.S.A.?
- ❑ What time of the day do you feel your best? Why?
- ❑ Which feeling is the most important? Why?
- ❑ Who or what makes you laugh?

FUTURE CHOICES
- ❑ What is something you really want but can't afford right now?
- ❑ What do you think is the best thing about being an adult?
- ❑ What will you be doing ____ years from now?
- ❑ What would you change if you could change the world?
- ❑ What is your greatest hope for the future?
- ❑ In the future, where would you most like to explore? Why?

IMAGINING
- ❑ If you had three wishes what would they be?
- ❑ If you had three wishes that had to be used to help others, what would they be?
- ❑ If you could invite four famous people to dinner, who would you invite? What would you discuss?
- ❑ What would your perfect bedroom look like?
- ❑ Where is another place you would like to live? Why?
- ❑ What would you do with $1000?
- ❑ If you could meet and talk with anyone in the world, who would it be?
- ❑ If you could participate in any event in history, what would it be?
- ❑ In which time in history would you prefer to live? Why?

Open-Ended Techniques

Kingore, B. (2005). *Assessment,* 3rd ed. Austin: Professional Associates Publishing.

STUDENTS' SELF-ASSESSMENT

The assessment and evaluation tools presented in this section accent students' analysis of their own work as well as the collaborative process of the students and teachers analyzing proficiencies. As Costa and Kallick accent,[27] *We must constantly remind ourselves that the ultimate purpose of education is to have students become self-evaluating. If students graduate from our schools still dependent upon others to tell them when they are adequate, good, or excellent, then we've missed the whole point of what education is about.*

Students use the Reading Review form (Figure 7.12) as an alternative to reading logs. On the form, students periodically reflect about a book they have read or are reading. The students' favorite part of the task is creating their own graphics for rating the book.

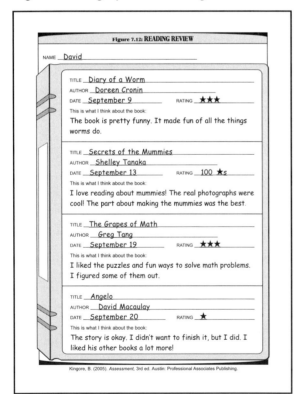

Kingore, B. (2005). *Assessment*, 3rd ed. Austin: Professional Associates Publishing.

Share with your class several examples of written reviews, such as television, movie, and book reviews. After discussing different kinds of ratings, allow students to create their own rating systems. Most students base their ratings on large numbers, such as *one million stars*. Some students, however, create more symbolic or abstract rating systems, like Kourtney's weather ratings and Michael's brain connections.

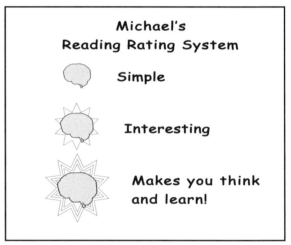

GRAPHIC ORGANIZERS FOR SELF-ASSESSMENT

Students' self-assessments can take many forms. Graphic organizers that teachers use for instruction can also be effective forms to prompt students' reflection. In the following example, the PMI strategy[28] is used to evaluate the first year of implementing portfolios in

[27] See Costa, A., & Kallick, B., 1992.
[28] See De Bono, E., 1993.

Kingore, B. (2005). *Assessment,* 3rd ed. Austin: Professional Associates Publishing.

Figure 7.12: READING REVIEW

NAME _____

Great Books!

TITLE _____

AUTHOR _____

DATE _____ RATING _____

This is what I think about the book:

TITLE _____

AUTHOR _____

DATE _____ RATING _____

This is what I think about the book:

TITLE _____

AUTHOR _____

DATE _____ RATING _____

This is what I think about the book:

TITLE _____

AUTHOR _____

DATE _____ RATING _____

This is what I think about the book:

Kingore, B. (2005). *Assessment,* 3rd ed. Austin: Professional Associates Publishing.

one middle school. The student's response shared here illustrates how the plus, minus, and interesting columns prompt critical thinking.

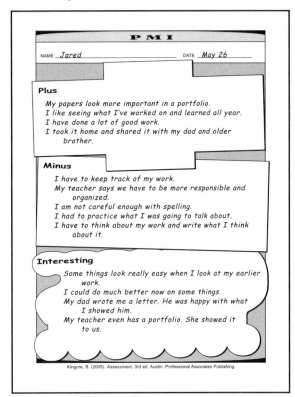

P M I

NAME _Jared_   DATE _May 26_

Plus

My papers look more important in a portfolio.
I like seeing what I've worked on and learned all year.
I have done a lot of good work.
I took it home and shared it with my dad and older
    brother.

Minus

I have to keep track of my work.
My teacher says we have to be more responsible and
    organized.
I am not careful enough with spelling.
I had to practice what I was going to talk about.
I have to think about my work and write what I think
    about it.

Interesting

Some things look really easy when I look at my earlier
    work.
I could do much better now on some things.
My dad wrote me a letter. He was happy with what
    I showed him.
My teacher even has a portfolio. She showed it
    to us.

Kingore, B. (2005). *Assessment*, 3rd ed. Austin: Professional Associates Publishing.

The PMI strategy is easily implemented by having students fold plain paper into thirds to create areas for organizing their responses. Students can turn paper horizontally for hand-writing ease.

Open-ended formats with less writing are effective for primary students and students with special learning needs. Both the Discussion Assessment (Figure 7.13) and the Teamwork Assessment (Figure 7.14) invite teachers to list the criteria specific to group tasks. The same forms can be used more than once as different criteria are listed when the tasks vary. The Teamwork Assessment uses thumbs-up graphics for students' assessments. The Discussion Assessment has blank places so a teacher can use a variety of assessment icons or words. Working individually on the Discussion Assessment or as a group on the Teamwork Assessment, students

assess the quality of their work when the task is complete. The discussion that ensues is reflective and often encourages the refinement of group interaction skills for future group work.

Figure 7.13: DISCUSSION ASSESSMENT

NAME _Gretchen_   DATE _March 15_
TOPIC _What can we do to help protect the environment?_

CRITERIA:	Below standard	C	B	A
1. *I read the assignment and prepared two key points.*				✓
2. *I made a positive contribution.*				✓
3. *I gave others a chance to participate, too.*			✓	
4. *I respected my classmates' ideas.*				✓
5. *I made my point promptly.*		✓		
6. *I asked questions that helped others think.*			✓	

How I prepared for the discussion:
I read the assignment and tried to think of two points and a question to share.

Something I liked:
Piggy-backing on each others' ideas worked well and was fun.

What I will do next time:
I will try to let other people talk more. I rambled, and others stopped listening to me.

Kingore, B. (2005). *Assessment*, 3rd ed. Austin: Professional Associates Publishing.

Figure 7.14: TEAMWORK ASSESSMENT

TEAM _Brian, Logan, Scott, Amelia, and Jess_
ASSIGNMENT _Building a newspaper bridge_
DATE _December 6_

CRITERIA:	👍	👎 (sideways)	👎
1. *We followed directions and planned well.*		✓	
2. *We helped each other problem solve.*	✓		
3. *We worked quietly together.*			✓
4. *We cooperated and encouraged each other.*	✓		
5. *We all gave ideas and helped each other.*	✓		
6. *Our bridge test was successful.*	✓		

What we enjoyed:
We liked working together to build and test the bridge.

What our team did well:
We all tried hard, and it was so much fun designing and building the bridge exactly like we planned. We really did well at being thoughtful and nice to each other.

How we need to improve:
We need to be more considerate to other groups. We got into trouble for being too noisy, but we were mostly loud because we got so excited about what we were doing.

Kingore, B. (2005). *Assessment*, 3rd ed. Austin: Professional Associates Publishing.

Kingore, B. (2005). *Assessment,* 3rd ed. Austin: Professional Associates Publishing.

Figure 7.13: DISCUSSION ASSESSMENT

NAME _____ DATE _____

TOPIC _____

CRITERIA:				
1.				
2.				
3.				
4.				
5.				
6.				

How I prepared for the discussion:

Something I liked:

What I will do next time:

Kingore, B. (2005). *Assessment,* 3rd ed. Austin: Professional Associates Publishing.

Open-Ended Techniques

Figure 7.14: TEAMWORK ASSESSMENT

TEAM _____

ASSIGNMENT _____

DATE _____

CRITERIA:	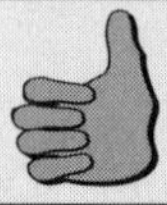 👍	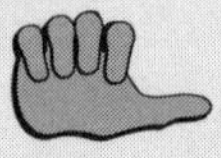 ✊	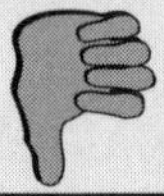 👎
1.			
2.			
3.			
4.			
5.			
6.			

What we enjoyed:

What our team did well:

How we need to improve:

GRAPHIC ORGANIZERS FOR EVALUATION

In addition to diagnosing students' strengths and needs, open-ended formats can be adapted to establish grades. The Editing Checklist Evaluation (Figure 7.15) and the Project Checklist Evaluation (Figure 7.16) illustrate that adding a scoring scale allows a holistic conclusion to be reached about the quality of the work. The teacher, with input from the students if desired, lists statements on the numbered lines of the form, describing the task and designating the attributes of the task. When the learning task is complete, the student self-evaluates by filling out the checklist, finishing the sentence-stem reflections, and circling a holistic interpretation of the level of quality attained. Then, the teacher uses the same copy of the form to complete an evaluation of the quality of the work. The Literature Evaluation (Figure 7.17) illustrates that evaluative scales can also be included on assessments that are composed of sentence stems.

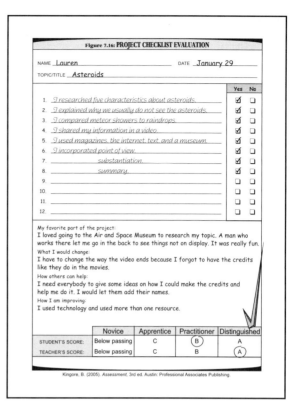

Adapt the forms to your grading needs by varying the scoring scale at the bottom of each form. Possible variations are included in the examples to prompt your thinking.

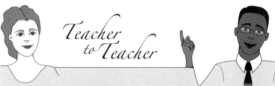

Using these forms as examples, encourage intermediate, middle school, and high school students to create their own open-ended assessment and evaluation forms. Shifting students from consumers to producers increases their involvement and sense of ownership in assessment procedures. Enhance their enjoyment of the task by allowing them to incorporate illustrations with clever or humorous phrases instead of more formal terminology.

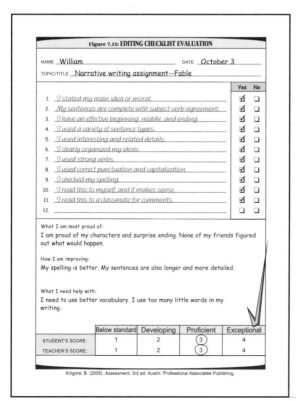

Kingore, B. (2005). *Assessment,* 3rd ed. Austin: Professional Associates Publishing.

Figure 7.15: EDITING CHECKLIST EVALUATION

NAME _____ DATE _____

TOPIC/TITLE _____

		Yes	No
1.	_____	☐	☐
2.	_____	☐	☐
3.	_____	☐	☐
4.	_____	☐	☐
5.	_____	☐	☐
6.	_____	☐	☐
7.	_____	☐	☐
8.	_____	☐	☐
9.	_____	☐	☐
10.	_____	☐	☐
11.	_____	☐	☐
12.	_____	☐	☐

What I am most proud of:

How I am improving:

What I need help with:

STUDENT'S SCORE:				
TEACHER'S SCORE:				

Kingore, B. (2005). *Assessment,* 3rd ed. Austin: Professional Associates Publishing.

Figure 7.16: PROJECT CHECKLIST EVALUATION

NAME _____ DATE _____

TOPIC/TITLE _____

	Yes	No
1. _____	☐	☐
2. _____	☐	☐
3. _____	☐	☐
4. _____	☐	☐
5. _____	☐	☐
6. _____	☐	☐
7. _____	☐	☐
8. _____	☐	☐
9. _____	☐	☐
10. _____	☐	☐
11. _____	☐	☐
12. _____	☐	☐

My favorite part of the project:

What I would change:

How others can help:

How I am improving:

STUDENT'S SCORE:				
TEACHER'S SCORE:				

Open-Ended Techniques

Figure 7.17: LITERATURE EVALUATION

NAME _____ DATE _____

TITLE _____

AUTHOR _____

I would compare this book to: _____

by: _____

Why:

The best things about this book:

How I demonstrated my learning:

Skills I used in my work:

STUDENT'S SCORE:				
TEACHER'S SCORE:				

Kingore, B. (2005). *Assessment,* 3rd ed. Austin: Professional Associates Publishing.

· CHAPTER 8 ·

Products:
Assessing and Differentiating

*Tell me I forget. Show me, I remember.
Involve me, I understand.*
—*Chinese Proverb*

Products result from *content* (the complexity of what students are to know) and *process* (how students use key skills and relate ideas as they make sense of the content). Students create products to demonstrate and extend what they learn. Thus, products are related to both learning activities and assessment. Well-designed product assignments have the potential to motivate students to excel[29] and encourage students to process information and apply skills in meaningful ways. The results assess students' learning and inform teachers.

Products include responses in the form of concrete items, physical actions, and verbal conclusions or summaries of understanding. Inherent within these products are more abstract outcomes from the students' work. These abstract products encompass enduring learning qualities such as frameworks of knowledge, strategies, attitudes, and self-efficacy (Tomlinson et al, 2002).

Products are an assessment tool when they provide concrete evidence of learning.

Through an effectively designed and completed product, students communicate their level of understanding. The product documents the student's achievement of the learning objectives.

Products are an evaluation tool when teachers evaluate the quality of the products and assign grades. However, teachers also assess product results to monitor and adjust instruction in order to ensure that all students experience continuous learning success. Another layer of assessment occurs when teachers evaluate students' work habits as students are engaged in the process of completing products. A final assessment application occurs when comparing a student's products completed over time. Both the student and teacher can use those products to assess how that student has grown and changed as a learner.

PRODUCT OPTIONS

Product options abound. To have value as assessment tools, however, product

---

[29] Research evidence, particularly that from Amabile (1983) and Csikszentmihalyi (1997), support that motivation to achieve increases when a student's interests are incorporated.

Kingore, B. (2005). *Assessment,* 3rd ed. Austin: Professional Associates Publishing.

assignments must be closely aligned to the learning objectives so understanding can be diagnosed. Exemplary products have an audience beyond the grading pen and stem from authentic tasks--representing the work of practitioners in a field. Teachers also seek products that can be efficiently prepared and involve students in respectful, equitable work.[30]

To increase the efficiency of determining appropriate product assignments, initiate or continue creating a list of products applicable to the curriculum and learning standards. Reflect upon the developing list, and ponder which product options:

- Are most appropriate for the students' ages, learning profiles, and interests.
- Are most applicable to the content.
- Actively engage students in applying and transferring acquired skills.
- Promote depth and complexity of content.
- Have diagnostic value.
- Are respectful, equitable work.
- Promote continuous learning success.
- Stem from the authentic problems and audiences.
- Require available materials and appropriate amounts of time.
- Encourage variety in applications.
- Are most enjoyable to facilitate.[31]

Students vary so dramatically in their strengths, needs, and best ways to learn that the differences are boggling in today's classrooms. To engage more students more of the time, classroom learning tasks need to offer as wide a variety in the types of products assigned as the variety represented by the students' learning profiles. When determining product assignments, teachers strive to incorporate a balance of learning modalities and intelligences. This balanced offering of product

assignments encourages students to demonstrate their best ways to learn and validates the significance of all modalities and intelligences. Students are more successful in learning tasks that respond to their readiness levels and incorporate their modality and intelligence strengths.[32]

Some educators, however, do not provide a balance of product offerings to students. Many inadvertently teach using products most related to their own strengths and passions. Still other teachers spend exorbitant amounts of time and energy seeking new products that their students have not experienced. They misinterpret variety to mean *fun* and end up on a product treadmill trying to find something new, sadly, sometimes inviting more fluff than substance that might interest students.

Products promote learning when they integrate students' best ways to learn and evolve from the curriculum and selected learning standards as authentic ways to demonstrate applications.

THE PRODUCT GRID

Teachers need a system to organize product options for learning with a concrete approach to product assignments that enables them to customize tasks effectively and efficiently. One example of a system for product options is a product grid. Participating teachers compliment the product grid system as one tool that helps more efficiently differentiate learning experiences and product assignments.

A product grid organizes multiple products appropriate to a class by encoding each product to learning modalities and multiple

---

[30] In Kingore (2004), Appendix B: Product Options for Differentiated Instruction presents a lengthy list of products designed for teachers to skim as a visual checklist to guide selection of the most appropriate product options for students.

[31] Adapted from Kingore, (2004), p. 23.

[32] See Vygotsky (1986), Csikszentmihalyi (1997), Grigorenko & Sternberg (1997), and Sternberg et al., (1998).

Kingore, B. (2005). *Assessment,* 3rd ed. Austin: Professional Associates Publishing.

intelligences.[33] As product options are deter-mined, they are listed in alphabetical order for quick reference. Each product is then coded to the modalities and intelligence preferences primarily required by the student to complete the product and present or share it with others.

In addition to matching the best ways for students to learn, the objective of a product grid is to replace simple, right-answer sheets that require little thinking with tasks that encourage active participation and challenge students to generate responses. To advance learning, the products must connect to content and invite students to apply and transfer acquired skills. The intent is not to entertain students but rather to engage them so appro-priately in learning experiences that enjoyment results. Experienced teachers report that these products also serve as springboards for increased discussion and interaction among students.

The following codes appear in the product grid examples in this chapter. If desired, vary the application of a product grid so it is more appropriate to students' needs by developing additional codes relating to inter-ests, culture, and gender.

Modality codes

V	=	visual
O/A	=	oral/auditory
W	=	written
K	=	kinesthetic

Multiple Intelligence codes

L	=	linguistic
L-M	=	logical-mathematical
N	=	naturalist
S	=	spatial
M	=	musical
B-K	=	bodily kinesthetic
Inter	=	interpersonal
Intra	=	intrapersonal

The products are coded to include the logical-mathematical and naturalist intelli-gences if the content of the products can incorporate specific logical-mathematical or naturalist content in the task. For example, the creation of a flow chart engages naturalistic intelligence when a student explains the life cycle of a rainforest butterfly or frog.

Most products incorporate interper-sonal intelligences when completed by a group of students; products encourage more intrapersonal intelligence when completed by an individual. Hence, both interpersonal intel-ligence and intrapersonal intelligence are marked for any product that could be completed equally well by either a group or an individual. As often as is appropriate, a teacher may begin a task assignment by stating to the class, *By yourself or with one or two other people...* Thus, students are sometimes given the choice to work alone or with others. As one wise gifted student observed, *You can't work with others all of the time without com-promising what you could really do.*

A PRODUCT GRID BLANK

A blank form for a product grid is provid-ed (Figure 8.1) so teachers can organize their instructional product options. Alphabetically list the products that are developmentally appro-priate to the students, most applicable to teaching, and useful to integrate learning stan-dards. Then, code each product to the learning modalities and multiple intelligences primarily required by students to complete and present that product.

[33] See Appendix B for a brief discussion of multiple intelligences.

Kingore, B. (2005). *Assessment,* 3rd ed. Austin: Professional Associates Publishing.

Figure 8.1: PRODUCT GRID FOR _____

	MODALITIES				MULTIPLE INTELLIGENCES							
	V	O/A	W	K	L	L-M	N	S	M	B-K	Inter	Intra

Kingore, B. (2005). *Assessment,* 3rd ed. Austin: Professional Associates Publishing.

PRODUCT GRID APPLICATIONS TO DIFFERENTIATE INSTRUCTION

Product grids provide six differentiation options.

PRODUCT-STUDENT MATCH

1 The teacher develops and uses a general product grid such as Figure 8.2 to more accurately prescribe a specific product appropriate to a student's learning profile, product preferences, and unique learning needs. The intent is to match product assignments to students' prior knowledge and learning rate.

LEARNING TASK EXTENSION

2 When a teacher skims a general product grid and a desired modality or intelligence is not engaged, the teacher ponders how the task might be varied to incorporate that need. For example, when a student makes a booklet about a topic, oral/auditory modes are not required. To address the needs of a highly auditory learner, a teacher might vary the task by: 1) allowing the student to record the booklet as a read-along book for others, 2) inviting the student to read the booklet to another class, or 3) arranging for the student to produce the booklet. In this manor, a product grid assists teachers' objective to select product assignments that orchestrate all of the modes of learning and intelligence preferences.

PRODUCT CHOICE

3 When preparing a lesson, the teacher may skim a list of products and select more than one option for students to use, all of which are appropriate to the learning task and the students. Product options allow each student some choice in how to demonstrate their learning, and the power of choice increases students' motivation to excel.

Figure 8.2: GENERAL PRODUCT GRID[34]

The grid lists products (acrostic, advertisement, analogy, annotated bibliography, audio tape, banner, bio poem, book or booklet, brochure, bulletin board, candidate platform/speech, cartoon or caricature, center (student made), chart, children's story (illustrated), choral reading, collection collage, comic strip, concept map (web), critique, cross section, dance, debate, demonstration, description, diagram (labeled), dialogue, diorama, display (labeled artifacts), documentary film, editorial, encyclopedia entry, essay, experiment, fable, family tree, film strip, flannel board presentation, flow chart, game, glossary, graph, handbook, illustration, informative speech, interview, invitation, jigsaw puzzle, journal/diary/learning log, lab report with illustrations, letter, list, magazine article, map (with legend), metaphor, mobile, model, mural, museum exhibit, mystery, newscast, newspaper, oral report, painting, panel discussion, pantomime, patterns, persuasive speech, photo essay, picture dictionary, poem, pop-up book, poster, puppet show (with music), questionnaire, rap, readers theater, real estate notice, rebus story, resume, reverse crossword puzzle, review (musical), rhyme, riddle, role play, salt map, satirical play, scavenger hunt, scrapbook, sculpture, simulation, soliloquy, song (original), speech, sports analysis, story (with illustrations), survey (with data graphed), symbols, TV program (with theme music), talent show, telegram, terrarium, time line, travelogue, trivia game, Venn diagram, video tape (with music), vignette, wordless book, written report) rated across Modalities (V, O/A, W, K) and Multiple Intelligences (L, L-M, N, S, M, B-K, Inter, Intra).

[34] Full-sized versions of the general product grid pages are included on the *Assessment Interactive CD-ROM*.

Kingore, B. (2005). *Assessment,* 3rd ed. Austin: Professional Associates Publishing.

CONTENT-SPECIFIC PRODUCTS

Teachers frequently request product grid examples that are specifically related to one subject area and/or grade level. Instead of a general product grid, the teacher brainstorms and organizes a list of products most applicable to a specific content area or topic for the class.

For example, which specific math products might increase critical thinking responses and help balance the use of computational exercises? In response to those requests, five specific product grids follow. These grids are customized for limited readers and writers (Figures 8.3A and 8.3B), primary students (Figure 8.4A and 8.4B), and the subject areas of language arts and social studies (Figure 8.5A and 8.5B), math (Figure 8.6A and 8.6B), and science (Figure 8.7A and 8.7B).

Most products are self-explanatory; however, some merit examples for clarification and application ideas. While many different content-related tasks are possible, some suggestions are offered to prompt your thinking of applications useful in your instruction.

Avoid losing a good instructional possibility when brainstorming product ideas alone or with others. Write quick notes of any application ideas that emerge. Focus on what students should learn and demonstrate as a result of this product experience.

TASK BOARDS

To save planning time and promote diversity in product responses, one or more teachers work as a team to prepare a list of content-specific products appropriate to the age, readiness levels, learning profiles, and strengths of the students. The teachers review their curriculum and teaching objectives to determine which products have the potential for rich instructional applications to the content. The products are open-ended and generic in order to match multiple learning topics, accomodate different learning styles, and allow teachers to assign them multiple times throughout the school year. The exact number of products on a task board is determined by the flexible thinking of the teacher.

Elaborate the products into clearly explained learning tasks that students select as appropriate to document their learning. Organize the tasks as a task board to post in the classroom and use for product assignments as needed throughout the year or to provide teacher-approved options for students who need replacement tasks when they have mastered the concepts and skills in the core curriculum. Figure 8.8 is one example of a task board with nine options for elementary and middle school students to select to demonstrate their understanding of a book they have read. Figure 8.9 provides six product options for elementary writing. Figure 8.10 is a math task board for young children. Figure 8.11 is an example of a task board for secondary history products.[35]

The task board options can be weighted for thinking level, complexity, and depth to align with the simple to more complex applications that are needed by specific students. The objective is to focus on a variety of product options useful over an extended period of time rather than to suggest that students have to select multiple products and complete multiple tasks for the same segment of learning.

[35] For additional prepared task boards, see Kingore, B., 2004.

Kingore, B. (2005). *Assessment,* 3rd ed. Austin: Professional Associates Publishing.

INDIVIDUALIZED PRODUCT GRIDS

To maximize student autonomy, use a copy of the class product grid to provide personalized product lists. To develop these lists, the teacher or the student assesses the student's modalities and pattern of intelligences.[36] On a copy of the class product grid, the teacher or the student then highlights three or four of the product grid columns that match the student's pattern of strengths. Next, the student skims down the list of products looking for those which are interesting and incorporate many highlighted strengths. Finally, the student lists those selected products to create an individualized product list.

Upper elementary and secondary students use individualized product lists when it is appropriate for them to choose which products they will complete to document their learning. The tool simplifies the determination of replacement tasks when the students has mastered the concepts and skills in the core curriculum. The products options can be weighted for depth and complexity to align with tiering objectives.

This option allows open-ended product selection as each student has a list of appropriate products to choose from to demonstrate achievement on any learning task. With this option, a student can use the list as needed all year. In a mixed-ability classroom, these product lists particularly help advanced and gifted students proceed independently with projects and self-directed study when pre-assessment validates that they have already mastered the core curriculum.

> *Use your individualized product list to choose how you will demonstrate your next learning achievement.*

Teachers question: *How do we determine grades when students are completing different products?* Product options for students do affect grading procedures. Seldom is an answer-key as effective as a rubric when different products are involved to demonstrate learning. Chapter 6 provides several rubric examples and a tool for generating rubics appropriate for product assignments. Chapter 3 includes a pictorial rubric generator that is applicable for evaluating young or ESL students.

Many products have the potential to serve as effective preassessments when used as repeated tasks. Acrostics, concept maps, flow charts, graphs, reports, time lines, and Venn diagrams are examples of products which can be completed and then repeated in the following manner for achievement comparisons.

1. Each student initially completes a product and records name, date, and score or grade on the product.
2. The student stores the product for comparison at a later date.
3. At teacher-designated times during instruction and/or after instruction is completed, the student retrieves the initial product and uses a different colored pen to embellish, delete, or correct items on the product. The use of a different color clarifies changes in the student's knowledge and understanding over time.
4. These products prompt productive achievement discussions between teacher and student, student to student, and between parent and child.

[36] See Appendix B for a simple, informal tool to assess multiple intelligences.

Kingore, B. (2005). *Assessment,* 3rd ed. Austin: Professional Associates Publishing.

Figure 8.3A: PRODUCT GRID FOR LIMITED READING AND WRITING SKILLS

	MODALITIES				MULTIPLE INTELLIGENCES							
	V	O/A	W	K	L	L-M	N	S	M	B-K	Inter	Intra
acrostic	•		•		•	•	•	•			•	•
alphabet chart for a topic	•		•		•	•	•	•			•	•
audio tape		•			•	•	•	•	•		•	•
chart	•		•		•	•	•	•			•	•
choral reading/readers theater	•	•	•		•	•	•		•		•	
collection collage	•			•	•		•	•		•	•	•
comic strip	•		•		•	•	•	•			•	•
concept or story map (web)	•		•		•	•	•	•			•	•
dance	•	•		•					•	•	•	•
demonstration	•	•	•	•	•	•	•	•	•	•	•	•
diorama	•			•	•	•	•	•		•	•	•
experiment	•		•	•	•	•	•				•	•
flannel board presentation	•	•		•	•	•	•			•	•	•
graph	•		•		•	•	•	•			•	•
illustration	•				•	•	•	•			•	•
interview		•	•		•	•	•				•	
jigsaw puzzle	•			•		•	•	•		•	•	•
list			•		•	•	•				•	•
mobile	•			•	•	•	•	•		•	•	•
mural/banner	•			•	•	•	•	•		•	•	•
museum exhibit/display	•		•	•	•	•	•	•		•	•	•
oral report		•		•	•	•	•	•			•	•
painting	•			•				•	•	•	•	•
pantomime				•		•				•	•	•
photograph or photo sequence	•			•	•	•	•	•		•	•	•
picture dictionary/scrapbook	•		•		•	•	•	•			•	•
picture book	•		•		•	•	•	•			•	•
play/puppet show	•	•	•	•	•	•	•	•	•	•	•	•
pop-up book	•		•	•	•	•	•	•		•	•	•
poster	•		•	•	•	•	•	•		•	•	•
rap/song		•		•	•				•	•	•	•
rebus story or sentence	•		•		•	•	•	•			•	•
riddle or rhyme		•	•		•	•					•	•
role play	•	•		•	•					•	•	
scavenger hunt	•		•	•	•	•	•			•	•	
scrapbook	•		•	•	•			•			•	•
sculpture	•			•					•	•		•
wordless book	•							•			•	•

Kingore, B. (2005). *Assessment,* 3rd ed. Austin: Professional Associates Publishing.

<table>
<tr><td>

Figure 8.3B:
PRODUCT EXAMPLES FOR LIMITED READING AND WRITING SKILLS

</td></tr>
</table>

Examples of potential products

- ACROSTIC--Using a concept or topic word, such as *families*, students brainstorm ideas as an adult writes significant words or phrases related to the topic that begin with each letter in the word.
- ALPHABET CHART FOR A TOPIC--For each letter of the alphabet, students brainstorm and list information to organize important facts and ideas about a topic.
- AUDIO TAPE--Record students retelling a folk tale or well-known story at the beginning, middle, and end of the year to hear and celebrate skill acquisitions and growth in story structure, vocabulary, and language fluency.
- CHORAL READING/READERS' THEATER-- Divide well-known poems or rhymes into parts for students to perform.
- COLLECTION COLLAGE--Students make a collage of items found in even numbers or items of a certain color, texture, size, or other category.
- DANCE--Students create a dance that demonstrates how different animals move, eat or communicate,
- DEMONSTRATION--Students demonstrate a simple sequence or task, such as how to get to school when it is raining.
- DIORAMA--Students: 1. Make a diorama illustrating a problem or solution in a story the class is reading, or 2. Make a social studies diorama interpreting life in a past time.
- FLANNEL BOARD PRESENTATION-- Students glue small velcro or sandpaper pieces to paper illustrations and place them on a flannel board to retell a story or sequence.
- GRAPH--Students graph how many classmates are: 1. Eating turkey on Thanksgiving or eating something else; 2. Having company at their house during the holidays or not having company; 3. Getting to school by walking, car, bus, bike, or another way.

- INTERVIEW--Students: 1. Tape record interviews with other students, 2. Interview family members to learn about family history, or 3. Interview people in school to learn about them and their jobs. Photograph the people being interviewed and display the photo as information is shared with others.
- MOBILE--Students create mobiles for different textures, such as rough, smooth, and tough, or for different categories, such as oviporus animals.
- PAINTING--Students paint: 1. A rainbow and explain its color sequence, or 2. A geometric figure with dots inside. *I painted a _____ with _____ dots inside.*
- PHOTOGRAPH OR PHOTO SEQUENCE-- 1. Using digital photographs of items around school, students describe a photo for others to identify. 2. Using several photographs of a learning experience at school, students place the photos in sequence as they retell the task.
- POSTER--Students create a poster using words and pictures to show others what they learned as they researched.
- RAP/SONG--Students use the tune for common songs, such as *The Farmer and the Dell*, to make up songs about math facts.
- REBUS STORY OR SENTENCE--Students use stickers or small cutouts of pictures in place of nouns in a sentence. Have them begin using simple patterns: *I want a [picture]. The [picture] can run.*
- RIDDLE OR RHYME--Students create riddles for others to solve about a topic being studied or people in the class. *I am the tallest and oldest person in the class. Who am I?*
- SCAVENGER HUNT--Students compute how many times a certain word appears on one page of the newspaper by highlighting that word each time they find it. Then, they compare results from several scavenger hunts.
- WORDLESS BOOK--1. Students tape record their version of a story for a wordless book and place their tape with the book in the reading center for others to enjoy. 2. Students dictate or write the words to accompany each page of a wordless book.

Kingore, B. (2005). *Assessment,* 3rd ed. Austin: Professional Associates Publishing.

Figure 8.4A: PRODUCT GRID FOR PRIMARY GRADES

	MODALITIES				MULTIPLE INTELLIGENCES							
	V	O/A	W	K	L	L-M	N	S	M	B-K	Inter	Intra
acrostic	•		•		•	•	•	•			•	•
alphabet book for a topic	•		•		•	•	•	•			•	•
audio tape		•			•	•	•	•	•		•	•
book or booklet	•		•		•	•	•	•			•	•
chart	•		•		•	•	•	•			•	•
choral reading/readers theater	•	•	•		•	•	•		•			
collection collage	•			•		•	•	•		•	•	
comic strip	•		•			•		•			•	•
concept or story map (web)	•		•		•	•	•	•			•	•
demonstration	•	•	•		•	•	•	•	•	•	•	•
diorama	•			•	•	•	•	•		•	•	•
experiment	•		•		•	•	•			•	•	•
fable		•	•		•	•	•				•	•
flannel board presentation	•	•		•	•	•	•	•		•	•	•
graph	•		•		•	•	•	•			•	•
illustration	•					•	•	•			•	•
interview		•	•		•	•	•				•	
invitation	•	•	•		•			•			•	•
jigsaw puzzle	•			•	•	•	•	•		•	•	•
journal/diary/learning log			•		•	•	•					•
letter			•		•	•	•					•
list			•		•	•	•				•	•
mobile	•			•	•	•	•	•		•	•	•
mural/banner	•			•		•	•	•		•	•	•
museum exhibit/display	•		•	•	•	•	•	•		•	•	•
newspaper	•		•		•	•	•	•			•	•
oral report		•		•	•	•	•	•			•	•
painting	•			•			•	•		•	•	•
photograph or photo sequence	•			•		•	•	•		•	•	•
picture dictionary/scrapbook	•		•		•	•	•	•			•	•
play/puppet show	•	•	•	•	•	•	•	•	•	•	•	•
poem/bio poem		•			•	•	•	•	•	•	•	•
pop-up book	•		•	•	•	•	•	•	•		•	•
poster	•		•	•	•	•	•	•			•	•
rap/performed rhyme/song		•		•	•	•		•	•	•	•	•
rebus story or sentence	•		•		•	•	•	•			•	•
riddle or rhyme		•	•		•	•					•	•
role play	•	•		•	•					•	•	
scavenger hunt	•		•	•	•	•	•				•	•
sculpture	•			•				•		•		•
story (with illustrations)	•	•	•		•	•	•	•			•	•
Venn diagram	•		•		•	•	•	•			•	•
wordless book	•						•				•	•

Kingore, B. (2005). *Assessment,* 3rd ed. Austin: Professional Associates Publishing.

Figure 8.4B:
PRODUCT EXAMPLES FOR PRIMARY GRADES

Examples of potential products

- ACROSTIC--1. Using a concept or topic word, such as *cooperation,* students brainstorm and write a significant word or phrase related to the topic that begins with each letter. 2. Using the title of a book the class is reading, students write events and details from the book.

- ALPHABET BOOK--Students write and illustrate an individual or small group alphabet book showing what they have learned about the topic being studied.

- AUDIO TAPE--Students record a book for the reading center and include a sound to designate when to turn the page.

- COLLECTION COLLAGE--Students work with others to create a collage for each color of the rainbow.

- COMIC STRIP--Students draw a comic strip in which one or two characters tell how to complete a simple process and sequence.

- CONCEPT STORY MAP (WEB)--Students create symbols for characters, settings, problems, and solutions and use them to map a book.

- FABLE--Students write and illustrate a fable using their favorite animal as the character and carefully plan their main idea as the moral of the story.

- INTERVIEW--Students interview five people to learn how they feel about spiders or insects and organize the results to share in class.

- INVITATION--Students write an invitation to the principal or other school personnel to come to their room to read the stories they created or to view other important completed work.

- JOURNAL / DIARY / LEARNING LOG--Each student compares three entries in his or her journal and explains one observation about his or her growth as a learner.

- LIST--As a class, list more precise words to say or write instead of simple, over-used words, such as *nice, said, good,* or *like.*

- MUSEUM EXHIBIT/DISPLAY--The class creates a three-dimensional museum exhibit to show what students have learned while researching life in the oceans. Each student completes a card to display beside one portion of the exhibit that explains important information.

- PHOTOGRAPH OR PHOTO SEQUENCE--Students use a digital or regular camera to take photographs of items around school and write descriptions of their photographs. Students then ask others to read the description and draw a picture of what was described without seeing the photograph. The students compare the drawing to the photograph and discuss similarities and differences.

- POSTER--Students make a poster called *Pairs* that shows different pairs of common things, such as hands, eyes, button holes, and twins.

- REBUS STORY OR SENTENCE--Students write a summary or retelling of the beginning, middle, and end of a book by drawing pictures or symbols to substitute for several nouns that are important to the story.

- ROLE PLAY--Read <u>Chrysanthemum</u>[37] by Kevin Henkes. With others, students role play different behaviors at school that would be *absolutely dreadful* and *absolutely perfect.*

- SCAVENGER HUNT--Students create a scavenger hunt for words on a cereal box, such as: *Find a word that means 'good;' Find a word that rhymes with 'cat;'* and *Count how many times the word 'in' is on the box.* They then challenge others to complete the scavenger hunt.

- SCULPTURE--Students make a paper sculpture using nineteen sizes of paper and five geometric shapes.

- VENN DIAGRAM--Students compare addition to subtraction, two dinosaurs, two characters, or two stories using an illustration for the Venn, such as a bow tie, a penguin with outstretched wings, or outlines of two dinosaurs overlapping slightly to create three areas for writing similarities and differences.

---

[37] Henkes, Kevin. (1996). *Chrysanthemum*. New York: HarperTrophy.

Kingore, B. (2005). *Assessment,* 3rd ed. Austin: Professional Associates Publishing.

Figure 8.5A: PRODUCT GRID FOR LANGUAGE ARTS AND SOCIAL STUDIES

	MODALITIES				MULTIPLE INTELLIGENCES							
	V	O/A	W	K	L	L-M	N	S	M	B-K	Inter	Intra
acrostic	•		•		•	•		•			•	•
advertisement/brochure	•	•	•	•	•					•	•	•
analogy/simile/metaphor		•	•		•	•	•				•	•
audio tape		•			•	•			•		•	•
book or illustrated story	•		•		•	•		•			•	•
bulletin board	•		•	•	•			•		•	•	•
cartoon or caricature	•				•			•			•	•
center (student made)	•	•	•	•	•	•		•		•	•	•
choral reading/readers theater	•	•	•	•	•	•		•	•		•	•
comic strip	•		•		•	•		•			•	•
concept or story map (web)	•		•		•	•	•	•			•	•
debate		•	•		•	•					•	
demonstration (labeled artifacts)	•	•	•	•	•	•	•	•	•	•	•	•
dialogue		•	•		•	•					•	
diorama	•			•	•	•	•	•		•	•	•
documentary film	•	•	•	•	•	•	•	•			•	•
editorial/essay/persuasive writing		•	•		•	•	•				•	•
fable (illustrated)	•	•	•		•	•	•	•			•	•
family tree	•		•		•						•	•
flannel board presentation	•	•		•		•		•		•	•	•
flow chart	•		•		•	•	•	•			•	•
game (original)	•	•	•	•	•	•				•	•	•
interview		•	•		•	•					•	•
jigsaw puzzle	•		•	•	•	•	•	•		•	•	•
journal/diary/learning log			•		•	•	•				•	•
letter/e-mail			•		•	•					•	•
magazine article			•		•	•					•	•
map/salt map (with legend)	•		•	•	•	•	•	•		•	•	•
mobile	•			•	•			•		•	•	•
model	•			•	•			•		•	•	•
mural	•			•	•		•	•		•	•	•
museum exhibit	•		•	•	•	•		•		•	•	•
newscast/TV program	•	•	•	•	•	•				•	•	•
newspaper	•				•	•	•			•	•	•
oral report/persuasive speech		•	•	•	•	•				•	•	•
panel discussion		•			•	•					•	
pantomime	•			•						•	•	•
photo essay	•			•		•	•	•		•	•	•
play/puppet show (with music)	•	•	•	•	•	•		•	•	•	•	•
poem/diamante/bio poem	•	•	•		•	•		•	•		•	•
pop-up book	•		•		•	•	•	•			•	•
poster/chart	•		•		•	•	•	•			•	•
rap/performed rhyme/song		•		•	•	•			•		•	•
rebus story	•		•		•	•		•			•	•
reverse crossword puzzle	•		•		•	•					•	•
role play	•	•		•	•	•				•	•	•
scavenger hunt	•		•	•	•	•	•			•	•	•
simulation	•	•	•	•	•	•	•	•		•	•	•
survey (with data graphed)	•		•		•	•	•				•	•
symbols	•				•		•	•				•
time line	•		•		•	•	•	•			•	•
travelogue	•				•	•	•	•			•	•
Venn diagram	•		•		•	•	•	•			•	•

Kingore, B. (2005). *Assessment,* 3rd ed. Austin: Professional Associates Publishing.

Figure 8.5B:
PRODUCT EXAMPLES FOR LANGUAGE ARTS AND SOCIAL STUDIES

Examples of potential products

- ACROSTIC--Students use a concept or topic word, such as *Africa* or *Apache*. They then brainstorm and write a significant word, phrase, or sentence related to the topic that begins with each letter.

- ADVERTISEMENT/BROCHURE--Students create: 1. An advertisement for an item used by a character or historical figure to solve a problem, including how it was used and its current value; or 2. An advertisement for a city or state they have studied, using words and illustrations that will make others want to visit that area.

- ANALOGY/SIMILE/METAPHOR--Students write direct analogies comparing a historical person or book character to a common object. *Martin Luther King, Jr. is like a broken clock because he ran out of time before he completed all the possibilities within him.*

- BULLETIN BOARD--Individuals or small groups of students make a bulletin board to highlight the publications and life of a favorite author who lived in or wrote about the time period or location being studied.

- CHORAL READING/READERS THEATER--Small groups transform a classic fable, short story, or poem into a readers theater to perform for parents or other classes.

- DEBATE--Students debate the censorship of books in school libraries, citing references for their research.

- EDITORIAL/ESSAY/PERSUASIVE WRITING--Each student writes an essay to the librarian, persuading the school to place a copy of a new book in the library. Students include supportive arguments explaining the book's literary merit and relevance to the student body.

- FAMILY TREE--Students interview their family members and develop a family tree that includes four or more generations. They then surround the family tree with pictures and maps of where different family members were born.

- FLOW CHART--Each student draws and labels a flow chart describing the sequence of events in a story the class is reading.

- INTERVIEW--In pairs, students simulate an interview between a reporter and a famous explorer or writer.

- JOURNAL/DIARY/LEARNING LOG--Students write journal entries for the main character of a novel, an explorer, or a historical figure.

- LETTER/E-MAIL--Students write a sequence of letters or e-mails between two main characters, discussing the book's main idea from the charcters' perspectives.

- MAGAZINE ARTICLE--Students write an article about living in one city, state, or country. They also take photographs, collect pictures, or draw illustrations to include in the article.

- NEWSPAPER--As a class, create a newspaper for the historical event being studied. Prompt students' thinking: *What is on the front page? What are the ads and sport events? Which businesses need more help?*

- PHOTO ESSAY--Students read Russell Freedman's <u>Lincoln: A Photobiography</u>[38] and then create a photobiography of the life in their community or a historical building in their city.

- POEM/DIAMANTE/BIO POEM--Students: 1. Create a bio poem for a historical figure or a character in a book; or 2. Write a diamante revealing two diverse perspectives of Manifest Destiny.

- TIME LINE--Students create a time line of dates significant to the social studies topic being studied. They then challenge others to label the time line in order to test their understanding of the topic.

- TRAVELOGUE--Students write travelogues from the perspective of early explorers as they pursue their travels and make their most important discoveries.

- VENN DIAGRAM--Students compare two countries by overlapping the outlines of their borders, creating three areas for writing similarities and differences.

[38] Freedman, Russell. (1989). *Lincoln: A Photobiography*. New York: Scott Foresman.

Kingore, B. (2005). *Assessment,* 3rd ed. Austin: Professional Associates Publishing.

Products

Figure 8.6A: PRODUCT GRID FOR MATHEMATICS

	MODALITIES				MULTIPLE INTELLIGENCES							
	V	O/A	W	K	L	L-M	N	S	M	B-K	Inter	Intra
acrostic	•		•		•	•		•			•	•
bio poem			•		•	•					•	•
bulletin board	•		•	•	•	•	•	•		•	•	•
center (student made)	•	•	•	•	•	•		•	•	•	•	•
chart/poster	•		•		•	•		•			•	•
children's story (illustrated)	•		•		•	•		•			•	•
collage	•			•		•		•		•	•	•
content puzzles	•		•	•	•	•		•			•	•
demonstration	•	•	•	•	•	•	•	•	•	•	•	•
diagram (labeled)	•				•	•	•	•			•	•
encyclopedia entry			•		•	•					•	•
error analysis	•		•		•	•					•	•
flow chart	•		•		•	•		•			•	•
game	•	•	•	•	•	•		•	•	•	•	•
glossary			•		•	•					•	•
graph	•		•		•	•		•			•	•
jigsaw puzzle	•			•	•	•		•			•	•
learning log			•		•	•						•
letter (math process)	•		•		•	•					•	•
list			•		•	•					•	•
math tracks	•		•	•	•	•		•			•	•
metaphor or simile	•	•	•		•	•					•	•
model	•			•	•	•	•	•	•	•	•	•
number challenge	•	•	•	•	•	•		•			•	•
number line	•		•	•	•	•		•			•	•
oral report/informative speech	•	•	•		•						•	•
patterns	•		•	•	•	•		•	•	•	•	•
questionnaire (data graphed)		•	•		•	•					•	
rap		•		•	•	•			•	•	•	•
recipe			•		•	•					•	•
reverse crossword puzzle	•		•		•	•		•			•	•
riddle		•	•		•	•					•	
scavenger hunt	•		•	•	•	•				•		
song (original)		•	•		•	•			•		•	•
story problem (original)	•		•		•	•		•			•	•
survey (with data graphed)	•		•		•	•	•	•				
test (original)	•	•	•		•	•		•			•	•
time line	•		•		•	•		•			•	
Venn diagram	•		•		•	•		•			•	•
written report			•		•	•					•	•

Kingore, B. (2005). *Assessment,* 3rd ed. Austin: Professional Associates Publishing.

Figure 8.6B:
PRODUCT EXAMPLES FOR MATHEMATICS

Examples of potential products

- ACROSTIC--Use a concept or topic word, such as *division* or *factorials*. Students brainstorm and write for each letter a significant word, phrase, or sentence related to the topic that begins with that letter.
- BIO POEM--Students create a bio poem for *integer*.
- BULLETIN BOARD--Create a bulletin board for students to post mathematical applications, such as: *Ways to Make 78;* or *Examples of Geometry in Architecture.*
- CENTER (STUDENT MADE)--Students use tangrams to create the ten digits and all the letters of the alphabet.
- CHILDREN'S STORY (ILLUSTRATED)--Students write and illustrate a story to explain a math concept. As examples, read Cindy Neuschwander's Sir Cumference series.[39]
- COLLAGE--Small groups of students organize collages showing fractions in daily life.
- CONTENT PUZZLES--Students write key math facts on a simple graphic outline and cut it into ten to fifteen puzzle pieces for others to put back together by correctly matching the problem and the solution.
- DEMONSTRATION--Students use manipulatives to demonstrate multiplication to a younger student.
- ERROR ANALYSIS--Students analyze a problem that is flawed, writing what is wrong and how to correct it.
- FLOW CHART--Students draw and label a flow chart that illustrates how to apply a specific math strategy or geometric proof.
- GAME--Students create a stock market game or math fact rodeo for others to play.
- LETTER (MATH PROCESS)--Students complete one math problem and then write a letter to someone explaining step-by-step how they completed that problem.
- MATH TRACKS--Students draw a long track on a paper and then write one number at the beginning of the track and a different number at the end. Starting at the first number, they use any appropriate operations (as simple as addition or complex as algebra) to create a continuous equation that concludes with the number at the end of the track.
- METAPHOR OR SIMILE--Students express a mathematical concept through a metaphor or simile, such as: *Addition is like compound words, and subtraction is like contractions.*
- NUMBER CHALLENGE--Set a challenge number for pairs of students to reach using dice and any appropriate math operation or formula (as simple as addition or complex as algebra).
- QUESTIONNAIRE--Students conduct questionnaires asking adults how math is needed in their jobs, and graph the results.
- REVERSE CROSSWORD PUZZLE--Provide the completed puzzle grid of numbers. Students write the math facts that resulted in those numbers.
- RIDDLE--Students develop simple or more complex riddles, such as: *I am an odd number larger than six and smaller than the square root of eighty-one.*
- SCAVENGER HUNT--Provide a list of math terms for students to find examples in the real world. Students then compare and discuss their findings.
- TEST (ORIGINAL)--Instead of taking a test, students write the test items for the math process or concept of study.
- WRITTEN REPORT--Students write: 1. A report about the real-life applications of a polygon; 2. A report regarding how and why different traffic and information signs are specific polygons; or 3. A report relating how geometry applies to baseball or some other sport.

[39] Neuschwander, Cindy. (1997). Sir Cumference and the First Round Table. (1999). Sir Cumference and the Dragon of Pi. (2002). The Great Knight of Angleland. (2003). Sir Cumference and the Sword in the Cone. Watertown, MA: Charlesbridge.

Kingore, B. (2005). *Assessment,* 3rd ed. Austin: Professional Associates Publishing.

Figure 8.7A: PRODUCT GRID FOR SCIENCE

	MODALITIES				MULTIPLE INTELLIGENCES							
	V	O/A	W	K	L	L-M	N	S	M	B-K	Inter	Intra
acrostic	•		•		•	•	•	•			•	•
audio tape		•			•	•	•		•		•	•
book/booklet	•		•		•	•	•	•			•	•
bulletin board	•		•	•	•	•	•	•			•	•
center (student made)	•	•	•	•	•	•	•	•	•	•	•	•
chart/poster	•		•	•	•	•	•	•			•	•
choral reading/readers theater		•	•	•	•	•	•				•	•
collection collage	•			•	•	•	•	•			•	•
comic strip	•		•		•	•	•	•			•	•
concept or story map (web)	•				•	•	•	•			•	•
critique		•	•		•	•	•				•	•
cross section	•				•	•	•	•			•	•
debate		•	•		•	•	•				•	•
demonstration (labeled artifacts)	•	•	•	•	•	•	•	•	•	•	•	•
description		•	•		•	•	•	•			•	•
diagram (labeled)	•		•		•	•	•	•			•	•
documentary film/film strip	•	•	•	•	•	•	•	•	•	•	•	•
editorial/essay/persuasive writing		•	•		•	•	•				•	•
encyclopedia entry	•		•		•	•	•				•	•
essay			•		•	•	•					•
experiment/demonstration	•	•	•	•	•	•	•	•			•	•
flannel board presentation	•	•		•	•	•	•	•		•	•	•
flow chart	•		•		•	•	•	•			•	•
game (original)	•		•	•	•	•	•	•	•	•	•	•
glossary			•		•	•	•	•			•	•
graph	•		•		•	•	•	•			•	•
handbook	•		•		•	•	•	•			•	•
interview		•	•		•	•	•				•	
lab report with illustrations	•		•		•	•	•	•			•	•
learning log			•									•
letter (science process)			•		•	•	•				•	•
list			•		•						•	•
mobile	•			•	•	•	•	•		•	•	•
model	•			•	•	•	•	•		•	•	•
museum exhibit/labeled display	•		•	•	•	•	•	•		•	•	•
panel discussion		•			•	•	•				•	
patterns	•		•	•	•	•	•	•	•		•	•
photo essay/sequence	•			•		•	•	•		•	•	•
picture dictionary	•		•		•	•	•	•			•	•
poem/diamante/bio poem	•	•	•		•	•	•		•		•	•
rap/song (original)		•	•	•	•	•	•		•	•	•	•
rebus story	•		•		•	•	•	•			•	•
report (oral or written)		•	•		•	•	•				•	•
reverse crossword puzzle	•		•		•	•	•	•			•	•
riddle/rhyme		•	•		•	•	•		•		•	•
role play	•	•		•	•	•	•				•	•
scavenger hunt	•		•	•	•	•	•	•			•	•
scrapbook	•		•		•	•	•	•			•	•
survey (with data graphed)	•		•		•	•	•	•			•	
terrarium	•			•			•	•			•	•
time line	•		•		•	•	•	•			•	•
Venn diagram	•		•		•	•	•	•			•	•

Kingore, B. (2005). *Assessment,* 3rd ed. Austin: Professional Associates Publishing.

Figure 8.7B:
PRODUCT EXAMPLES FOR SCIENCE

Examples of potential products

- ACROSTIC--Using a concept or topic word such as *photosynthesis,* students brainstorm and write for each letter a scientific word, phrase, or sentence related to the topic that begins with that letter.
- AUDIO TAPE--Students record the sounds of a season or species for others to identify.
- BULLETIN BOARD--Students compare and contrast: 1. States of matter; or 2. Life forms in Antarctica with life in the Arctic Ocean.
- CENTER (STUDENT MADE)--Students collect and categorize items that magnets do or do not attract.
- CHART/POSTER--Students illustrate and label the physics principles demonstrated by amusement park attractions.
- CHORAL READING /READERS THEATER--In small groups, students perform one or more of the choral readings about insects in Joyful Noise: Poems for Two Voices[40] by Paul Fleischman and use that format to organize facts about other animals or plants.
- COLLECTION COLLAGE--Students use a digital camera to complete a collage of photographs of simple and complex machines found at home.
- CRITIQUE--Students write a critique about how the scientific method was applied during a specific experiment conducted in class.
- DEBATE--Students organize a class debate on the issues of DNA research or using animals for research studies.
- ENCYCLOPEDIA ENTRY--Students write and illustrate a fictitious encyclopedia entry about a newly discovered life form on another planet, including specific information about its anatomy, habitat, behavior, and life cycle.
- EXPERIMENT/DEMONSTRATION--Students demonstrate how to use and interpret the results from a piece of scientific equipment,
such as a magnet or compound microscope.
- FLOW CHART--Students use a flow chart to demonstrate a life cycle, such as a butterfly or frog.
- GRAPH--Students graph the weather in their area for one month. They then compare it to a Farmer's Almanac 100 years earlier and record three observations or conclusions.
- MOBILE--In small groups, students create mobiles that represents the relationship of our solar system or galaxy to the latest discoveries in space.
- MODEL--Using common items as symbols, students construct a DNA chain and explain the reasoning behind the symbols they chose.
- POEM / DIAMANTE / BIO POEM--Students compose a diamante contrasting two opposite forces in nature.
- REVERSE CROSSWORD PUZZLE--Students write science terms in the grid and then challenge others to write the descriptors that result in those terms.
- RIDDLE/RHYME--Students create simple or more complex riddles using science concepts, such as: *I magnify things you can not see and focus them when you look through me.*
- SCAVENGER HUNT--Students conduct a scavenger hunt to identify and quantify the chemicals found in their kitchens.
- TERRARIUM--Students establish a terrarium and write out the sequence of procedures they used to complete it.
- TIME LINE--Students complete a time line mapping of the progression of a major tropical storm and then compare their results with others in the class to interpret similarities.
- VENN DIAGRAM--Students: 1. Over-lap four circles to create a four-way Venn that compares the similarities and differences of four biomes; or 2. Use a Venn diagram to compare the attributes of two species or the same species living in two different biomes.

Products

[40] Fleischman, Paul. (1992). *Joyful Noise: Poems for Two Voices.* New York: HarperCollins.

Kingore, B. (2005). *Assessment,* 3rd ed. Austin: Professional Associates Publishing.

Figure 8.8: LITERATURE TASK BOARD FOR ELEMENTARY AND MIDDLE SCHOOL

Create an artifact bag for your book. In a paper sack, include six to ten items with a log book explaining how each symbolically represents a character, problem, key event, or solution from the story.	Make an illustrated chart to compare five causes and their effects in the story. Rank them from most to least significant in the story and explain your rankings.	Draw a story board with captions or a comic strip with speech balloons to sequence the major events and ideas in the story.
Write a telephone or e-mail dialogue between two of the characters. Have their conversations reveal their traits and the main ideas of the story.	**Free Choice** Design your own book response.	Construct a diorama of the most significant scenes. Use details to incorporate as much story content as possible. Include a display card to explain your diorama to others.
Imagine that the main characters are members of your school. Create a yearbook entry for each and include a picture, their school activities, what they would be voted, and a quotation.	Create three analogies about the main characters in the story. What would each be if each character were a different country, a piece of furniture, or an animal? Illustrate and explain each analogy.	Create a concept map which includes the sequence, problem, solution, and main idea of the story. Incorporate different symbols for the events and characters.

Kingore, B. (2005). *Assessment,* 3rd ed. Austin: Professional Associates Publishing.

Figure 8.9: WRITING TASK BOARD FOR ELEMENTARY

Make a list of ten things to which you would say, "Yes!"	Pretend you are the tallest person in the world. Write about what you can do and the problems you have.	Write three things you would do to make the world a better place.
Create your favorite pizza! Write the directions for someone to make it for you.	Write a letter to complain about a product or event. OR Write a letter to compliment someone.	Write about your favorite toy when you were younger.

Kingore, B. (2005). *Assessment,* 3rd ed. Austin: Professional Associates Publishing.

Figure 8.10: MATH TASK BOARD FOR PRIMARY

Graph the favorite color of ten classmates.	Show three ways to solve this problem. (Post the problem here.)	Create a paper chain of number sentences that result in the number: _____ (Post the number here.)
Write and illustrate a number story problem that has candy and three people in it.	Use the tune to *Farmer in the Dell.* Create several verses to the song using math facts.	Write a letter to a classmate explaining how to complete this problem. (Post the problem here.)

Kingore, B. (2005). *Assessment,* 3rd ed. Austin: Professional Associates Publishing.

Products

Figure 8.11: HISTORY TASK BOARD FOR SECONDARY

1 Complete a four-way Venn diagram comparing different social, economical, and political trends of the time period or culture being studied.	**2** Using the word *HISTORY* as an acrostic, explain the major ideas related to the: ❑ Period, ❑ Culture, ❑ Historical figure, or ❑ Event that is being studied.	**3** Write a news report about one of the main events during the period being studied as if it were ten years after it occurred. Explain the impact that it has had.
4 Write and illustrate: ❑ The travelogue and map of an explorer, or ❑ The log of an inventor from the period or culture being studied.	**5** **Free Choice** Design your own response.	**6** Create a timeline of the dates most significant to this topic of study with symbols representing important people, places, and events. Challenge others to label the timeline.
7 Describe how the historical person, event, or issue being studied would be different today. Explain your thinking.	**8** Create a newspaper for the historical period or culture being studied. Include a front page, a business page, and a social-living page with advertisements and letters to the editor.	**9** Using a choral reading format of two voices, write a comparison of opposing viewpoints for the following issue. (Post the issue here.)

Kingore, B. (2005). *Assessment,* 3rd ed. Austin: Professional Associates Publishing.

· CHAPTER 9 ·

Integrating and Assessing Learning Standards

Standards are important resources for teachers but have little meaning until teachers and administartors take true ownership of them.

—Judy Carr & Douglas Harris

Learning standards are a national phenomenon. Virtually every state education department and national professional group advocate academic standards. These standards result from a reexamination of important achievement expectations and are based upon a significant body of nation-wide research and best practices instead of more random preferences. This research provides guidance to reshape curriculum and assessment into a coherent plan that incorporates standards and promotes student achievement.

Standards are articulated in the form of objectives and prescribed in terms of concepts, skills, or attitudes to promote student excellence. District-wide teams of teachers interpret these standards and translate them into classroom learning elements with achievement targets that guide students' development of proficiency. The intent is for standards to be seamlessly woven into instruction so they are natural rather than an isolated segment of learning or testing.

DEFINITIONS

Standards describe the desired results of students' educational experiences. They are statements identifying essential knowledge (what students should know) and skills (what students should be able to do). They are a consensus that clarifies expectations and quality. Throughout this chapter, *standards* and *learning standards* are used interchangeably for variety.

Benchmarks describe the steps along a K-12 continuum required to reach the standards. They are more specific, concrete statements to interpret standards into an instructional framework guiding classroom applications and assessments. Criteria are determined, often in the form of checklists or rubrics, to assess benchmarks.

Standards-based is a descriptor to suggest that curriculum components, including learning materials, processes, products, and

Learning Standards

assessments, have been aligned to relate to standards and to each other. The curriculum is specifically designed to focus on identified standards and ensure that all students have access to that knowledge and skill.

STANDARDS ASSESSMENT AND EVALUATION

Students' achievement of standards is evaluated at the classroom level and the results compared at school, district, state, and national levels. Rubrics and standardized tests are largely used to measure the standards and provide samples of students' learning of the curriculum. The test is not the curriculum although some standardized test scores have such high stakes that they seem to drive the curriculum.

District personnel analyze student achievement data from these standardized tests to determine what works and what is not an effective practice in order to initiate proactive steps to better students learning--at least as measured though standardized tests. Evaluating standards promotes changes in curriculum, instruction, assessment, and the data collection process.

In addition to evaluation through rubrics and standardized tests, standards are more informally and continually assessed in the classroom to focus attention on the quality of instruction and level of student achievement. This assessment of achievement employs multiple techniques to gather data and guide instruction. Such techniques include observation, checklists, conferences, and product assessment. Rubrics are used both to assess the steps toward reaching standards and to evaluate achievement levels.

Assessing learning standards requires that they are clearly understood by all participants and that all students have clear access

to opportunities to learn. In standards-based classrooms, standards provide a common language to discuss and assess achievement; they clarify learning targets by specifying skills and outcomes.

Preassess students' mastery of standards and benchmarks within a segment of learning. The scored preassessment is stored as written documentation of achievement levels and skill needs. Each student can complete and attach to this product a list of learning standards and benchmarks showing areas of mastery as demonstrated by the preassessment. This process enables a productive instructional focus without redundant skill practice.

Teachers sometimes ponder whether all of the emphasis on standards is really worthwhile. One recent experience provided a concrete answer to me.

After teaching for several years, I had accumulated a great number of student examples. When moving to a new location, it seemed timely to review the mass and determine how much to continue saving. In so doing, I came across some examples of a writing experience students had completed over fifteen years before. As I reviewed what had certainly been strong examples at that time, I realized how sophisticated we have become with current writing standards. These twelve-year-old students' achievements were typical of our expectations in writing with fourth or fifth grade students today!

While some might interpret this example as pushing down the curriculum. I was reassured of the power of best practices and

Kingore, B. (2005). *Assessment,* 3rd ed. Austin: Professional Associates Publishing.

higher expectations. With standards, we know so much more about quality writing and how to guide students to that level. Standards can guide achievement.

IMPLEMENTING A STANDARDS-BASED CURRICULUM IN THE CLASSROOM

Teachers' have the pivotal responsibility for integrating and assessing students' achievement of the applicable standards for their grade levels and content areas. In a standards-based classroom, teachers incorporate standards in several different ways.

1. *Learning tasks are selected as vehicles to implement the curriculum and standards.*
2. *Standards are correlated across content areas.*
3. *Standards are clearly communicated in kid-friendly language.*
4. *Students share the responsibility to document their achievement of standards.*
5. *Rubrics are correlated to state or district learning standards.*
6. *Standards are communicated to the parents.*
7. *Standards are communicated on grading reports.*

1. Learning tasks are selected as vehicles to implement the curriculum and standards.

In a standards-based classroom, activities are more than just *something students do.* Learning experiences are analyzed for potential instructional applications that will integrate standards within the curriculum. Learning tasks are then selected and planned to develop or extend the standards and other learning

objectives in the curriculum. These learning tasks are evaluated with rubrics.[41]

To accomplish this integration of standards and activities, sequence the curriculum topics or learning segments. Next, analyze intended outcomes and applicable standards before *reasoning in reverse* to select learning experiences with the potential to enable students to reach that objective. *I want students to learn these skills and concepts during this unit. The learning experiences to best achieve that outcome include...*

For each topic or segment of learning, list related standards and learning experiences to document when specific skills and concepts are integrated throughout the unit (Figure 9.1: Content Standards Plan). Then, when asked to map where in the curriculum a standard is addressed and taught, teachers have an efficient vehicle to communicate that information.

2. Standards are correlated across content areas.

Seek as many ways as possible to integrate standards across content areas. Common wisdom such as *every teacher is a teacher of reading* and informal statements referencing *writing across the curriculum* are examples of the standards in one content area being reinforced in another subject. In some schools, it is productive to concretely analyze implementations of standards across the curriculum rather than leave such correlations to chance. Using the information in a content plan, such as Figure 9.1, teachers can build upon that information by correlating their content area segments of learning to the skills and concepts of another content area.

On Figure 9.2: Standards Grid, list selected learning activities for a topic or segment of learning. Then, list applicable standards

---

[41]See Chapter 3 for examples of rubrics and processes for generating rubrics.

Kingore, B. (2005). *Assessment,* 3rd ed. Austin: Professional Associates Publishing.

Figure 9.1: CONTENT STANDARDS PLAN

CONTENT AREA _____   DATE _____

TOPIC/LEARNING SEGMENT _____

Standards:	Learning Experiences:

Kingore, B. (2005). *Assessment,* 3rd ed. Austin: Professional Associates Publishing.

Figure 9.2 STANDARDS GRID

STANDARDS FOR: _Writing_

ACTIVITIES:
A: _Skill sheet applications_
B: _Cooperative problem solving_
C: _Creating story problems_
D: _Computer applications_
E: _Math is sports project_
F: _____
G: _____

STANDARDS FOR: _Mathematics_	Writes to inform, express thoughts, influence, or entertain	Demonstrates a command of the conventions of spelling, capitalization, and punctuation.	Recognizes and applies appropriate organization of ideas in written text.	Writes in complete sentences using correct, varied, and effective sentence construction.	Applies standard grammar and usage, including subject-verb agreement and parts of speech.	Employs appropriate and precise word choices	Uses prepositional phrases to elaborate written work.	Uses conjunctions to connect ideas meaningfully.
Uses place value to represent whole numbers (to 1,000,000,000) and decimals (to 0.001)	E	E	E	E	E	E	E	E
Uses equivalent fractions in problem-solving solutions	B C	B C	C	B C	C	C	C	C
Compares two fractional quantities using common denominators								
Relates decimals to fractions to the thousandths								
Adds, subtracts, multiplies, and divides with whole numbers, fractions and decimals	C E	C E	C E	C E	C E	C E	C E	C E
Identifies prime factors and common factors of whole numbers.								
Estimates to determine reasonable results.	B		B					

Kingore, B. (2005). Assessment, 3rd ed. Austin: Professional Associates Publishing.

or benchmarks for two content areas. In each cell where standards intersect, record which activities apply. An example plotting writing skills in math is provided.

3. Standards are clearly communicated in kid-friendly language.

As a class learning experience, involve students in determining the key words of each learning standard or benchmark and then restating that objective into kid-friendly language. This activity accents the relevancy of the standards to the learning objectives in the classroom and provides students some ownership in applying those standards to their learning. For example, a standard, such as *The student is expected to find similarities and differences across texts such as in treatment or organization,* might be simplified for students' daily reference to *Identifies similarities and diffferences.*

Kingore, B. (2005). *Assessment,* 3rd ed. Austin: Professional Associates Publishing.

Figure 9.2
STANDARDS GRID

ACTIVITIES:

A: _____

B: _____

C: _____

D: _____

E: _____

F: _____

G: _____

STANDARDS FOR: _____

STANDARDS FOR: _____

Kingore, B. (2005). *Assessment,* 3rd ed. Austin: Professional Associates Publishing.

Learning Standards

In early childhood classrooms, teachers may conclude that this task is too difficult for young learners. In that case, teachers determine which key words to post without children's interpretations. However, the children are still involved in referring to and using the posted standards.

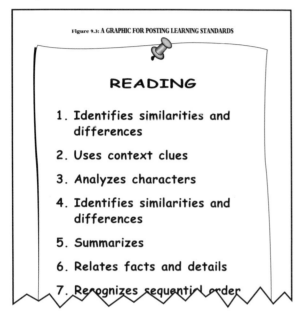

Figure 9.3: A GRAPHIC FOR POSTING LEARNING STANDARDS

READING

1. Identifies similarities and differences
2. Uses context clues
3. Analyzes characters
4. Identifies similarities and differences
5. Summarizes
6. Relates facts and details
7. Recognizes sequential order

Post the students' interpretations on a simple graphic such as Figure 9.3 for frequent reference during learning tasks. Laminating this standards graphic allows it to be a reference tool throughout the school year. For example, when teaching a skill or concept to a small group, check that skill on the posted standards graphic to emphasize its application. When students are working at a learning station or center, post the applicable standards graphic, check the skills or concepts to be practiced, and require students to conclude their center experience by briefly noting in a learning log or on a sentence stem strip how they incorporated those skills or concepts in their work at the center.

4. Students share the responsibility to document their achievement of standards.

Teachers and students co-share the responsibility to document the students' achievement of learning standards. To increase students' active involvement in assessing their learning, use standards-based product captions, checklists, and sentence stems.

1. Standards Product Captions

Key words for learning standards can be incorporated on captions strips that students use to assess a product for their portfolio. In addition to reflection, these caption alternatives require each student to be responsible for analyzing and then checking the skills or concepts applied in that work. As adults assess products, these captions document a student's learning so that redundant learning experiences can be avoided.

Using a standards-based caption, such as Figure 9.4, fill in one or more skills before duplicating the form for students to use. Or, students can fill in the specific skills as they assess their work.

As an alternative format, use Figure 9.5 to list the standards for a content area before the form is duplicated. In this manner, all of the standards are listed so the student assesses which ones are demonstrated in a specific piece of work by checking one or more of the standards-based skills.

2. Standards Checklists

Provide students with a checklist that details required learning standards for a content area. Students check a standard and record the graded product they completed that documents their level of achievement on each

Figure 9.6: STANDARDS REFLECTION

NAME *Cindy*   DATE *October 13*

This work shows my ability with standard # *1 & 3* because *I discussed three similarities and three differences between the antagonists and protagonists in the two novels.*

Figure 9.3: A GRAPHIC FOR POSTING LEARNING STANDARDS

Kingore, B. (2005). *Assessment,* 3rd ed. Austin: Professional Associates Publishing.

Figure 9.4: CAN DO SKILLS!

Can do!

NAME _____   DATE _____

This work shows that I can _____

_____

_____

I think _____

_____

_____

I demonstrated these skills:

☐ _____   ☐ _____

☐ _____   ☐ _____

☐ _____   ☐ _____

Kingore, B. (2005). *Assessment,* 3rd ed. Austin: Professional Associates Publishing.

✂ -

standard. The products are typically those graded with a shared rubric and are included with the checklist as substantiation.

The checklist is a useful reference when assessing products to document standards achievement. It is an efficient tool to organize examples of all of the standards in the students' portfolio selections.

Use a Standards Checklist as a simple way to organize a set of products documenting achievement of learning standards. Students glue the checklist on the outside of a manila folder and place products inside the folder in the order of the items on the checklist. This folder can be stored in the regular portfolio or in students' work folders.

Writing: Standards

Standards	Product	Grade
☐ Legible handwriting		
☐ Prepositional phrases		
☐ Complete complex sentences		
☐ Appropriate voice and style		
☐ Literary devices		
☐ Transitions; conjunctions		
☐ Cohesive organization		
☐ Logical support of ideas		
☐ Vivid, precise wording		
☐ Subject-verb agreement		

3.Standards Reflection

Provide sentence stems to prompt students' reflection about a learning standard application. Sentence strips, such as Figure 9.6, can be duplicated for students to complete and then attach to their work. These brief

Kingore, B. (2005). *Assessment,* 3rd ed. Austin: Professional Associates Publishing.

Figure 9.5: STANDARDS FOR _____

NAME _____ DATE _____

This work shows that I can _____

_____

_____

I think _____

_____

_____

I demonstrated these standards:

☐ _____

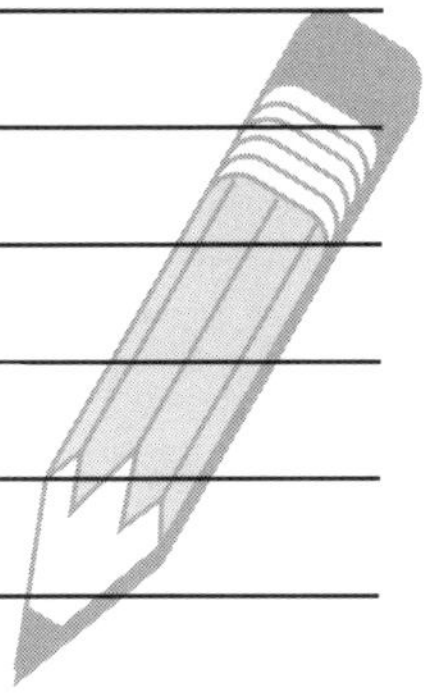

☐ _____

☐ _____

☐ _____

☐ _____

☐ _____

☐ _____

☐ _____

☐ _____

☐ _____

☐ _____

☐ _____

☐ _____

☐ _____

☐ _____

Learning Standards

Kingore, B. (2005). *Assessment,* 3rd ed. Austin: Professional Associates Publishing.

Figure 9.6: STANDARDS REFLECTION

NAME _____   DATE _____

This work shows my ability with standard #_____ because _____

_____

_____

_____

Kingore, B. (2005). *Assessment,* 3rd ed. Austin: Professional Associates Publishing.

✂ ---

statements are a communication device to clarify learning accomplishments within any product and are not limited to use on products selected for the portfolio. Teachers can request that students write a reflective sentence to staple on a product that is completed 1) during independent work to be turned in for grading, 2) during centers, or 3) for the Standards Checklist Folder.

5. *Rubrics are correlated to state or district learning standards.*

When standards are integrated into instruction, it follows logically to incorporate the skills of the standards as assessment levels on a rubric. While any rubric can be correlated to

Learn✏ **Writing Rubric**			
😞	😐	🙂	😃
I did not follow directions. I did not work.	My writing is neat and legible. I wrote complete sentences and paragraphs that vary to match meaning and purpose. My writing is clearly developed using precise words and vivid images with no major errors.	My writing is legible. I clearly developed a main idea and details. My paragraphs are complete and vary to match meaning and purpose. My capitalization and punctuation enhance meaning. I used precise words and vivid images with no major errors.	My writing is legible with no major errors. My major ideas and details are clear and organized. I added, deleted, combined, and rearranged my writing to revise it. I use prepositional phrases. I used precise adjectives.
Novice	Apprentice	Intermediate	Skilled

learning standards, one effective device is a holistic standards rubric prominently displayed as a poster in the classroom. This poster concretely illustrates students' skill development over time though ascending skills or standards written on cards. Each card level is placed in the pocket chart of the poster when it is appropriate to express that level of challenge.*

The Standards Rubric takes the form of a poster in order to eliminate the need for paper copies and to post it where it is easily viewed by everyone in the room. Furthermore, anyone visiting the room can immediately identify current learning objectives.

The rubric is developmental because it begins with simpler levels of proficiencies and then increases achievement levels over time as skills develop. With primary children, simple icons and captions can be used to enhance the visual appeal and enable the poster rubric to be read and understood. More complex levels are appropriate for older students. Examples of ascending skills on rubric cards are shared in Figure 9.7 for typical first grade and fifth grade writing standards.

*Construction procedures for a Standards rubric poster are detailed in Appendix E.

Kingore, B. (2005). *Assessment,* 3rd ed. Austin: Professional Associates Publishing.

Figure 9.7: **WRITING SKILLS**

First grade beginning writing skill examples			
I did not try. I did not work. *Card 1*	I drew a picture. I wrote some letters. *Card 2*	I neatly drew a picture. I wrote several letters. I wrote my name and the date. *Card 3*	My picture is neat and colorful. I can tell or write about it. I wrote my name, date, and other important words. *Card 4*
I wrote a sentence about my picture. I used capital and lowercase letters. I sounded out some words. *Card 5*	I wrote more than one sentence. I used capital letters, lowercase letters, and periods or question marks in my sentences. I sounded out some words. *Card 6*	My writing is neat and legible. My sentences are interesting. I used capitalization and punctuation correctly most times. I sounded out and spelled most of the words I used. *Card 7*	I wrote carefully and used good spacing. I wrote several interesting sentences. I used capitalization and punctuation correctly. I spelled my high-frequency words correctly. *Card 8*

Fifth grade beginning writing skill examples			
I did not follow directions. I did not work. *Card 1*	My writing is neat and legible. I wrote complete sentences and paragraphs that vary to match meaning and purpose. My writing is clearly developed with no major errors. *Card 2*	My writing is legible. I clearly developed a main idea and details. My paragraphs are complete and vary to match meaning and purpose. My capitalization and punctuation enhance meaning. I used effective words with no major errors. *Card 3*	My writing is legible with no major errors. My major ideas and details are clear and organized. I revised my writing. I used prepositional phrases. I used precise verbs and adjectives. *Card 4*
My writing is legible with no major errors. I elaborated with details that increase interest and meaning. I added, deleted, combined, and rearranged my writing to revise it. My prepositional phrases and conjunctions elaborate ideas. I used vivid adjectives, verbs, and adverbs. *Card 5*	My writing is legible with no major errors. I use compound sentences with vivid words and images. My prepositional phrases and conjunctions elaborate ideas and increase interest. I used transitions. I edited grammar, usage, and spelling. *Card 6*	My writing is legible with no major errors. I use complex sentences with vivid words and images. My writing is related and interesting. My introduction and conclusion are strong. I used effective transitions. I edited grammar, usage, and spelling. *Card 7*	My writing is legible with no major errors; spelling is proficient. My composition has clearly related, well-developed ideas. My introduction and conclusion add clarity, depth, and interest. My writing is generally organized and smooth; transitions link ideas. I edited effectively. *Card 8*

Kingore, B. (2005). *Assessment,* 3rd ed. Austin: Professional Associates Publishing.

Learning Standards

To translate any content area learning standards into a rubric format, initially refer to district standards to determine the desired levels and kinds of skills for the beginning of the school year. List those skills on one card to signal the grade-level proficiencies. (Card number four delineates that level on the shared first- and fifth-grade writing examples.) Next, determine the ascending levels of skills that build to the proficiencies on card four. Those skill levels are listed on cards one, two, and three.

Cards five through eight or more list the levels of skill proficiencies to be developed next. When students are proficient at level four, reorder the cards. Level one might remain the same if the teacher wants to accent that a lack of effort will result in low achievement in the class. Card two is removed; shift the third and fourth cards down, and add card five as the new proficiency goal in the fourth position. Later, as skills accelerate, the card levels shift again and card six is placed in the rubric poster. Continue the process throughout the year by developing additional cards as skills reach new levels.

A Standards Rubric is effective for students' goal setting and self-assessment. Students can refer to the poster before starting a learning task to set the level they intend to achieve. After completion of the task, students again reference the rubric to self-assess and record on their work the level they achieved.

6. Standards are communicated to the parents.

Parents demonstrate an increased level of concern about the quality of schools because of news stories and headlines. They express a legitimate interest in understanding how national and state learning standards affect their child's achievement. For example, at a recent parent session in Michigan, parents expressed frustration because they did not know what their children *should* be learning. They felt they had no way to gauge accomplishments or needs and wanted to know how to find out that information. The school district's wise response was to translate the district learning standards into parent terminology and provide copies to parents.

Once parents understand the importance of standards, they need an overview of the scope and sequence of selected standards-based learning elements to comprehend what their child is to learn next and how to support the school's effort. Communicating standards helps parents refocus their thinking about their child's learning from the negative *what is wrong* to constructive feedback that guides *what are the learning needs* and *what do we do to support those needs.* Actively involved parents want to know: *Which skills and concepts do I watch for and discuss with my child?* Figure 9.8: A Parent's Role in Supporting Learning Standards provides some guidance.

7. Standards are communicated on grading reports.

Marzano stresses that...*a single letter grade or percentage score is not a good way to report student achievement in any subject area because it simply cannot present the level of detailed feedback necessary for effective learning.*[42] He challenges educators to explore standards-based alternatives. One example he poses is a reporting system based upon a list of content-area standards with a four-point scale. Student achievement is reported by marking the four-point scale for each standard and then calculating an overall achievement score for that subject, such as in Figure 9.9.

[42]See Marzano, 2000.

Figure 9.8: A PARENT'S ROLE IN SUPPORTING LEARNING STANDARDS

Here are some ideas for how you can become more informed about learning standards and involved in your child's learning.

- Be aware of the school's learning expectations for your child.
- Request a copy of the standards for the grade level.
- Ask questions about a standard or practice you do not understand.
- Notice and discuss how a standards-based environment changes the school practices of the past.
- Focus on the learning rather than just attend to the grade. Discuss with your child:

> *What did you learn doing this?*
> *What is something you are pleased with about your work?*
> *What skills were you working on for this task?* (In standards-based classrooms, learning objectives are openly discussed with students.)

- Model reading and writing at home by personally engaging in authentic reading and writing tasks, such as reading books or newspapers, visiting a library with your child, and writing notes to your child.
- Seek ways to use math experiences at home, such as counting or measurement tasks, math-related games, and software.
- Be an advocate rather than an advisory.
- Acknowledge effective practices when you see them.

Kingore, B. (2005). *Assessment,* 3rd ed. Austin: Professional Associates Publishing.

Learning Standards

This approach would communicate more clearly, however, if a rubric were used instead of only a four-point score (Figure 9.10). The rubric would clarify the differences in the degrees on the scale to better substantiate student achievement. Educators will rightfully view the development of these standard rubrics as a major task. However, the ensuing professional conversations and clarifications about achievement are a substantially valuable result of the process.

Letter grades and percentage scores are so ingrained into our society that any departure is likely to be viewed with disdain by parents and community members in general. Hence, rather than replace report card grades, standard reports can be useful in interpreting or clarifying the grade designation to parents. If the traditional reporting card is continued, a list of standards could accompany it with student achievements marked for each standard.

Kingore, B. (2005). *Assessment,* 3rd ed. Austin: Professional Associates Publishing.

Figure 9.9: VOCAL MUSIC STANDARDS

Standard 1--Music Appreciation	STANDARDS RATING			
1.1--Form opinions about music	1	2	3	4
1.2--Communication				
1.2a--Describe musical events	1	2	3	4
1.2b--Discuss music across the curriculum	1	2	3	4
Standard 2--Vocal Performance				
1.1--Sing diatonic melody	1	2	3	4
1.2--Perform rhythmic patterns	1	2	3	4
Standard 3--Notation	1	2	3	4
Standard 4--Composition	1	2	3	4

Figure 9.10: VOCAL MUSIC STANDARDS

	STANDARDS RATING			
	1	2	3	4
Standard 1--Music Appreciation				
1.1--Form opinions about music	Does not express opinions	Does not support opinions	Expresses and supports valid opinions	Supports opinions by comparing/contracting musical styles
1.2--Communication 1.2a--Describe musical events	Unable to identify events such as form or climax of a piece	Identifies events and form with help	Describes the form and events in a piece	Uses musical terminology to compare genres and events
1.2b--Discuss music across the curriculum	Unable to discuss	Discusses relationships to history	Identifies several relationships to art and history	Parallels the development of music with culture, history, and other subjects.
Standard 2--Vocal Performance 1.1--Sing diatonic melody	Uses a speaking voice	Sings less than 50% of the pitches correctly	Sings diatonic melody in tune	Uses an appropriate voice; sings in tune; excellent tone quality
1.2--Perform rhythmic patterns	Lacks rhythm	Performs pattern with help	Performs pattern correctly without help	Performs pattern fluently
Standard 3--Notation	Can not identify age-appropriate musical symbols	Identifies age-appropriate symbols with help	Names and writes age-appropriate musical symbols	Names and writes musical symbols fluently
Standard 4--Composition	Unable to compose	Composes with extensive help	Can compose and perform when given a musical framework	Writes and improvises original music

Kingore, B. (2005). *Assessment,* 3rd ed. Austin: Professional Associates Publishing.

· CHAPTER 10 ·

Communication with Parents

What you're not up on, you're down on.
—Dutch Adage

Parents frequently do not understand the portfolio or authentic assessment process because they have never experienced it themselves. Educators need to communicate with parents to help them understand that this assessment process provides a greater depth of information than report cards or standardized tests alone. For example, parent conferences that support information by sharing specific student products enable parents to gain a clearer understanding of their child's patterns of strengths, learning needs, interests, and progress than any report card can communicate. Moreover, the actual work that students complete over time provides richer and more authentic means than tests alone of assessing what they are learning and the depth of their thinking.

With the guidance of educators, parents can understand how authentic assessment supports the work students do and inspires students to have high expectations for themselves. Share information about assessment with parents through meetings, letters, and articles.

PROCEDURES FOR PARENT COMMUNICATION

PLAN A MEETING WITH PARENTS TO DISCUSS ASSESSMENT

Hold a meeting for the parents of the students in your class. Check the following suggestions that you want to incorporate in the meeting to maximize the opportunity for parents to become more informed. List additional ideas that more specifically address the needs of your students.

Parent Meeting Agenda

❑ Explain authentic assessment and discuss the educational benefits it provides in the classroom.
❑ Provide an overview of your assessment plans and include specific information about the children's involvement and responsibilities.
❑ Model the portfolio process that will be used, as many adults benefit from seeing concrete examples.

❑ Use an overhead transparency of a student's repeated tasks from the beginning, middle, and end of a previous year to demonstrate to parents how products document growth and level of achievement.

❑ If you used portfolios last year, have a former student work with you to role play a portfolio conference between a student and a teacher or parent.

❑ Discuss when parents will have an opportunities to review students' portfolios and conference with you and/or their child about what has been learned.

❑ Inform parents about the assessment process at the end of the year and what will happen to the portfolio their child has developed.

❑ _____
❑ _____
❑ _____
❑ _____

The more concretely and interactively you can illustrate the portfolio process, the more informed the parents will be.

RECOMMEND THAT PARENTS TALK WITH THEIR CHILDREN ABOUT WORK AT SCHOOL

Parents can learn much from their child's perceptions of learning experiences. Encourage parents to ask questions and talk with their children about their work at school. Many times, a student's excitement about learning increases parental interest in the process.

Over time, parents and children benefit from the student conferencing with parents to share items in the portfolio and discuss what the student has learned and achieved. Specific suggestions for student-involved parent conferences and portfolio exhibitions for parents are shared in Chapter 5.

ENCOURAGE PARENTS TO READ ARTICLES ABOUT ASSESSMENT

Share articles about authentic assessment with parents. An introductory article for parents is reprinted at the end of this chapter and may be copied to share with the parents of your students.

PROVIDE A SERIES OF INFORMATIVE LETTERS TO PARENTS

Over time, share a series of letters with parents to broaden their knowledge about portfolios and authentic assessments. Plan several letters to use at different times throughout the year. Keeping parents informed about assessments increases the likelihood that they will understand and support the process.

Several sample letters are included. These letters are not necessarily intended for copying and sending home, but rather as examples of potential content to include in your letters. Busy teachers can more quickly produce the letters they need if they have samples to look at and revise.

Overview of Parent Letters

• *Introducing the Portfolio Process*
Figure 10.1 is most effectively used when you begin portfolios. Determine which areas of the curriculum you intend to focus on in the portfolios and inform parents of those areas.

• *Product Selection*
The product selection letter, Figure 10.2, accents the value of the analytical process involved in selecting items for the portfolios. Sharing specific criteria that children use as they select an item helps parents understand that portfolios are more than just collections of students' best work.

- *Products Completed at Home*
  Figure 10.3 is effectively used as an invitation for home participation after the portfolio process is established. Students' learning does not stop when the school day finishes. Some children, particularly young children, limited-English students, or those with special learning needs, complete work at home that offers significant information about their interests and talents. This letter acknowledges the important role that home environments play in a child's learning and invites some items completed at home to be added to the portfolio at school.[43] However, Figure 10.3 also addresses the problem of work done at home being completed by someone other than the student alone.

- *Student-Parent Conferencing*
  Figure 10.4 helps parents understand their role in a conference. It prepares them to more effectively and positively interact with the student as the student's work is shared. Posing specific questions to ask during the sharing process helps parents maintain a positive experience for the child. When using this letter, consider also providing a copy of the Portfolio response Letter (Figure 5.1) to guide parents' writing to their child

PLAN SPECIAL PORTFOLIO OCCASIONS, AND INVITE THE PARENTS TO PARTICIPATE

Another effective parent communication device is to plan special occasions for the parents to share the portfolios. While many opportunities exist, three examples are outlined here.

1. Parents are invited to review and discuss their child's portfolio at home. Their child takes the portfolio home overnight and then returns it the next day. This is especially valuable to working parents in home environments where the portfolio will be safe and respected overnight. In specific cases where a teacher deems by his or her best judgement that a portfolio should not be sent home, copies of the work can be sent in place of the originals.

2. A second option is to organize a student-led portfolio exhibition at school so parents can come to share the child's portfolio. This alternative often works well during lunch time or some evening events, such as Curriculum Night.

3. A third option is to invite parents to celebrate the bound portfolio book when it arrives at home at the end of the year.

Prepare invitations to parents that inform them of these special portfolio events. Three samples are included in Figures 10.5 through 10.7 that invite parents to share the portfolio with their child at home, to come to school for a portfolio exhibition, or to celebrate the bound portfolio book at the end of the year. Blank copies of several borders to use for your own invitations are included in Appendix C.

SEEKING INFORMATION FROM PARENTS

Parents know a great deal about their child. Some parents express frustration because they have information they would like to share with teachers yet worry if teachers would welcome such input. Consider providing a forum for this valuable exchange of information. One useful way to access this information is to use the communication form in Figure 10.8, From Parent to School.

[43] If desired, include captions such as those found in Chapter 4 for use at home.

Kingore, B. (2005). *Assessment,* 3rd ed. Austin: Professional Associates Publishing.

Figure 10.1: INTRODUCING THE PORTFOLIO PROCESS

DATE: _____,

Dear _____,

This year, your child will develop a portfolio of learning experiences throughout the school year. Just as professional writers and artists maintain a portfolio to showcase their accomplishments, student portfolios help us gain a better understanding of children's patterns of strengths, needs, interests, and progress. The actual work that students complete over time provides a richer and more authentic means than tests alone to assess how capable they are, what they are learning, and the depth of their thinking.

Collaboratively, your child and I will select many products for the portfolio in the following curriculum areas:

- _____
- _____
- _____
- _____

The portfolio will contain both first drafts and refined pieces to document how your child thinks, works, and how much your child is learning. The students will manage their own portfolios to develop organization skills and extend their responsibility and ownership in their work.

The portfolio process involves collection, selection, and reflection. Students first collect their completed work for several days before they review it and select a product for their portfolio. Then, each student reflects about the selected product and attaches a caption to explain why that product was added to the portfolio. The products not selected for their portfolio are sent home. At the end of the year, this most exciting portfolio will be bound and sent home for your family to keep.

During the year, there will be informal sharing and conferencing opportunities for you to examine the work in progress. Through this portfolio, you will discover what your child knows about his or her own learning, and you will enjoy the concrete examples that demonstrate the growth your child makes this year.

Sincerely,

Kingore, B. (2005). *Assessment,* 3rd ed. Austin: Professional Associates Publishing.

Figure 10.2: PRODUCT SELECTION

DATE: _____,

Dear _____,

Each student has designed a portfolio, and we have started to select the contents from our learning experiences. You may remember that the portfolio process involves collection, selection and reflection. Students continue to collect their completed work at school for several days before the students and/or I review it to select a product for their portfolio. Then each student reflects on the selected product and attaches a caption to explain why that product was added to the portfolio. Items not selected for the portfolio are taken home for your immediate review.

Through product selection for their portfolios, students increase their awareness of their capacity for self-reflection and making judgments. As students determine which products to include, they learn to think about important evaluation criteria such as:

- What does this product document about your learning?
- What examples should be kept in your portfolio to best represent your growth throughout the year?
- Which products best document current achievements of learning standards?
- Which pieces demonstrate something significant that you think, feel, or care about your work?
- Which products show growth with important skills or concepts you have worked on?
- Which products demonstrate progress you have made in a specific subject area?
- What makes a piece satisfying to you?

Judging the merits of one's own work is a life skill that your child is practicing and refining through the portfolio process. Please contact me at school if you have questions or would like to have further information about this important part of our learning environment.

Sincerely,

Kingore, B. (2005). *Assessment,* 3rd ed. Austin: Professional Associates Publishing.

Communication with Parents

Figure 10.3: PRODUCTS COMPLETED AT HOME

DATE: _____,

Dear _____,

    Some of you have asked what you can do at home to help us identify your child's special learning interests and talents. Each reporting period, encourage your child to bring one example from home to include in his or her portfolio that shows some work your child initiated at home or a product that is especially well done. Hopefully, these products will be completed not as homework, but because your child is enjoying learning. You may send a photograph of the product if it is a three-dimensional item such as a model, construction, or sculpture. Other examples may include:

- Writings,
- Collections,
- A child-developed science experiment,
- Tape recordings or photographs of drama or musical productions,
- Drawings, paintings, or original photographs,
- Original math problems or graphs,
- Self-initiated projects, and
- Photocopies of awards.

    It is very important to your child's self-esteem that you send products that were completed by your child alone. We want children to feel proud of their work because they have tried hard to do their best. When others complete work for children, it is harder for children to feel proud and confident. They learn, instead, to depend on others to do for them and that they can never do well enough alone. That is not the life message parents want children to learn. From time to time, praise your child's efforts and encourage your child to select a product that he or she worked on alone and has done well to include in the portfolio at school.

    Please always be sure your child's name and the date are written on the back of the product. Complete with your child a brief note to attach to the product to help us better understand what your child thinks about that product.

    Thank you for all you do at home to encourage your child to value learning. Please contact me at school if I can help you or answer questions.

                    Sincerely,

Kingore, B. (2005). *Assessment,* 3rd ed. Austin: Professional Associates Publishing.

Figure 10.4: STUDENT-PARENT CONFERENCEING

DATE: _____,

Dear _____,

Your child is prepared to share his or her learning experiences with you. Each child has selected some products to discuss, but ask about additional products as you wish. As you review the work together, please remember that your child has worked very hard to complete this. It shows how much has been learned and accomplished since the beginning of this school year.

Consider the following suggestions to ensure a positive experience for your child.

1. Try to listen carefully and encourage your child to talk more than you. Careful listening helps you understand your child's accomplishments and how he or she feels about them.
2. Let your child lead the portfolio sharing. Ask: "What do you want to show me first?"
3. Continue asking questions that let your child explain the products and learning process to you. Ask open-ended questions such as:
   a. What is your favorite piece in your portfolio?
   b. What is something that makes you feel especially proud of what you have learned?
   c. What is something that was hard to do?
   d. How did you get your idea for this work?
4. Notice and respond to as many positive points as possible. Continue to comment on the strengths and improvements you observe in your child's work. Encouragement will help your child know you are proud of what she or he has learned. Your positive feedback will help your child feel eager to share with you again at a later time. Too many negative comments cause some children to want to hide their work instead of sharing it with others.
5. When you and your child finish reviewing the portfolio, consider writing a note to your child about the experience. This is a special opportunity to write some words of recognition to your child. Many children highly value these notes and save them in the portfolio.

If you have questions or concerns about anything you see or hear, please contact me at school so we can discuss them together. Thank you for participating in your child's education.

Sincerely,

Kingore, B. (2005). *Assessment,* 3rd ed. Austin: Professional Associates Publishing.

Communication with Parents

Figure 10.5: PORTFOLIO EXHIBITION

DATE: _____

Dear _____,

    You are invited to a portfolio exhibition at school. Please come to our class on:

_____

Your child has prepared a portfolio of valued accomplishments and would like to spend about 15 minutes showing you how much is being learned.

                        Sincerely,

Kingore, B. (2005). *Assessment,* 3rd ed. Austin: Professional Associates Publishing.

Figure 10.6: THE PORTFOLIO BOOK

DATE: _____,

Dear _____,

    Your child is bringing you a treasured book on _____. It is the portfolio book we have worked on all year to provide an organized record of accomplishments and growth. This work is very important to the children and they feel so proud of themselves for all they have learned. We hope you will celebrate this special book with your child and grant it a special place in your hearts and on your bookshelf.

    This book now belongs to your family to keep and enjoy over the years. Look forward to a portfolio book every year to herald your child's learning.

                        Sincerely,

Kingore, B. (2005). *Assessment,* 3rd ed. Austin: Professional Associates Publishing.

Figure 10.7: PORTFOLIO SHARING WITH PARENTS

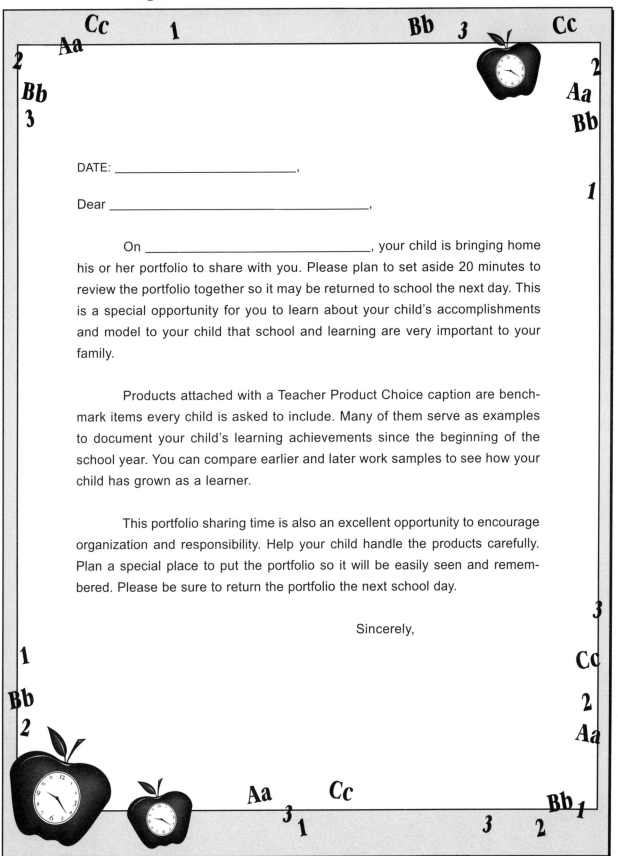

DATE: _____,

Dear _____,

On _____, your child is bringing home his or her portfolio to share with you. Please plan to set aside 20 minutes to review the portfolio together so it may be returned to school the next day. This is a special opportunity for you to learn about your child's accomplishments and model to your child that school and learning are very important to your family.

Products attached with a Teacher Product Choice caption are benchmark items every child is asked to include. Many of them serve as examples to document your child's learning achievements since the beginning of the school year. You can compare earlier and later work samples to see how your child has grown as a learner.

This portfolio sharing time is also an excellent opportunity to encourage organization and responsibility. Help your child handle the products carefully. Plan a special place to put the portfolio so it will be easily seen and remembered. Please be sure to return the portfolio the next school day.

Sincerely,

Kingore, B. (2005). *Assessment,* 3rd ed. Austin: Professional Associates Publishing.

Communication with Parents

Figure 10.8: FROM PARENT TO SCHOOL

The purpose of this communication form is to use your experienced observations to help us better know your child and how to best assist and advance learning at school. Continue writing on the back if you need more space. Please return this to school by: _____.

CHILD'S NAME _____   DATE _____

YOUR NAME _____

What do you want us to understand about your child?
Is there something special about his or her needs that we should know?

Describe how your child feels about school.

Describe your child's special interests or abilities.

List any organizations or groups in which your child is involved.

What does your child like to do at home?

What responsibilities does your child have at home?

Describe your child's organization at home and how she or he cares for things.

In what ways do you feel we can best help your child at school?

List three or four words that best describe your child.

Is there anything else that you would like to share about your child?

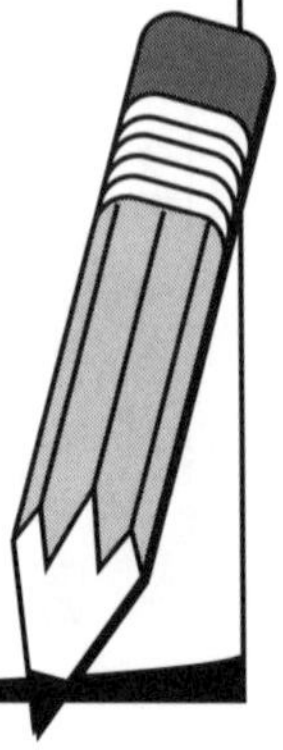

Kingore, B. (2005). *Assessment,* 3rd ed. Austin: Professional Associates Publishing.

Figure 10.9:

Introducing Parents to Student-Managed Portfolios:

A collaborative effort toward authentic assessment

The products that children produce throughout the school year help parents and educators gain a better understanding of children's needs, interests, and progress. The actual work that children complete over time provides a richer and more authentic way than tests alone to assess what they are learning and the depth of their thinking.

Thus, in many schools across the nation, educators and students collaborate to collect and store a selection of each student's products in curriculum areas such as writing, math, reading, social studies, science, and/or art. This collection is called a portfolio and may contain first drafts as well as refined pieces to better show how a child thinks, works, and how much the child is learning.

DEFINITION

A portfolio is a systematic collection of student work selected largely by that student to provide information about the student's attitudes, motivations, level of achievement, and growth over time.

Currently, parents and schools view standardized test results as indicators of children's abilities and achievements. However, standardized tests typically only measure right answers rather than high-level thinking skills and responses such as problem solving, flexibility in thinking, organization, and decision making. Instead of debating whether standardized tests or portfolios are better indicators, professional educators are working to effectively use both to provide a more complete picture of the multiple facets of a child's abilities and needs.

Portfolios are largely managed by the children to develop their organization skills and extend their responsibility and ownership in their work. Children are encouraged to produce quality work, value their own progress, and select products for their portfolio that document what they are learning.

PRODUCT SELECTION

Not every product a child completes is placed in the portfolio. Children typically keep their work at school for several days and then review it to select a product for their portfolio. Each product placed in the portfolio has the child's name and date on it so growth over time can be determined. Each product also has a caption or brief note attached to explain in the child's own words why this product was selected. The products not selected for the portfolio are sent home so parents consistently have examples of the student's work.

Children also produce things at home that show their interests and talents. Throughout the year, parents may encourage children to take to school a few examples of what they have done well at home to include in their portfolio.

It is very important to a child's self-esteem, however, that parents send products which children have completed by themselves. We want children to feel proud of their work because they have tried hard to do their best. When others complete work for children, it is harder for children to feel proud and confident. They learn, instead, to depend on others to do for them because they can never do well enough alone. That is not the life message parents want children to learn.

PORTFOLIO USE

Educators use the portfolio process to teach students to critique their work and reflect

Kingore, B. (2005). *Assessment,* 3rd ed. Austin: Professional Associates Publishing.

Communication with Parents

on its merits. When children are reviewing their work to select a product to go in their portfolios, teachers prompt students' analysis and decision-making skills by asking them to think about questions such as the following.

- What makes a high-quality product?
- What examples do you want to keep in your portfolio to represent what you are learning throughout the year?
- Which products document your achievements of learning standards?
- How does this product show something important that you think?
- How does this product show something important that you have learned?
- How does this product demonstrate the progress you've made in a specific topic or subject area?

During the year, the portfolio may be used in several productive and informative ways. A teacher can discuss a child's portfolio with the child to help clarify the child's growth, celebrate current achievement, and establish future learning goals. A child might also discuss his or her portfolio with a peer to celebrate a success and share ideas for future products. Furthermore, during a conference, the portfolio becomes a useful tool to concretely illustrate to parents the learning achievements and needs of the child.

At the year's end, in many portfolio projects, the teacher collaboratively reviews the portfolio with the student to select a few representative products to place in a School Career Portfolio. This portfolio showcases the student's growth, quality work, and highest achievements; it typically is added to each school year to provide a window to the child's thinking and achievements over several school years. Some schools bind this School Career Portfolio and present it to the students when they move out of the district or graduate from that school.

Each year, the portfolio products not placed in the School Career Portfolio may be bound together and taken home at the end of the school year for parents and children to keep. This organized book of products is treasured by parents and children alike. As one parent commented: "Now I can throw away a whole drawer full of papers. The whole year is in this one book!"

When most parents were in school themselves, their teachers did not use product portfolios as a key focus of their educational assessment. Thus, this process is relatively new and frequently not understood by parents who have never experienced it for themselves. Be willing to learn about portfolios because this process has a tremendous potential to add importance to the work children do and inspire them toward higher expectations for themselves. Portfolios can also help parents increase their awareness of the abilities and needs of their children. Parents are encouraged to read, ask questions, and talk to children about the portfolio process. It is an exciting experience!

SELECTED RESOURCES

Farr, R. & Tone, B. (1998). *Portfolio and Portfolio Assessment.* Ft. Worth: Harcourt Brace College Publishers.

Kingore, B. (2001). Parent assessment: Developing a portfolio to document your child's talents. In *The Kingore Observation Inventory (KOI),* 2nd ed. Austin: Professional Associates Publishing. 63-64.

Paulson, F., Paulson, P., & Meyer, C. (1991). What Makes a Portfolio a Portfolio? *Educational Leadership*, 48, (2) 60-64.

Stenmark, J. (1991). Math Portfolios: A New Form of Assessment. *Teaching K-8*, (5) 62-64.

• CHAPTER 11 •

The End of the Year

A hard beginning maketh a good ending.
—John Heywood, *Proverbs*

Educators often wonder what to do with portfolios at the end of the year. For optimum value, the portfolio process should continue over several years. However, my work with many schools revealed that passing the entire portfolio on to next year's teacher was not productive. Portfolios that grow an inch each year get large rather quickly. So those portfolios were often stuck away in a closet. Teachers reported that they did not need to review that much from the past to prepare them to effectively work with their new class.

Thus, the recommended process at the end of the year is to select only a few products for next year's teacher to help guide instructional planning. The remaining portfolio items are sent home as a portfolio book. At the end of the year, then, the natural closure of the students' assessment process and learning experiences involves either selecting products for the School Career Portfolio or encouraging high school students to evaluate items for a Professional Portfolio, and then gathering the remaining products into individual students' books.

THE SCHOOL CAREER PORTFOLIO

One value of a portfolio is its effectiveness in documenting a student's learning development and achievements over time. School Career Portfolios maximize the potential of this value without excessive volumes of products. At the end of each school year, select a few products from the yearly portfolio to go into the School Career Portfolio, and send it to next year's teacher. The remaining products in the yearly portfolio are bound together in a book that goes home as a keepsake. This publishing process is elaborated later in this chapter.

The School Career Portfolio is typically a file folder to which products are added each year. It is usually stored with the cumulative file or with the current home room teacher and can be bound and presented to each student at graduation or at the end of the portfolio process. As another option, use a computer disk or CD-ROM to store the School Career Portfolio.

Kingore, B. (2005). *Assessment,* 3rd ed. Austin: Professional Associates Publishing.

To avoid excessive work for any one person, arrange for the scanning of the selected products to be completed by each student as a learning experience during computer lab times.

A table of contents is initiated to list the title, date, and location of each product within the School Career Portfolio. The student continues to add new products and update the table of contents until the end of each school year.

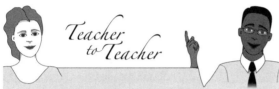

If students hand-write the table of contents, over time it presents a clear view of their handwriting development.

CRITERIA FOR INCLUDING PRODUCTS IN THE SCHOOL CAREER PORTFOLIO

Primary Grades

Three pieces are chosen to document growth and achievement. The teacher is primarily responsible for the choices and includes one piece from the beginning, middle and end of the year. Frequently, one additional special piece or *best piece* is also included.

Intermediate, Middle School, and High School

Four to six pieces are chosen to document growth, learning standards, thinking process, and highest academic accomplishments. The student and teacher collaboratively select the products. Growth and achievement are typically validated by insuring that products are chosen from throughout the school year

and have captions attached explaining the learning standards integrated within the work. Growth in thinking process skills are shown through the student's metacognitive reflection about a learning process or task, such as a completed written piece with its first draft attached. The student's choice for highest academic accomplishment or *best piece* is accompanied by the student's written reflection discussing the work and why it is considered the highest accomplishment for the year.

USES FOR THE SCHOOL CAREER PORTFOLIO

- ### Documents the student's learning achievements
  When continued over several years, the school career portfolio documents the student's changes as a learner and enhances self-worth as the student discovers how much she or he has achieved.

- ### Guides instruction
  This portfolio guides a teacher's instructional decisions about the long-term development and learning needs of each student. The teacher is able to review the concrete product examples in the portfolio instead of only the numbers, letters, grades, and percentages typical of reporting files.

- ### Represents students
  At the beginning of the school year, students can choose one piece from their School Career Portfolios to share with their new class as an introduction of themselves and their achievements.

- ### Celebrates total school experience
  At graduation or the end of the portfolio process, the School Career Portfolio may be bound and then presented to the student as a wonderful closure and valued heirloom.

Kingore, B. (2005). *Assessment,* 3rd ed. Austin: Professional Associates Publishing.

When the School Career Portfolio is completed, have students create a special title page for it that includes a title, symbol, and explanation of how this portfolio represents the student.

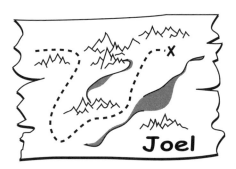

Joel

I decided to use just my name for a title and a map for my symbol because I see my portfolio as a map of my school days. It plots my learning travels. This represents most of my life and the learning experiences that have brought me to where I am right now. I already know I am going to enjoy looking back at this portfolio later.

Joel, High School Senior

THE PROFESSIONAL PORTFOLIO

In high school, especially during the junior and senior years, students begin restructuring their portfolios to develop a School Career or Professional Portfolio. Products from the yearly portfolio and the School Career Portfolio can be evaluated for inclusion in the Professional Portfolio. The purpose of this portfolio is to demonstrate how a student's different experiences, achievements, and talents translate into the specific abilities required in the future. This portfolio

simultaneously prepares students for the process of job placement and/or college admission interviews, as it results in products to feature at either interview.

Rather than follow a generic formula for what to include, each Professional Portfolio should be as unique as the individual who develops it. The items in the portfolio should specifically relate to the talents, interests, and aspirations of the student. The products should focus on the abilities and skills required where the student intends to work or apply to college rather than attempt to present a global view of talents that might fit any situation.

Reflective Questions to Guide Selection

What am I consistently good at that I want to demonstrate in my portfolio?

What products best reflect my preparation for my career choice?

What products might an employer or college want to view in order to evaluate my talents and potential?

Which pieces are most satisfying to me? How are they effective or important?

What am I doing to continue the development of my talents and accomplish my goals?

For maximum impact, the Professional Portfolio should be concise, neat, and clearly organized. Keeping the portfolio concise means it is more likely to be viewed willingly by busy interviewers. It also requires that the student be thoughtful about which items to select instead of mindlessly including everything. A neat portfolio is important to convey an image of pride and care in preparation. Clear organization is vital because the portfolio

Kingore, B. (2005). *Assessment,* 3rd ed. Austin: Professional Associates Publishing.

The End of the Year

is intended to clearly communicate with others. Develop a table of contents to guide the reader. Use subdivisions as the main categories by which the student wants to represent herself or himself to others. Subheadings can further delineate specific talents.

Think an inch. Purchase an attractive one or two inch binder for use as a Professional Portfolio. Develop a table of contents, and use tabs to clearly mark the subdivisions within the portfolio. Make every item easy to find. Use a three-ring plastic sleeve to hold special products so those items do not have to be hole punched.

PUBLISHING THE YEARLY PORTFOLIO IN THE ELEMENTARY AND SECONDARY GRADES

Products not selected for the School Career Portfolio are bound and sent home as a keepsake. Parents and students love having these books as a record of learning experiences and growth. To begin the publishing process, encourage students to analyze the parts of trade books and build as many of those features into their portfolio books as is appropriate. The more these portfolio books are made to look like published books the better. They should look as important as they are! The following are examples of ideas incorporated into portfolio books by some classes.

CONTENTS OF PUBLISHED PORTFOLIO BOOKS

Book Cover
If they have not already done so, students design a front and back cover for their portfo-

lio book. As an alternative, they cut apart their portfolio container folder or envelope on the fold line to create the front and back cover of their book.

Title Page
Students write a title page complete with an inventive publishing company incorporating the school's name and the copyright year for their book. The teacher is often named as the Executive Editor. Title examples include *My Treasury from Mrs. Wilhelm's Second Grade* and *The Life and Times of Kent Matthew in Seventh Grade*.

Table of Contents
Students use copies of a simple Table of Contents form, such as Figures 11.1 and 11.2, or develop their own organizational formats. If the portfolio contents are organized chronologically, students write the names of the months, list their products in order, and complete the table for their portfolio book. If the contents are organized by areas of the curriculum, the table of contents should reflect that organization.

Figure 11.1: TABLE OF CONTENTS

Writing	PAGE
• Autobiography	1
• Best Piece: "A Walk in the Past"	4
• Repeated Task: Persuasive Paragraphs	6
Reading	
• Author Study: Laurence Yep	8
• Reading Review Log	9
• Poetry Project	16
Math	
• Division Mastery Test	18
• Photo Essay: Fractions in the World	19
• Repeated Task: Hardest Math Problem	22
Social Studies	
• Regional Map of the US	23
• Davy Crockett Report	24
• Time Line	27
Science	
• Weather Unit	28
• Experiment in Electricity	29
• Plant Diagram	30
Music/Art	
• Family Portrait--Watercolors	34
• Animal Sculpture	35
• Music Sight Reading: Beginning and End of Year	36

Kingore, B. (2005). *Assessment*, 3rd ed. Austin: Professional Associates Publishing.

Kingore, B. (2005). *Assessment,* 3rd ed. Austin: Professional Associates Publishing.

Figure 11.1: TABLE OF CONTENTS

PAGE

- _____
- _____
- _____
- _____
- _____
- _____
- _____

- _____
- _____
- _____
- _____
- _____
- _____
- _____

- _____
- _____
- _____
- _____
- _____
- _____
- _____

The End of the Year

Kingore, B. (2005). *Assessment,* 3rd ed. Austin: Professional Associates Publishing.

Figure 11.2: TABLE OF CONTENTS

PAGE

- _____ _____
- _____ _____
- _____ _____

- _____ _____
- _____ _____
- _____ _____

- _____ _____
- _____ _____
- _____ _____

- _____ _____
- _____ _____
- _____ _____

- _____ _____
- _____ _____
- _____ _____

- _____ _____
- _____ _____
- _____ _____

Kingore, B. (2005). *Assessment,* 3rd ed. Austin: Professional Associates Publishing.

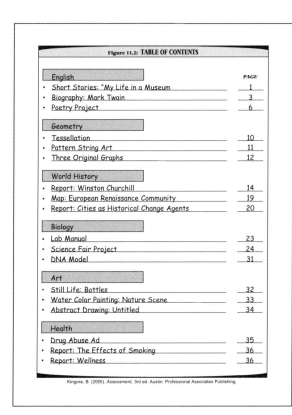

Kingore, B. (2005). *Assessment*, 3rd ed. Austin: Professional Associates Publishing.

Once students create a table of contents for their portfolio, they begin to use the table of contents in other books with renewed interest and ability.

About the Author

Just as information about the author is included on the book jacket of many published books, each student writes an About the Author paragraph or page. One example of a form is shared as Figure 11.3. Including a personal or school photograph on the page is an attractive idea. The photograph is an added delight when students later look back at these special books. An About the Illustrator page may also be included by some students who like to talk about themselves in multiple roles.

Dedication Page

Students might also include a dedication page in their portfolio books. It is interesting to see to whom students dedicate their books. They sometimes dedicate their book to their teacher, a wonderful validation of the caring and hard work teachers expend to help students achieve success in learning.

Highlights of the Year

Highlights of the Year is another page students love to have in their books. Students list on this page events during the school year which they most enjoyed or want to remember. It is fascinating to read what each student chooses as Highlights of the Year. The students' selected highlights are seldom the educational aims on which we have spent the most time!

Letter of Recommendation[44]

Letters of recommendation are an important component when working with secondary students on their professional portfolios, but these letters can be a welcomed addition to a portfolio book for any age of student. Students may ask a friend, family member or significant adult to write a letter of recommendation for them. It is interesting over time to look back on these encouraging statements.

Friends and Classmates

One or two pages for the autographs of friends and learning colleagues is a great interactive addition to these books if your school does not have a yearbook. Just as high school students have a yearbook signing time, classes have portfolio book signings during which classmates write graffiti-style messages to one another.

---

[44] When including letters of recommendation, teachers usually suggest students use individuals other than the teacher. Writing large numbers of recommendation letters for students at the end of the year may not be a prudent task for busy teachers.

Figure 11.3: ABOUT THE AUTHOR

NAME _____

DATE _____

PHOTOGRAPH OR SYMBOL	FAVORITES
	MUSICIAN: _____
	ALBUM: _____
	ARTIST: _____
	MOVIE: _____
	ACTOR: _____
	SPORT: _____
	ATHLETE: _____
	HOBBY: _____
	FOOD: _____

Three words that others would use to describe me:

Two books I love and how each has influenced me:

Something I have done that makes me proud:

Something I want to do in the future:

Kingore, B. (2005). *Assessment,* 3rd ed. Austin: Professional Associates Publishing.

Reflections through the Years

Consider placing one or two pages at the end of the portfolio book that provide a space to add notes over time. In later years, as students revisit this particular portfolio book, they can record the date and write themselves a note about how they now feel about the contents or the process. As one third grader expressed: *It will be fun to look back at this when I'm old and in middle school!*

Binding

Finally, the yearly portfolio books are bound in some way, such as using plastic bindings, three-hole punching the pages and placing them in a notebook, or three-hole punching and using metal rings or yarn to hold the pages together. It is exciting to see the pride students demonstrate in these finished portfolio books!

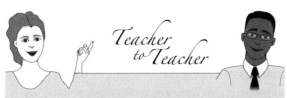

Arrange for a parent volunteer or aide to complete the process of binding the portfolios. There is too much for you to do toward the end of the year to expend your energy and time in binding books. If you are a perfectionist and need the books finished perfectly, choose a parent who is also a perfectionist and model for that parent how to accomplish exactly what you want.

If many classes in your building have portfolios, avoid frustration by coordinating the use of the publishing or binding materials and equipment so everyone is not trying to complete the process at the same time.

CELEBRATING THE PUBLISHED PORTFOLIO BOOKS

The portfolio has been a year-long process and a significant part of students' learning environment. Use the bound portfolio books to reach closure on this process. Consider organizing a portfolio celebration with the students before the books are taken home. If appropriate, plan refreshments together for the celebration.

When the bound portfolio books are handed back to the students, you will see excited smiles and everyone looking around to see how the books turned out. Since it is obvious they are eager to talk together about the books, group the students in pairs or trios and encourage them to share their book with their classmates. Most groups will talk incessantly and be genuinely impressed with each other's work. The portfolio books serve as a self-esteem boost and confidence builder. Consider providing time for students to autograph each others' books.

When finalizing the publications, send a letter to the parents announcing when each book will arrive at home and that it represents significant learning accomplishments from the entire year. A sample letter is included in Chapter 10 (Figure 10.6). Consider elaborating this letter with several comments from your students about their books. Their enthusiastic comments are infectious to others' enthusiasm and help establish a positive attitude toward sharing what has been learned as the books are celebrated together at home.

Videotape your class as they share their bound books and talk about them together. It will be a great motivator for introducing next year's class to your portfolio process.

Kingore, B. (2005). *Assessment,* 3rd ed. Austin: Professional Associates Publishing.

PUBLISHING THE YEARLY PORTFOLIO IN EARLY CHILDHOOD

Early childhood learners have fewer products in their portfolios because much of their learning is process oriented without a product. At the end of the year, their portfolio books will be thin. But teachers still report that the parents are thrilled to get the bound books. The young children are also thrilled because they love their work to look important. The following is a typical list of the contents of their bound books.

Consider laminating the front and back covers of the bound portfolios to protect them for years to come. There is no need to laminate each page of the book. Laminating every page adds expense and extensive preparation time to the process yet does not result in longer-lasting books.

CONTENTS OF PUBLISHED PORTFOLIO BOOKS FOR YOUNG CHILDREN

Book Cover

Many different choices for the cover are possible, but a favorite idea is to use pictures the child has completed at the beginning and the end of the year for the front and back covers of the bound portfolio. For example, the front cover might be a picture of the student or the student's family drawn at the beginning of year and dated; the back cover might be a picture of the same subject drawn at the end of year and dated. Figures 11.4 and 11.5 are examples of graphic organizers that children can write and draw on to create a front and back cover of a portfolio.

Table of Contents

This can be a listing of specific products for each child's book using the blank chronological Table of Contents in Figure 11.1. However, some teachers prefer to simply duplicate a list of topics studied during the year with the dates each topic was completed so parents have a chronological overview of how the products relate to the learning experiences.

Poem

Include a poem that addresses the philosophy of your class. Dorothy Law Nolte's *Children Learn What They Live*, Leila P. Fagg's *Play Today?*, and Helen E. Buckley's *The Painting* are good examples to consider. Parents benefit from these gentle reminders of developmentally appropriate practices and expectations for young children.

Products

The products selected during the year by the child and the teacher are placed here in chronological order to demonstrate the child's growth throughout the year.

About the Author

Use the About the Author form (Figure 11.6) to record the child's ideas and include a current photograph from home or school. Adding their thumb print is fun, because children know from television that everyone's fingerprint is different. The sentence prompts can be completed by the children writing in their temporary (invented) spelling or by Big Buddies, aides, or parent volunteers who act as scribes for the children.

If colored ink pads are not available, let the children color the thumb print area of their thumb with a marker, and then press it on the paper.

Figure 11.4: PORTFOLIO FRONT COVER

Kingore, B. (2005). Assessment, 3rd ed. Austin: Professional Associates Publishing.

Figure 11.5: PORTFOLIO BACK COVER

I drew this picture.

DATE _____

The End

Friends and Classmates

Young learners love collecting signatures from other kids. Provide one or two pages for children to collect the autographs of friends and classmates.

Binding[45]

Bind these portfolio books by using plastic bindings, three-hole punching and placing pages in a notebook, or three-hole punching and using metal rings or yarn to hold the pages together. Young children are proud of these special books!

Several primary teachers reported using the About the Author (Figure 11.6) with small groups of students as a teacher-directed language arts activity at the beginning of the year. This initial task is a preassessment informing teachers of many aspects of children's readiness, such as oral language development and emergent literacy skills. The form is then used again at the end of the school year. This application produces two important portfolio products and is an interesting way to assess children's changing view of their abilities and preferences at school.

CELEBRATING PUBLISHED PORTFOLIO BOOKS WITH YOUNG CHILDREN

Plan a celebration sharing the finished books with the children before the books are taken home. If appropriate, plan a class activity to make refreshments together for your portfolio book party.

Young children are so surprised at their books! They look at each page as if they had never seen it before! Pair the children and let them *read* their book to a classmate. Use a large piece of chart paper and record the children's comments and reactions as a language experience. Their responses document the pleasure and self-esteem enhancement the portfolio books bring to each author.

When preparing the books to take home, send a letter to the parents announcing when each book is to arrive at home and what it represents.[46] As a language arts task, add to your letter several comments from the children about their books to infect their parents with children's enthusiasm for their accomplishments.

> *My mom will be so proud of this.*
>
> *You know I did this--*
> *all by myself I did this.*
>
> *Want me to read my book to you?*
>
> *This is my important paper stuff.*
>
> *I like my book best.*

Referring to her drawing of her family at the beginning and end of the year, one child told her teacher:

> *My family looks funny when I was a baby.*
> *Now they look good.*

---

[45] Refer to the implementation tip for binding discussed in this chapter at the end of the *Publishing the Yearly Portfolio in the Elementary and Secondary Grades* section.

[46] Figure 10.6 is a sample letter.

Kingore, B. (2005). *Assessment,* 3rd ed. Austin: Professional Associates Publishing.

Figure 11.6: ABOUT THE AUTHOR

NAME _____

DATE _____

My Thumbprint:

My Picture:

My favorite thing at school:

My favorite book: _____

By: _____

Something I like to do and why:

Something I do not like to do and why:

I want to be:

Kingore, B. (2005). *Assessment,* 3rd ed. Austin: Professional Associates Publishing.

Appendices and References

· APPENDIX A ·
A Sequence for Implementing Portfolios

Whether as members of an assessment committee or working by yourself, use the following suggestions to guide decisions regarding a sequence for portfolio implementation. Taking time to plan your implementation will increase success and may save hours of frustration later. Prioritize by developing your portfolio definition and determining what you would initially like to accomplish with portfolios. Then, plan how you might best organize the process so it begins smoothly and operates effectively. Next, focus on the kinds and levels of communication needed among educators, parents, and students. With those decisions made, plan how to best model the process to students to prompt their enthusiasm about developing their own portfolios. You also need to plan how to integrate the process into your regular classroom routine so you avoid portfolios becoming something extra to do.

1. PRIORITIZE

- Develop your own definition of portfolios to clearly communicate your intentions.
- List what you would like to do and what you would like to accomplish through implementing portfolios; prioritize that list.
- Avoid trying to do too much at once. You don't have to do it all now. Begin small. Let the process develop and grow with time and experience.
- Allow your portfolios to reflect the personal goals, styles, strengths, and needs of you and your class.

2. ORGANIZE

If you are not confident with organization and management procedures, revisit this listing after you have read Chapter 2: Organizing Portfolios.

- Determine your portfolio containers, collection folders, filing system, storage location, and management procedures.
- Decide the number of products which may be selected, the time, day, and process for the selection.
- Determine when students' work will go home and communicate that schedule to parents.
- Prepare needed forms and collect needed materials.
- Plan the first item for students to file in their portfolio so the process begins smoothly and quickly. For example, determine a specific repeated task for students to complete and file the first week you implement portfolios.

3. COMMUNICATE

Communicate with other teachers and administrators

- Share articles, books, and information about portfolios.
- Form a network with other interested educators to nurture ideas as you share successes and concerns or problems. Plan to meet regularly--don't leave it to chance. We are all too busy for communication to occur if we don't schedule interaction times.
- Discuss together how to use portfolios to validate the variety of modalities, styles, and intelligences represented by the students in your classes.
- Constantly ask: *Is there an easier way to do this?*
- Discuss together how to best use portfo-

Kingore, B. (2005). *Assessment,* 3rd ed. Austin: Professional Associates Publishing.

lios to document grades, student learning, and achievement.

• Begin an ongoing "Need to Know" list. Write down the questions that occur to you so you can network with and learn from other professionals using portfolios.

Communicate with parents

• Share brief articles about portfolios and authentic assessment.

• Regularly send informative letters to parents. Consider developing one letter a month as a beginning goal to keep parents informed about students' progress and the use of portfolios in your classroom.

• Hold meetings with parents during which you model portfolios, have students share their portfolios, discuss the process, and note the growth and pride the students demonstrate. Accent to parents: *Through your child's portfolio, you will be better informed about their child's strengths, achievements, and needs because you will see concrete examples.*

Communicate with students

• Explain to students what a portfolio is in your class, the reasons for developing a portfolio, and what benefits it provides. Discuss how older students in some states use portfolios for job interviews and college entrances. Explain how adults use portfolios for job advancement or to obtain a new job.

• Discuss ownership, choice, and pride. Say to students: *Your portfolio will become the finest book you have ever developed. It represents you when you are not available to represent yourself. You will be making choices from the work you produce to represent the most important things you learn and the things most significant to you. Years in the future, you will be able to look back through this portfolio to remember and celebrate your learning.*

4. MODEL

Someone modeling a portfolio can inspire students' interest and enthusiasm in developing their own portfolios. People always smile and almost glow when they present and discuss the items in their portfolio. Thus, modeling is a powerful asset because pride of accomplishment shines through. Students see for themselves what portfolios can become.

If you and your students have not developed portfolios before, use these options to model portfolios.

Product Show and Tell

• Hold a product show and tell by asking students to bring in any piece of work they produced in school before this year. Each student then explains any of the following factors that are appropriate.
   - CIRCUMSTANCES--How or why was the piece produced?
   - TIME--When was it done? How much time and effort was involved?
   - RATIONALE--Why was that piece chosen? Why was it saved?
   - REFLECTION--What does it mean to the student now?

Professional Portfolios

• Ask an adult to model her or his professional portfolio for the class. Artists, models, and authors (professional or amateur) typically have a selection of products and materials which represent their greatest professional accomplishments. Ask one or more to show their portfolio, share why it is important to them, and discuss why some pieces were selected over others. List which criteria these adults deemed important in their portfolio selections. Later, your class can discuss these criteria in terms of what selections they might make for their own portfolios.

Kingore, B. (2005). *Assessment,* 3rd ed. Austin: Professional Associates Publishing.

If you have implemented portfolios in your classes before but this year's students have not had portfolios, consider using this option.

Portfolio Panel

- Invite students from last year's class to present and discuss their portfolios with this year's students. This panel can accent the process and how they feel about portfolios. Discuss how individual and different the portfolios are because they reflect personal strengths and choices.
- Encourage this year's class to ask questions. Then together, develop a list of possible criteria to guide the selection of portfolio items.

If this year's students have developed portfolios before, model the continuation of portfolios by using their previous selections.

Peer Product Sharing

- Have each student select one item from last year's portfolio or from their School Career Portfolio to share in this class as an introduction to themselves and their achievements.
- Discuss what is satisfying to them about their portfolios. Elicit their suggestions for making portfolios even more significant this year.

5. INTEGRATE

Portfolios should reflect the instructional decisions and authentic learning experiences in your class. Make portfolios a part of the regular routine in your class rather than something extra to do.

- Establish a specific time each week for portfolio selection and maintain your schedule.
- Consider setting up a bulletin board to showcase portfolio selections. One example of a portfolio selection bulletin board is presented in Chapter 2.
- Integrate portfolios as a part of authentic learning experiences in your class. Analyze where the different parts of your portfolio process best fit your instruction. For example, students' product selections and reflections about their learning provide an effective closure to a topic of study.
- Integrate portfolios into students' daily learning experiences. Frequently discuss criteria for quality work and students' reactions to what they are learning.
- Integrate portfolios with assessment goals and topic objectives. Consider how you can use portfolios to document students' learning accomplishments.
- Integrate portfolios with instructional decisions. How do portfolios enable you to showcase the kind of instructional experiences you believe best benefit students? How do portfolios support your use of a wide array of learning tasks beyond simple fill-in-the-blank responses?
- Relate portfolios to students' strengths and needs. Integrate multiple modalities and multiple intelligences in the product opportunities available to students.

6. IMPLEMENT

- Teach the process to students. Over time, help them practice and refine their collection, selection, and reflection procedures.
- Reflect often on the effectiveness of the process. Discuss with students what they think is working well and what needs to be changed. Elicit their opinions regarding which products or projects should be continued with next year's class and why certain products are not effective learning experiences.
- Revise your procedures as needed. Is there an easier or more efficient way?
- Plan your next step. What will you incorporate next so the process develops and expands?

Kingore, B. (2005). *Assessment,* 3rd ed. Austin: Professional Associates Publishing.

· APPENDIX B ·
Pictorial Rubric Poster

MATERIALS:
- **Two (or more) pieces of posterboard**
- **A title and criteria icons**
- **Crayons, markers, or colored paper**
- **Glue**
- **Velcro**

Especially when working with young children, rather than provide a paper copy of a pictorial rubric for each child, teachers can enlarge the pictures to create a rubric poster for the wall. On colored paper, print the full-sized versions of the Pictorial Rubric Generator icons,[47] or develop unique icons that address the specific needs of the students or task. When creating additional criteria icons, encourage students to draw images to represent the ascending levels of the criteria. This will save teacher preparation time, increase students' ownership in the assessment process, and better communicate the different criteria levels to the students.

Cut the first piece of posterboard according to the dotted lines on the diagram. These cuts result in five pieces to be used as the five-inch-tall criteria strips. On one side, glue a criterion icon and the three corresponding pictured levels onto each strip. On the back of each strip, attach a piece of velcro at each end. Ensure the velcro is in the same place on each strip so the strips are interchangeable on the poster. Four strips will fit on the finished rubric poster at one time, but create many of them to be able to quickly adjust to different tasks throughout the day without requiring multiple rubrics.

The second piece of posterboard is the foundation of the rubric. Create a title and attach it to the top four inches of the poster. Then, attach the velcro pieces that will hold the criteria strips in place. On each criterion strip, with the velcro pieces in place (leaving the fricative sides of each piece of velcro exposed), press each strip onto the poster backing so the velcro pieces adhere to each other.

The velcro pieces hold each criterion strip in place on the poster and allow the criteria to be easily changed in order to match any learning experience. Be careful to place the velcro strips in the same place on each criteria strip and on the poster to ensure they align in any sequence.

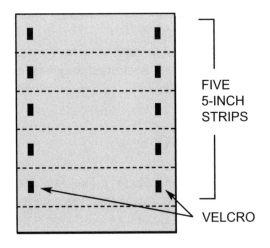

FIVE
5-INCH
STRIPS

VELCRO

---

[47] Full-sized versions of the icon are included on an interactive CD-ROM, Kingore, 2005. See Chapter 3 for more information about the Pictorial Rubric Generator.

· APPENDIX C ·
Borders

Border pages are fun to use and add visual appeal to communications and projects. Many teachers report that they do not have a computer in their classroom and they have difficulty accessing graphic packages. Therefore, the pages in this appendix may be used for any purpose, such as:

- Communicationg with parents,
- Invitations to school and classroom events,
- Announcements,
- Learning experiences,
- Project descriptions,
- Cover sheets, and
- Many portfolio applications.

Some of the border designs are included in Chapter 10 as example letters to parents.

Kingore, B. (2005). *Assessment,* 3rd ed. Austin: Professional Associates Publishing.

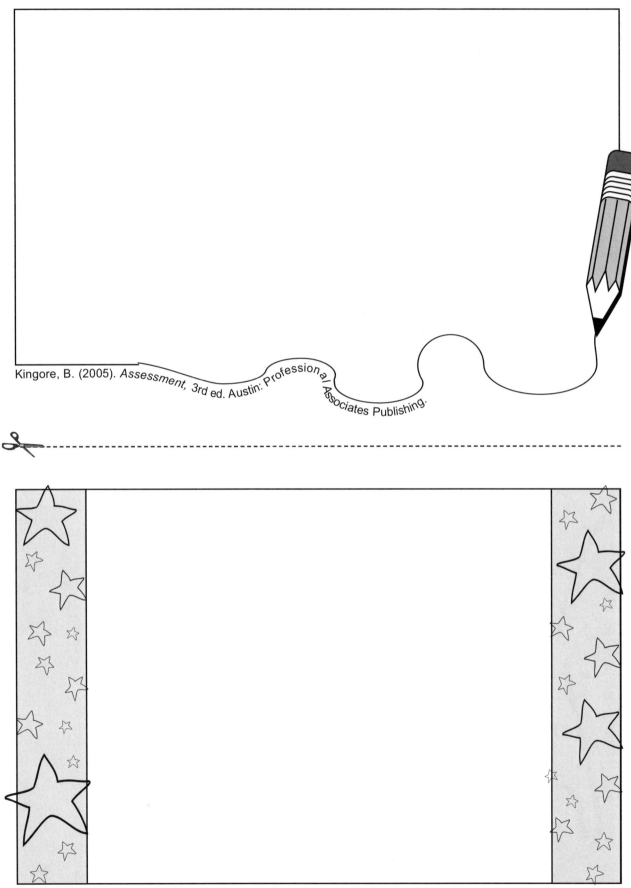

Kingore, B. (2005). *Assessment,* 3rd ed. Austin: Professional Associates Publishing.

Kingore, B. (2005). *Assessment,* 3rd ed. Austin: Professional Associates Publishing.

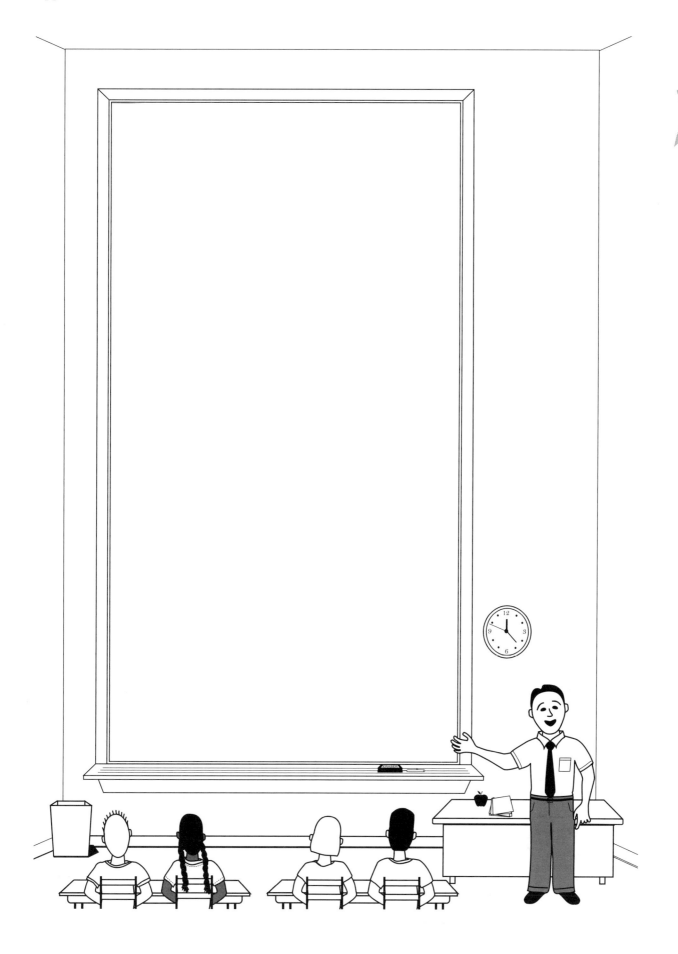

Kingore, B. (2005). *Assessment,* 3rd ed. Austin: Professional Associates Publishing.

· APPENDIX D ·
Assessing Multiple Intelligences

Researchers are reexamining the definition of intelligence. One theory, offered by Harvard University professor Howard Gardner,* proposes different kinds of intelligence that are all equal in value and importance. Gardner's theory originally consisted of seven intelligences, but in 1995, he added an eighth intelligence-- naturalist. The following is a brief overview of these eight intelligences.

* **Linguistic**
  Is sensitivity to spoken or written language
* **Logical-Mathematical**
  Reasons with logical or numerical patterns
* **Naturalist**
  Recognizes species of plants or animals
* **Spatial**
  Visualizes, forms a mental image, and perceives configurations
* **Musical**
  Produces and appreciates rhythm and musical expression
* **Bodily-Kinesthetic**
  Problem solves with body movement
* **Interpersonal**
  Understands other people and works effectively with them; other-driven
* **Intrapersonal**
  Is sensitive to one's own feelings, thoughts, and desires; self-driven

Gardner defines intelligence as the ability to solve problems or create things valued in a culture (1996). Everyone possibly has all of these intelligences, but each person typically has high areas in one or more.

It is important to understand each student's pattern of intelligences. From Gardner's perspective, "it is more important to discover areas of strength and to build on them than it is to fret too much about areas of weakness" (1995). As minority populations continue to increase, schools need to recognize and appreciate diversity in learning since different cultures value different abilities. Encourage students to use strengths not traditionally accented in classrooms to succeed. Observe and analyze the intelligences that children favor while learning or applying what they learned. Use that insight to provide learning experiences which incorporate that pattern of strength to help all students view themselves as capable.

Only to the degree that instruction offers opportunities for the highest levels of performance on a wide range of student-selected contents and products can the portfolio process support the search for multiple talents and diverse abilities.

Intermediate, middle school, and high school teachers find that students increase self-understanding when they analyze their own patterns of intelligences. Students are typically fascinated with learning more about how they best succeed and why some learning tasks are harder for them. Simple tools, such as My Pattern of Intelligences on the next page, can help students informally determine their multiple intelligences. These tools were piloted with hundreds of educators in workshops and multiple upper-elementary through high school students in classrooms across the country. Most people reported that their personal pattern of intelligences included three or four of the eight multiple intelligences. Students can apply that insight to the Product Grids in Chapter 8.

*Gardner, H. (1996, Spring). Your child's intelligence(s). *Scholastic Parent & Child,* 32-37.

Kingore, B. (2005). *Assessment,* 3rd ed. Austin: Professional Associates Publishing.

MY PATTERN OF INTELLIGENCES

NAME _____ DATE _____

Analyze your multiple intelligences by rating how each intelligence is like you on a scale from 1 to 10 (with 10 being extremely high). What pattern do you see about your ways to be smart?

Linguistic
Writing, word plays, reading, speeches, oral presentations, effectively uses words to teach others

Logical/Mathematical
Problem solving, math, logic problems, tangrams, analyzes, likes to create new math problems

Naturalist
Science, nature, exploring outdoors, categorizing, interested in birds and animals

Spatial
Graphic organizers, drawing, visualizing, maps, implementing graphics when teaching others

Bodily/Kinesthetic
Manipulating physical objects, body movement, role play, prefers to be in motion

Musical
Rhythm, rap, sing or play instruments, prefers to have music playing while learning, creates songs

Interpersonal
Collaboration, solving human conflicts, group skills, prefers to talk with others to solve problems

Intrapersonal
Self-sufficient, self-understanding, journals, diaries, prefers to think alone to solve problems

The areas in which you scored the highest suggest your pattern of intelligences. These may be the strengths that most help you learn, succeed in solving problems, and complete classroom products. What do you think are your strengths in the intelligences you scored highest?

INTELLIGENCE   STRENGTH

• _____ _____

• _____ _____

• _____ _____

Kingore, B. (2005). *Assessment*, 3rd ed. Austin: Professional Associates Publishing.

· APPENDIX E ·
Standards Rubric Poster

Appendices and References

MATERIALS:
- **Two pieces of posterboard**
- **A title bar, faces or icons, and captions**
- **Text for at least four cards to begin**
- **Crayons, markers, or colored paper**
- **Glue**

Cut the first piece of the posterboard according to the dotted lines on the diagram. These cuts result in one strip for the pocket of the poster and six cards. The six cards display the skill proficiencies, and ascending skills or standards are written on each of the six cards to place in the poster when it is appropriate to express that level of challenge. (Using the front and back of each card creates 12 cards for ascending skill levels.) *Customize the skills to reflect the needs and levels of the class as well as the relevant standards.*

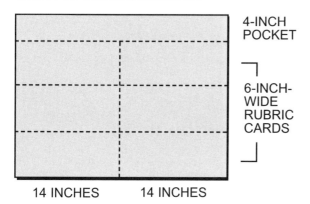

4-INCH POCKET

6-INCH-WIDE RUBRIC CARDS

14 INCHES   14 INCHES

The second piece of posterboard is the foundation of the Standards Rubric Poster. Create a title to communicate the purpose of the rubric, and glue faces or other icons onto the poster. Glue corresponding captions onto the pocket strip to clearly communicate the proficiency levels to the students. Develop captions that focus on either effort or achievement, and attach them to the four-inch strip. Then, create a pocket for the caption cards by stapling the pocket strip onto the bottom of the poster as well as between each card.[48]

Select captions that best communicate the instructional priorities. For example, some teachers prefer to emphasize the learning effort a child demonstrates at school. Other teachers want to accent the level of accomplishment a child experiences. Write the captions using language that will communicate clearly to the students.

Use markers to draw faces, other icons, or grading scores, and then, color each caption to match its corresponding descriptor. (To save time coloring, create the icons and captions on four differently colored pieces of paper.) These matching colors help clarify the evaluation levels to young learners. Even young children know that *I did not work* is not the desired behavior because the unhappy face and that caption use the same color. Finally, personalize the Pocket Chart Poster with additional color and designs. Consider including students in the creation of the rubric to save time and give the students more ownership in the assessment process.

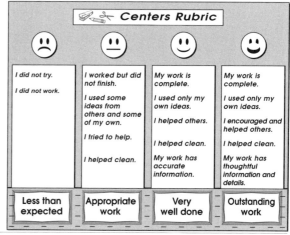

[48] Face pieces, customizable captions, title icons, and formatted cards are included in Kingore, 2005.

Kingore, B. (2005). *Assessment,* 3rd ed. Austin: Professional Associates Publishing.

References

Amabile, T. M. (1983). *The social psychology of creativity.* New York: Springer-Verlag.

Baker, L., & Brown, A. L. (1984). Cognitive monitoring in reading. In J. Flood (Ed.), *Understanding reading comprehension* (pp. 21-44). Newark, DE: International Reading Association.

Betts, G. & Kercher, J. (1999). *Autonomous learner model: Optimizing ability.* Greeley, CO: ALPS Publishing.

Carr, J. F. & Harris, D. E. (2001). *Succeeding with standards: Lining curriculum, asessment, and action planning.* Alexandria, VA: Association for Supervision, Curriculum and Development.

Cooper. J. D. & Kiger, N. D. (2002). *Literacy: Helping children construct meaning, 5th ed.* Boston: Houghton Mifflin.

Costa, A. L., & Kallick, B. (1992). Reassessing assessment. In A. L. Costa, J. A. Bellanca, & R. Fogarty (Eds.), *If minds matter: A foreword to the future, Volume 11* (pp. 275-280). Palatine, IL: IRI/Skylight.

Csikszentmihalyi, M. (1997). *Creative flow and the psychology of discovery and invention.* New York: Harper Collins.

De Bono, E. (1993). *Teach your child how to think.* New York: Penguin Books.

Farr, R. & Tone, B. (1998). *Portfolio and performance asessment.* Ft. Worth: Harcourt Brace College Publishers.

Gardner, H. (1996, Spring). Your child's intelligence(s). *Scholastic Parent & Child,* 32-37.

Gardner, H. (1993). *Multiple intelligences: Theory in practice.* New York: Basic Books.

Grigorenko, E., & Sterberg, R. (1997). Styles of thinking, abilities, and academic performance. *Exceptional Children,* 63, 295-312.

Kingore, B. (2005). *Assessment interactive CD-ROM.* Austin: Professional Associates Publishing.

Kingore, B. (2004). *Differentiation: Simplified, realistic, and effective.* Austin: Professional Associates Publishing.

Kingore, B., Ed. (2002). *Reading strategies for advanced primary readers.* Austin: Texas Education Agency.

Kingore, B. (2001). *Kingore observation inventory (KOI), 2nd ed.* Austin: Professional Associates Publishing.

Marzano, R. (2000). *Transforming classroom grading.* Alexandria, VA: Association for Supervision, Curriculum and Development.

Ministry of Education. (1991). *Supporting learning: Understanding and assessing the progress of children in the primary program; A resource for parents and teachers.* British Columbia, Canada.

Paulson, F. L., P. Paulson & C. Meyer. (1991, February). What makes a portfolio a portfolio? *Educational Leadership,* 60-63.

Popham, J.W. (1997, October). What's wrong--and what's right--with rubrics. *Educational Leadership*, 72-75.

Stenmark, J. K., Bush, W. S., & Allen, C. (2001). *Classroom assessment for school mathematics, K-12* Reston, VA: NCTM.

Sternberg, R., Torff, & Grigorenko. (1998). Teaching triarchically improves student achievement. *Journal of Educational Psychology, 90.* 374-384.

Stiggins, R. (2001). *Student-involved classroom assessment, 2nd ed.* Upper Saddle River, NJ: Merrill Prentice Hall.

Tomlinson, C. (2003). *Fulfilling the promise of the differentiated classroom.* Alexandria, VA: Association for Supervision, Curriculum and Development.

Tomlinson, C., Kaplan, S., Renzulli, J., Purcell, J., Leppien J., & Burns, D. (2002). *The parallel curriculum: A design to develop high potential and challenge high-ability learners.* Thousand Oaks, CA: Corwin Press.

Vygotsky, L. (1962). *Thought and language.* Cambridge: MIT Press.

Index

•Q•

•R•

•S•

Index

Assessment Interactive CD-ROM

Dr. Bertie Kingore
ID CODE: BK-06

Grades: K - 12

This fully interactive and customizable CD-ROM provides the forms from the *Assessment* book, almost all of which are **completely customizable**. Included are:

- The pictorial rubric generator to build rubrics as posters or handouts for young learners or ESL students,
- An expanded rubric generator to choose from dozens of customizable criteria or write your own, creating an endless number of rubrics on the computer in minutes, and
- Over 130 completely customizable self-evaluations, assessments, interviews, conference forms, goal-setting forms, product grids, borders, and parent letters!

PO Box 28056 • Austin, Texas 78755-8056
Toll free phone/fax: **866-335-1460**
www.kingore.com